How to Get into Commercials

How to Get into Commercials

A COMPLETE GUIDE FOR BREAKING INTO AND
SUCCEEDING IN THE LUCRATIVE WORLD OF
TV AND RADIO COMMERCIALS BY ONE OF THE
NATION'S LEADING CASTING DIRECTORS

by Vangie Hayes
with Gloria Hainline

BARNES & NOBLE BOOKS

A DIVISION OF HARPER & ROW, PUBLISHERS

New York, Cambridge, Philadelphia, San Francisco,
London, Mexico City, São Paulo, Singapore, Sydney

A hardcover edition of this book is published by Harper & Row, Publishers, Inc.

HOW TO GET INTO COMMERCIALS. Copyright © 1983 by Vangie Hayes. All rights reserved. Printed in the United States of America. No part of this book may be used or reproduced in any manner whatsoever without written permission except in the case of brief quotations embodied in critical articles and reviews. For information address Harper & Row, Publishers, Inc., 10 East 53rd Street, New York, N.Y. 10022. Published simultaneously in Canada by Fitzhenry & Whiteside Limited, Toronto.

First BARNES & NOBLE BOOKS edition published 1985.

Library of Congress Cataloging in Publication Data

Hayes, Vangie.
    How to get into commercials.
    Includes index.
    1. Acting for Television–Vocational guidance.
2. Television advertising–Vocational guidance.
3. Radio advertising–Vocational guidance.   4. Radio
broadcasting–Vocational guidance.   I. Hainline, Gloria.
II. Title.
PN1992.8.A3H35   1983   791.45′028′02373   81-47230
ISBN 0-06-014888-8
ISBN 0-06-463704-2 (pbk.)

85 86 87 88 89 10 9 8 7 6 5 4 3 2 1

Contents

A section of photographs follows page 152.

Introduction

This is not a "how to win fame and fortune quickly and easily" book. But it could help you do both.

You could be like Susan Spilker, who started out as a bookkeeper for an L.A. agent and, thanks to her red hair and acting lessons, was sent on a rush casting call and is now making over $100,000 a year. You could be like theater actress Jan Miner (Madge The Manicurist), who did one commercial for Palmolive Liquid and many dollars and almost twenty years later is still advising her customers to dip their fingers into a bowl of Palmolive Liquid. Or you could be like Grant Schaft, Arizona State student, who was picked up by a research company looking for Close-up toothpaste users, chosen for the commercial, spotted by an L.A. agent, and is now on his way to a promising career. You could even take a leap from commercials to stardom. Diane Keaton, Sandy Duncan, Tom Selleck, and others did.

It's all possible. But making it big is only a small part of what this book is about. It's more about what comes before you make it big. I want to tell you all you need to know—all the steps you need to follow to become a successful television performer.

I'm a casting director, and people constantly ask me, "How can I get into commercials?" This question—and you people who have asked it—motivated me to write this book. I felt I could use my inside view to guide a beginner. And I wanted to do it as if I were sitting face-to-face with you. I wanted to personally help you type yourself, to carefully and thoroughly help you organize your venture as you would a business, and to inform you honestly about the rewards and drawbacks along the way. The more know-how you have, the better your chances of getting your share of the $350 million paid to commercial performers each year. That's why I wanted to cover even the smallest details of becoming a television performer.

But it was not just the beginner with whom I wanted to talk in this book—but also you the professional. Each chapter contains specific information that will help you get more commercials and improve the quality of your performance.

As I began to put my notes together, I discovered I wanted to impart more information than merely "how to." I wanted to show the business of being a television-commercial performer as it is— to present the profession as not only fun, monetarily rewarding, but also one worthy of a serious striving toward excellence. Most TV commercials whiz by in a twinkling of an eye—a half-sweep of the second hand of a watch. But that thirty-second spot is the result of months of planning, days of preparation, hours of shooting, and years of experience—and it can influence the life of virtually everyone involved in its making (and the viewer, too). Whether you are making a career out of TV commercials or doing just one commercial, there is hardly any other field that offers so many opportunities to find out about yourself and to grow. Am I being idealistic? Maybe. But that's the way I feel about it. And that's what I hope this book is about.

In the following chapters, I will take you through every phase of getting yourself together—i.e., finding your type; preparing; getting your pictures; putting your résumé together; handling interviews and auditions; getting an agent; handling business relationships, money, unions; getting your children and even your pets and your home into commercials.

The first chapters up to "Day of the Shoot" apply to almost everyone. I suggest they be not only read through but used as you would a workbook. You may want to jump to those chapters that apply specifically to you—e.g., "You Have Such an Interesting Voice." No matter how you use this book, I sincerely hope the chapters ahead will help you find your way to a casting director's office, to an audition, and ultimately to the other side of your TV screen, performing in a TV commercial.

Good luck.

Vangie Hayes

How to Get into Commercials

1

I Could Be in That Commercial

It's very curious, but whenever I go to a party or to a friend's house, someone always seems to be auditioning. The businessman next to me at a dinner party discovers I'm a casting director and suddenly his voice deepens. When I visit friends, their children parade before me unusually well groomed. Recently, the daughter of one of my friends confessed that when she and her sister were teen-agers, they used to freshly wash and brush their hair, all with hopes I'd see them as Breck shampoo types (the fact that I didn't cast Breck commercials didn't matter).

I find that almost everyone has a secret ambition to do a commercial. Many have a Lana-Turner-discovered-in-a-drugstore feeling about it. It could happen to them.

Now, I happen to feel there's a commercial for everyone, but I also feel it requires a lot more than a secret ambition. The fact that you're reading this book shows you have the first requisite. You don't just dream about doing a commercial, you want to find out how you go about it. More than likely you watch TV commercials convinced you could judge as well as that woman from

Atlanta which detergent takes out ground-in dirt, or that you could act the part of a hardhat pouring a glass of beer with as much anticipation as one of those macho guys, or that your kids could consume snacks as enthusiastically as any of the striped-T-shirt crowd. Okay, let's see if you're right. Let's look at who the people in those commercials are and see if you could really be one of them.

Who Are the People Who Perform in Commercials?

If you had asked me five or ten years ago, I'd have said that if you weren't a professional actor or actress, you wouldn't have a chance to do a commercial. Actually, there's a certain irony there. In the late Forties and early Fifties when commercials first started, actors and actresses with theatrical backgrounds didn't want to do them; they looked down at commercials. Casting directors used "models" exclusively. Although some were actually model models, the term also included character people, housewife types—any talent.

In the Sixties that changed. Probably because of the good money in commercials and the chance to support their careers, actors and actresses began to enter the field. Eventually, we had such a great pool to dip into, they made up 80 percent of our casting choices. With the development of "testimonial" commercials in the Seventies, that again changed. Although actors and actresses still dominate the field, there's a whole new cast of characters doing commercials.

Let's look at who they are.

Many of the people in commercials today are called "real people." You usually see them in testimonial commercials making a statement about a product, oohing and ahhing over its demonstrable superiority. "That's amazing!" exclaims the housewife. "I don't believe it . . . I'm amazed!" Most of this group are found by research companies whose business it is to go around the country and discover people who use their products. Some are selected from letters they have sent to manufacturers, praising their products.

People who own their own businesses—e.g., Tom Carvel, the Carvel ice cream man; and Frank Perdue, the chicken man—are another well-represented group. And then there are the celebrities—e.g., Lauren Bacall (High Point), Muhammad Ali (d-Con Roach Spray), Michael Landon (Kodak), Telly Savalas (Ford). And there are some not so well-known experts in their fields—e.g., chefs, beauty experts, auto mechanics, gymnasts, and scuba divers.

As new ideas come into vogue—for instance, as more women enter professions—new commercial types are created.

As you can see, chances are excellent there's a place for you. After all, practically all of the people you see on TV commercials started with the same thought you have: I could do that commercial.

How a TV Commercial Is Born—And Your Part in It

As you read on, you will get a more detailed picture of the process of making a TV commercial. (Specifically, I refer you to chapter 14.) Of course, there are variations in the process, but briefly here's how it works.

The manufacturer of a product (the client) goes to his advertising agency, the people whose job it is to design and produce ads, with an assignment to create a TV commercial. The agency's creative department—creative head, copywriter, and art director—get to work and come up with ideas based on product information and consumer research. The copywriter then writes a script and the art director visualizes it—that is, sketches a storyboard, a series of panels depicting the scenes of the commercial. (See illustration on pp. 164–65.) This storyboard becomes the master plan of the commercial and the focus of all the subsequent activity. Once the agency's principals (creative head, account representative) approve it, the account man, who is liaison between the creative department and manufacturer, presents it to the client. Upon client approval, the storyboard is given to the agency producer, the production overseer, who sends it to film houses for bids.

WHERE YOU COME IN

Even before the film company is selected, the casting director (that's my job) begins to search out talent for the roles depicted on the storyboard. He or she usually refers to his/her picture file and talent lists, and then puts out a call to agents who handle actors and models and whose function it is to find them jobs and negotiate contracts. In the case of the testimonial commercial, the people selected by research groups are notified directly.

The next step is the audition, which is usually taped. These tapes are often viewed and judged by as many as sixteen different people before a selection is made.

By this time, the film company has been selected and the day of the shoot has been set. The TV commercial is then shot at a studio, and afterward edited and distributed to TV stations.

Although the process may have variations, your first stop as a performer usually will be the casting director's office.

The Joys of Being a Casting Director

I'll let you in on a secret about casting directors. Nothing gives us more fun and satisfaction than discovering new talent. I become electrified when someone walks into my office and I can say, "My God, that's it!"

I get so excited, I almost become possessive of my find. If, say, a terrific actress comes in without an agent and asks me to help her find one, my instinct is to keep her for our own accounts. If an agent sends someone to me for a reading and he or she is really good, I'm tempted to keep it my secret. (I do, incidentally, resist such temptations.)

If at an audition some of the people involved in the selection don't share my enthusiasm for the talent, they simply go down in my estimation. If it turns out that my discovery is perfect for a client, it's really a red-letter day. Sandy Duncan is a good example. When she came in for an interview, I was taken at once by her bubbly personality, talent, whimsy, charm—and if these qualities weren't enough, she had perfect teeth. I couldn't wait to send her around to the people on the Colgate account.

AND MORE JOYS

On a par with finding *the one,* there is the satisfaction a casting director gets watching people develop. One of the first lessons I learned when I started was never to count people out. I remember this would-be commercial actress came in to see me and everything about her seemed wrong—nose too long, thick glasses, crooked teeth, hair a mousy shade of brown. I thought the best favor I could do her was to suggest she give up. The next time I saw her, she was in an off-Broadway show. She had metamorphosed amazingly. Her hair was lighter, her glasses were gone, her teeth were capped, her nose had been fixed. Naturally, I called her back.

But it's not only seeing people's appearances improve that's rewarding, it's also watching them grow, gain confidence, become pros who know their craft.

The third big joy in the life of a TV casting director is watching the fun people have doing a commercial. Getting in front of the cameras can be the most exciting experience of their lives. Their fantasies have come true. They come out of the shooting proud of themselves. "Hey, I did it! I'm in a TV commercial!" For me, it's like a bonus.

The Exciting Life of a TV-Commercial Performer

The world of TV commercials is stimulating, creative, hectic, lucrative, glamorous, frustrating, and a lot of good, hard work—but it's never dull. In all my years as a casting director, I have seldom watched someone do a commercial who was not caught up in it.

Even if you do just one commercial, you are in for an enriching experience. You will get an inside view, be a part of what it takes to make a TV commercial. You will find yourself in the hub of the TV-commercial world—agents' offices, photographers' studios, advertising agencies, audition rooms, studio sets. You will meet the many interesting people who populate this world—actors, models, advertising-agency people, film-company people, body-beautiful people, makeup people, business people. You may have a chance to travel. Because it was winter here and summer there, we recently sent Dan Haggerty (Grizzly Adams) to New Zealand to do a Nestea commercial.

And then, seeing yourself on tape, seeing yourself with different people, and getting different feedback from people is an excellent way to become aware of yourself and develop your craft. It's hardly the luck of the draw that the people who are the best actors or actresses in other areas usually win the commercial. If you can do *A Thousand Clowns,* you certainly can do advertising copy.

"Yes," You Say, "But What Are My Chances?"

Your chances are usually as good as you are. Some people can walk into a casting director's office and by the time they reach the desk they have won the commercial. This is true of someone with a fabulous face and figure, and a personality to match.

Granted, your entry into the field may not be as spectacular, but if you're a good commercial type, have talent, work at it, come in for the interview well prepared, appropriately dressed, full of concentration, energy, and openness, you have a good chance of getting into commercials and working yourself up to a successful career. Remember, there are lots of commercials made each year. Why not one costarring you? I say "costarring" because in commercials the product is always the star.

What It Takes

If I had just a few golden words to offer, they would be: Take your work seriously, and yourself not so seriously.

If you come into an audition with a chip on your shoulder, with an I'm-not-really-here-doing-this attitude, if you look at a commercial as an easy way to make a few extra dollars while you become another Robert Redford or Jane Fonda, forget it. People will pick up your attitude and chances are they'll not want to fight through it to get you straightened out. Result: No job.

In my experience, the people who succeed have a businesslike, positive attitude. They work at getting jobs. They have stick-to-itiveness, imagination—if one thing doesn't work, they'll try something else. They make the rounds, accept rejection without being touchy, and they call back. They work on themselves: They take acting lessons, speech lessons, classes; they keep themselves physically in shape.

With me, a little charm and a lot of humor go a long way. The person who comes in with a relaxed attitude, who lives in the here and now, and who doesn't make me feel like an ogre for not having a particular commercial to offer is the one who makes me really stop and take note.

Occupational Hazards

If there's one big occupational hazard, it's rejection. It comes with the territory. Some people never take the first step because of that fear of being turned down. I suggest you scratch the word "rejection" and substitute the word "opinion." This is a business full of subjective opinions.

A casting director may not always spot a winner. I can personally vouch for that. I recently interviewed an eager young woman who wanted to do commercials and eventually to get into a soap. Although she was very attractive, she was a little on the heavy side for commercials. She told me that she and a girlfriend lived in the Village and that they both had a sweet tooth and loved to fill up on bakery delights.

Since she'd come to me for advice, I gave her the benefit of my wisdom and began to pontificate. She should take responsibility for losing weight. As she was just starting and it was a competitive business, she should not think of getting any work for two years. And so on.

A couple of weeks later, I went on vacation. When I came back, I discovered another casting director in my department had hired her for a big commercial—just as she was. Six months later "my protégée" phoned and told me she'd just gotten a running part in a soap opera. The last time I heard from her, she was buying a town house. I goofed on that one, but I've never been happier to be wrong.

In this business, success is not guaranteed—rejection is. I know actors and actresses who tell me they always come in second or third but never land the part. It's like that old advertising slogan, "Always a bridesmaid but never a bride." Nevertheless, I wait for the day they will come in and tell me they got a commercial. Those who persist usually do have their day. On the other hand, if you sense there might be a reason for your rejections, and it's not overwhelming, you can always check yourself out, improve your appearance and your acting approach—in short, pick yourself up, dust yourself off, and start all over again.

Again, I'd like to repeat the theme of this book: You have a chance to get into commercials. If I didn't believe that there are many opportunities, I wouldn't have written this book. Now, before we get on with the business of getting started—finding your type—I recommend you take the following test.

DO I HAVE WHAT IT TAKES?

1. Do people tell me, "You're so easy to get along with," or do they say, "You're overly sensitive"?

2. Will I try what the other person suggests?

3. Can I take rejection? Can I take "no" on the phone, put it

in perspective without wanting to slam the phone down and mentally kill the rejecter?

    4. Am I a natural salesperson?

    5. Will I go out and try different ways to make contacts instead of sitting home and waiting for Steven Spielberg to appear at the door?

    6. Will I refuse to give up after a few auditions if I don't win one?

    7. Am I curious? (It helps to learn about a product or what's needed in a scene.)

    8. Will I keep working on a scene?

    9. Do I try to get things done right away? Do I welcome obstacles as a challenge rather than something to get me off the hook?

    10. Do I come up with solutions?

    11. Do I make the first move toward people?

    12. Do I always look well groomed?

    13. Do I tell my contacts what I can do for their business rather than how they can help me pay the rent?

    14. Am I willing to reveal my feelings?

    15. Do I have a regular job or income to hold me over while I'm going on interviews and auditions?

    16. Do I initiate action rather than have someone tell me what to do?

    17. Would I rather be on stage or part of the audience?

    18. Do I enjoy working on myself—exercising, keeping in shape?

    19. Am I open to new situations, meeting new people?

    20. Can I take not being in control, not knowing what will happen next?

If you answer yes to eighteen out of twenty questions, you have a winning attitude. Read on.

Where Do You Fit In?

HOW TO KNOW YOUR TYPE

Let's say you were to walk into my office for a general interview. How would I look at you? What do I look for?

I don't even have to think about it. I know what I would do automatically. (I do it all the time.) I would ask myself if you were the commercial type—that is, if you were an attractive person, open, enthusiastic, with healthy looks, energy, warmth—the kind of person you see on TV commercials.

The second question I would immediately ask myself is what specific type you are. A running monologue usually goes on in my head in a first interview. He's a perfect truck-driver type—look at those muscles. She's lovely—good bone structure—a cosmetic type—wonder if she can do a couple of lines.

Sometimes the type is apparent on sight. Other times I have to work a little at it. I may say to myself, She's not very attractive, but she does have a warmth—could be a good interviewer. Or, He's a little old for the average spokesperson type, but we did recently have a call for a druggist in that age group.

At any rate, I always make an effort to place the candidate. As a casting director, finding people who represent a type is my job. I even find myself typing people in the street or at parties. I once approached a woman in an Italian restaurant. At the time, we were casting for a mother-in-law type who was sure no one could cook pasta for her son like she did. This woman—who was indeed Italian—was perfect for the role. Headwaiters and cabdrivers, incidentally, are often tapped for interviews because they are so true to type.

Getting to Know You

Once I know your type, I can proceed with the interview. A general interview is more or less a get-acquainted affair and so I would have no specific commercial to offer you. Nevertheless, the next thing I'd ask myself is how you match up with my agency's accounts. Would you be a good spokesperson for Kodak? Would you be a good voice-over for Ford?

As we chatted on, I would see other things about you—notice you had an engaging smile, or beautiful, expressive hands, or a nervous mannerism, or a captivating voice but with a slight lisp. Inevitably, your background would come up and I might discover you're an expert swimmer or an amateur magician.

In time, I would give you a sample commercial to read and probably discover even more about you. You may show a comedic side, or have character-type possibilities, or display a spokesperson's authority. But chances are, if you first struck me as a housewife type, that will be my lasting impression. In the TV world, that's a plus. In real life, a housewife might also be a femme fatale, a poetic dreamer, or an assertive department-store buyer; but in TV commercials, a housewife is a housewife is a housewife, and should be instantly recognizable as one. The commercial message depends on it—and your success, it follows, depends on it as well.

The Thirty-Second Identification

Today, most commercials run thirty seconds. That's not much time to do a selling job, so naturally a sponsor doesn't want to waste a second of it on anything but the product.

When you consider that an actor speaks for and is identified with the product, and that he is on camera close up but a few seconds, you can see why it's so important that the viewer (potential consumer) instantly recognize the role the actor is playing. Even before the product appears, the viewer should say, "That's a housewife," or a lumberjack, or a fashion model, or a newspaper man. If the viewer has to spend time figuring out who the character is, the message may be lost.

Thus, if you don't look the part, you don't get the part. There's no way around it. As a TV performer, you must be your type in the flesh. Makeup, wardrobe, lighting, and other theatrical tricks can change the way you look on the stage, but in TV they don't work. Unlike the theater, there's not enough distance to help create illusion. The close-up camera is blunt. It tells the barefaced truth. You must be true to type or you won't work in commercials.

Now that that's been said, let's get down to the very important business of finding and working on your type.

What Are the Most Common Types?

Generally, types are based on the specific market the manufacturer hopes to reach. If the product is a detergent, the type chosen to sell it would be a housewife.

As new markets develop, so do "new" types. With the graying of America, we see many more older people doing commercials—but again the specific market makes a difference in type: Whereas grandmothers were once stereotypes—little old ladies with cameo brooches—today they are shown as attractive, involved people, people with the income to spend money on a particular product or service.

Most TV-commercial types, however, are classic. If you've watched commercials for any length of time, you're familiar with them. For the purposes of this chapter, we will concentrate on the following adult types. (I'll discuss various child types in chapter 17.)

Housewife
Young Husband/Father
Young Woman-Next-Door
Cosmetic Model—Female
Fashion Models—Male, Female
Plus 12 Sizes
Glamour—Female
Handsome Man Type
Career Woman
Young Mother
"Real People"—Nonprofessional-Man-on-the-Street/
                Woman-in-the-Laundry Types
Character—   *Blue-Collars*—movers, truck drivers,
                    waitresses
               Professional—businesswomen, business-
                    men, professors, lawyers, teachers
Comedian/Comedienne
Spokesperson
Voice-Over
Celebrities
Celebrity Look-alikes
Experts—Including Athletes
Owner of a Business

Your TV Set—Watch and Compare

Now you're ready to discover where you belong in the world of
TV-commercial types. The best thing for you to do is to watch
TV. Watch frequently and carefully. Observe the wide spectrum
of products advertised. Notice the range of types. In one day's
viewing, you will see celebrities like Bill Cosby, beautiful cosmetic
models like actress Lauren Hutton, character actors like Mr.
Whipple, and a host of real people—housewives, etc—not to
mention infants and puppy dogs.

    Once you have an idea of the types, cast yourself in a commer-
cial. Find the performer you're most like. Compare your looks,

hairstyle, dress, personality. Be selective. Pinpoint your type. If you think you're a housewife, ask yourself whether you are a healthy Ivory Soap type or an older mother type. If you envision yourself as a macho type, figure out whether you're a model or a blue-collar-worker type.

Do Not Overlook Other Endowments

If you're a woman with hands that could fondle a man's face and inspire a legion of them to buy a particular shaving cream, or if you're a man with the kind of hair a woman would love to muss, do look into the body-parts category.

Although as a rule body-part commercials are done by special models (Linda Rose, who made a fortune as a hand model, is a good example), you don't have to specialize to do one. Body-part modeling, you'll find, is a good way to pick up extra money while you're waiting for a job as a principal in a commercial. With all the close-ups of legs, hands, hair, in commercials, there's plenty of work around. Besides, your special endowment may help you get a commercial. Say you're up for a housewife part, the fact that you have good hands and know how to use them will automatically give you an edge. (If you're interested in knowing more, see "Body Parts" on p. 238.)

A Warning About Typing Yourself

Above all, don't fantasize in typing yourself. It sometimes happens that someone will walk into my office and say, "I see myself as a cosmetic model" at the very same time I am saying, "Now there's a pleasant young housewife." If you're going out for the wrong part, it could waste time and lose opportunities.

Professional Requirements for Types

Before you match up your type with a casting director's type requirements, I suggest you follow this dictum:

Choose a type that will work for you, and one for which there are a lot of calls.

It's quite possible you may find you fit into more than one slot. Although later on this may be to your advantage, in the beginning I would recommend you concentrate on one category.

Now let's look at the major types in depth and see which of them best represent your type.

ARE YOU A HOUSEWIFE?

You're in luck if you're in this category. You're one of the most sought-after commercial types. Last year advertisers spent more than $60 billion promoting household products, and the projection for the coming years is even higher. What's more, the age range in this category, 18–40, is the broadest, and the degree of attractiveness most varied. You'll work.

Of course, you will have to meet general requirements. You must be average-looking—not too chic, not too glamorous or exotic-looking, but still have a little character. You must be the fashionable weight and height. You must be able to deliver lines. And you must look like the kitchen you're in is yours, the family you're concerned about, yours. In short, you must have the stamp and stature of a contemporary housewife.

To illustrate the possibilities within this category, below are typical casting calls (talent requests sent out by casting directors to agents). You will notice that references are sometimes made to current movie stars, a common practice in trying to describe a type.

We need someone around 30, pleasant, attractive—has one or two lines to deliver—should be believable.

We need someone around 20—should have a warm, teasing, human quality—be good with kids.

We need two housewives—to distinguish between them, we could have one Goldie Hawn type and the other a Marsha Mason type.

Sometimes the call really narrows the field. Here's one that recently went out on a Pride wax housewife commercial: "We need a young charactery woman—has to be able to move pretty well as she'll have to dance with a mop."

See the photo of Beverly Place, who was tapped by a research scout as an Ivory Soap user and good commercial prospect. Her most noticeable quality is a natural wholesomeness. You'd believe she could be your next-door neighbor, and you'd like it if she were.

ARE YOU THE YOUNG HUSBAND OR THE YOUNG FATHER TYPE?

A good representative of this type was the young Alan Alda, who, incidentally, started in commercials. In other words, to qualify in this category you should have a vulnerable look, with perhaps a slightly comic quality. You should be so warm, cute, and lovable, you could make a wife forgive you for sneaking a slice of her unfrosted cake, or cause your pregnant wife concern over your sympathetic labor pains. Good looks are also important, but you should not be too handsome—a smidgen of character is a big plus. Age range: 25–35. Height: 5'7"–6'1". Weight: average.

ARE YOU THE YOUNG WOMAN-NEXT-DOOR TYPE?

If just yesterday you were a cheerleader, you're probably perfect for this category. You would fit right into a fast-food or soft-drink commercial. You might play the part of a stewardess, bank teller, or woman on a date. The look here is young (18–25) and bouncy, very bouncy. Your look can be pretty to a little kookie, just so long as it's natural—hair natural, makeup natural. You're less glamorous than the cosmetic model; still, if you're a model, you might well fit in. No problem if you're under 5'7".

Important: If you can top all this with acting ability, you've got it made.

ARE YOU A COSMETIC MODEL?

This is one of the most difficult categories to cast, and therefore one of the best-paying. It's not unusual for models in New York and Los Angeles to make $2,000 a day. The stars make even more! When you consider that perfection is the major criterion, it's really not extravagant.

To get into this area, you must be extremely photogenic—have classically beautiful hair, eyes, nose, mouth, skin. Cheryl Tiegs, Christie Brinkley, Kelly Emberg, and Cristina Ferrare are prime examples. You must be able to relate to the camera—project energy, sex, excitement.

Near impossible? There's more. Often, you must fulfill specific product requirements. A Revlon commercial, for instance, calls for a sophisticated type, a Bonne Belle commercial for a wholesome type. To be a Clairol model, not only must you have beautiful, silky, thick hair, it must be a specific shade of dark blond or light brown. To do a Close-up commercial, not only must you have an enchanting smile, every tooth must be the exact same length and shade of white, and you must show a certain number of teeth. Believe me, perfect teeth are hard to find. While working on the Close-up account, I looked at so many teeth, I began to feel like a dentist.

If you have all this going for you, a couple of inches off in height (5'8") may be overlooked, but unfortunately that's about the only concession made in this category. Check the strict requirements below and see if you qualify. For your sake and for all of us casting directors who cast cosmetic commercials, I hope you do.

Hair: thick, shiny, contemporary length (better on the long side)

Eyes: large; thick lashes; light, medium color; well-delineated iris and pupil

Teeth: even, white (not gray or yellow), wide arch

Complexion: flawless

FASHION MODELS (MALE, FEMALE)

Jeans have made this category burst out at the seams, for men as well as women. Rear views, at least at this writing, are as prevalent on the tube as midafternoon reruns. Even the younger teen-age models have gotten into the act. The trendsetter, of course, has been Brooke Shields, who at age 15 stirred the fashion industry with her naughty but nice Calvin Klein commercial: "Wanna know what comes between me an' my Calvins? Nothing." She's now a celebrity in her own right and has just signed a million-dollar contract with Calvin Klein. With such a success story, naturally imitations abound (as do unplucked eyebrows), but, of course, there is only one Brooke Shields.

Generally, whatever your sex, you must be attractive, natural, healthy-looking, and move well to fit into this category. Your figure, as you might guess, is the key element. Females should be tall, slim, leggy, well proportioned. If you're short- or long-waisted, it could be a problem with some manufacturers. Male models should be slim with narrow hips. In either case, you should be able to step into a perfect size, without alterations. However, the product may call for variations in size—a particular jean style may require a narrower hip and wider waist.

SPECIFIC QUALIFICATIONS FOR MEN
- Model or macho man
- Age 20–30
- 6′
- Perfect 40R

SPECIFIC QUALIFICATIONS FOR WOMEN
- Under 30
- Over 5′7″
- Sizes 7, 8, 9, or possibly 10
- Measurements 34-24-34 (approx)

PLUS-12 SIZES

If you're not the ideal tall, slim model type, you have a better-than-ever chance to be a fashion model. Today the size 12-plus group makes up more than one-third of the population. As the manufacturer is naturally interested in reaching this market, the call for models in extra sizes has grown and keeps growing.

ARE YOU A GLAMOUR GAL?

You know whether this is your category. Your mirror and enough turned heads have told you so.

Although physical requirements for glamour gals are less rigid than for fashion or cosmetic models, the overall impact required is hard to measure up to. Advertisers look for a kind of stunning overall effect—full hair, a great smile, a pretty face, and a breathtaking figure. It doesn't matter whether you're a blonde, brunette, or redhead—what counts is your ability to project a sexy, intriguing, or mysterious quality.

Good examples of glamour-gal types are found in commercials aimed at men—ads for men's toiletries, automobiles, vacation or travel services, wines, beers, etc. As a glamour gal, you may or may not deliver a line, but if you do, it must stick. See the photograph of Erin Gray.

ARE YOU THE HANDSOME MAN TYPE?

You're in demand for all kinds of commercials if you're in this category. You're good-looking, macho, romantic, and quite sexy. If you're a male model type, you will appear in ads for men's toiletries and other male-oriented commercials. You will escort beautiful women in perfume commercials. If you're the perfect 40 R size used in catalog modeling (see chapter 16 for explanation), you may also do fashion commercials. If you're a more handsome, rugged type, you will probably appear as the dashing hero in women's-product commercials. In the latter case, your chances of winning a commercial are enhanced if you have athletic prowess—i.e., can ride a motorcycle, play tennis, dance expertly. In all cases, you must be at least 6′ tall. Tom Selleck, currently the lead in "Magnum P.I.," is a good example of this type. He recently starred in one of our Close-up commercials.

ARE YOU A CAREER WOMAN?

This category has "come a long way, baby." Today, more and more manufacturers and services are trying to woo this rapidly growing market.

To get a job as a TV career woman, you must meet a specific set of qualifications. You should be between 25 and 55, bright, down-to-earth, and project an image of energy, authority. Your look should be attractive, businesslike, not overly sexy or glamorous. And as this type is often a spokesperson or has dialogue, you should also be able to deliver lines.

ARE YOU A YOUNG MOTHER?

Are you pretty, natural-looking, slim, average height, age 18–34? Do you have a fresh, radiant look about you? Are you a *Redbook* mother? If so, you could answer this casting call.

Although the category is similar to the young housewife type, it usually calls for someone just a bit younger. Often commercials will have a 30-year-old mother give advice to a 22-year-old mother. However, with a new product, one that the older mother might not have heard about, the roles may well be reversed, with the young mother the informant.

In any event, both the young mothers are identifiable by a quality of softness. We think of white, pink, and blue when we see them, and we share their delight in recent motherhood.

ARE YOU ONE OF THE REAL PEOPLE?

Practically everybody but actors and models qualifies in this category. You don't have to be beautiful or handsome or come in a perfect size, shape, age, or even have much talent to fit into this category. All you need do is use the product or service advertised. Real people, plain and simple, are the consumer-at-large. As one of them, you are valuable to advertisers who are looking for people to make a personal statement about a product.

Sound easy? It is easier than most, but still there are some requirements. To find out if you're right, ask yourself these questions: Do I get so enthusiastic about a product that I want to pass the word around? Am I qualified to make a personal statement about the product? (Am I a housewife with a large family who really knows which laundry detergent gets out ground-in dirt, or do I suffer from an ailment like arthritis, and can I sincerely demonstrate how a pain reliever actually helps me lift a heavy skillet?)

Authenticity and sincerity are the key words in this category. The people chosen are those who inspire confidence, who are really themselves, down to their regional dialect.

ARE YOU A CHARACTER/COMEDIAN/ COMEDIENNE TYPE?

The broadest range of types falls under this heading. A casting call for a character can be for a young man with a funny look (something interesting or memorable) about him, or a woman whose look says "head nurse," or a Lily Tomlin type.

Character types in TV commercials are often defined by occupation. Here an actor or actress has a wide choice of roles. An actor who can play a construction worker can also be a stagehand or a moving man. An actress who can play a nightclub singer may also be a beautician or an astrologer. In all cases, the actor or actress must instantly put across the role he/she is playing.

Many character types fall into the more comic vein. Balding "Uncle Fred," nearsighted "Aunt Margaret," or gramps and grandma are examples of mildly comic characters. People who play these parts are usually physically distinguishable and expressive.

And then there are the much more broadly played comedic character parts. Nancy Walker is the perfect example of a diner waitress done with a great deal of fun.

Comedians like Rich Little (7-Up) and George Burns (Ray-O-Vac batteries) also come under this broad category. As their comic character personas are pronounced, they usually play themselves. Rarely is the average stand-up comedian used, as there is no time to do a routine.

All in all, if you strike people as funny, it's a pretty good clue that this is your category.

ARE YOU A SPOKESPERSON?

Although the character played by Charley Welch who drives the wagon in the Pepperidge Farm commercials qualifies as a spokesperson—that is, a representative who speaks for a company—I would like to focus on the more commonly used spokesperson: the person who could be an executive in the company.

To qualify in this category, you should be between the ages of 30 and 50, pleasant, attractive, successful-looking. If you're an actor or announcer, or fit into the career-woman category, you have a better chance of doing this kind of commercial.

Training is important, for you must have the authority to be the voice of the manufacturer. Your manner should be confident, self-possessed (most of the men have deep, strong voices). Your delivery should be intelligent, forceful, and objective. You should be able to convince the viewer of a product's efficiency, not simply by using it but by demonstrating its superiority. When you say "we," people should envision a whole company.

DO YOU HAVE THE VOICE TO DO TV VOICE-OVER OR RADIO COMMERCIALS?

Unseen performers make up this category. Representatives of this type are the sultry, insinuating voice over a cosmetic commercial; the brisk, authoritative voice over a corporation commercial; the announcer coming in on the tag end with a call to buy the product; and virtually every voice delivering a radio commercial.

It's obvious your voice is the herald of success in this area. If it's distinctive, if people often comment about what a beautiful voice you have, this might well be your niche. But don't be fooled—although it may seem the easiest of all categories, it's not. You must be able to speak as if to one person (the old-style pompous talking-at-you narrations are a thing of the past). You must be able to articulate well, be warm, friendly, convincing. It is really a fine craft. Many of the people who do this kind of commercial work have had years of radio experience or have had a great deal of voice and speech training.

As in the other categories, it's important that product and type (in this case your voice) should complement each other. For instance, the voice delivering a food commercial should sound appetizing. Ed Herlihy, who has done Kraft commercials for more than twenty years, can make one almost taste the food. By the same token, Joe Sirola for "I love New York" can make you want to pack your bags for the Big Apple immediately.

Some of the great voice-over actors, like Norman Rose, Alexander Scourby, and Joe Sirola, rarely appear in front of the camera, but they've made a lot of money just on their voices.

ARE YOU A CELEBRITY?

You don't have to be a Lauren Bacall, Michael Landon, or Muhammad Ali to be a TV-commercial celebrity. You needn't even have accomplished some spectacular feat such as climbing up the World Trade Center as George Willig did; nor do you have to be a Dallas cheerleader. Of course, such accomplishments do make you more interesting to an advertiser.

But the fact is, with cable, regional, or local television, there's room for many kinds of celebrities. Big fish in little ponds are also welcome. You may be one. Have you won a Queen of the Lilacs contest? Or are you the best logroller or the best arm-wrestler in your area? The possibilities are endless.

Whatever your claim to fame, you'll probably find the fringe benefits surprising. Doing a commercial is an excellent way to promote yourself, an invaluable way to make contacts for your career or avocation. And then there's the money you will receive for doing the commercial. Of course, the amount of publicity and how well you're known will determine how much. All in all, however, it's a profitable area to look into. Naturally, you will have to connect your area of prominence with a product. John McEnroe and Prince racquets, for example, were a natural.

ARE YOU A CELEBRITY LOOK-ALIKE OR SOUND-ALIKE?

Look-alikes need not be sound-alikes, although it helps if they are. Richard Mixon, who both looks and sounds like the former president, is a prime example of someone who has his subject down to a "let me say this about that." Still, it's enough to be just a look-alike (do commercials with no lines) or sound-alike (do voice-over only) to make it in this comparatively new field. In recent years, not only have look-alikes appeared in more and more TV commercials, they are much in demand for personal appearances at supermarket openings and such events. It's become such a popular area that Ron Smith, an agent who handles look-alikes exclusively, has offices on both coasts.

Of course, looking like someone is not enough. Celebrity look-alikes must mirror their subjects' mannerisms as skillfully as the famous impersonator Rich Little. Many of the look-alikes you see in TV commercials have spent a great deal of time and study perfecting their characters.

Topicality, of course, is important in this category. If you're a dead ringer for Fred Allen, it won't help you much, unless he has a revival. Of course, if you're the spittin' image of Ronald or Nancy Reagan, you've got it made—at least at this writing.

ARE YOU AN EXPERT?

Experts are often known only in their fields. For example, top winetaster Paul Henderson, who appears in the California Cellars Wine commercial, is hardly a household name; still, when he compares Taylor's Chablis with other wines, you believe he can judge the difference. Theoretically, this is true of any expert, whether a scientist, dog breeder, body builder, hairdresser, or teacher. Their authority comes through. It's the reason this type is so valuable to advertisers.

If you're interested in this category, don't let the word "expert" throw you. You don't have to be in the big leagues to qualify. It's enough to be known locally or in the trade. If you do something better than anyone else, have a special way of doing it, and have gained some fame, you're a candidate.

One more thing: Before you start making contacts (see chapter 9), think about tying in your expertise with a product. For example, at present I'm involved in casting a caterer who has used Lubriderm, a hand cream. Who can give a more convincing testimonial than a cook who washes her hands all day?

Note: Whatever your area of expertise, you must have tangible proof of your ability and skill—i.e., examples of your work, awards, or current publicity.

COULD YOU DO YOUR OWN COMMERCIAL?

You own your own company. You think, Nobody knows my product or could sell it better than I. You may be right. But there are a few small hitches. One, can you project your passion and knowledge? Two, can you do it and be yourself completely?

Actually, playing oneself is one of the hardest things for a performer to do. Actors and actresses are hired to appear in commercials because the average person is too self-conscious. Still, if you meet the tough requisites, if you're yourself to your gravelly voice or twinkly look, the rest almost magically falls into place. Tom Carvel, Frank Perdue, and Gloria Vanderbilt are living proof. If I had to cast the likes of them, I would be hard put. These people are unique.

One caution before you cast yourself in your own commercial: Even if you're sure you could tell your story honestly, or that you have what it takes to become another Lee Iacocca, Chairman of Chrysler Corporation, consult experts in the field first. Ask your advertising agency for its frank opinion. If they agree you can do it, be open to coaching. You'll find the rewards many. Your do-it-yourself commercial could help put you on a more personal basis with your customers—indeed, even make you something of a celebrity. It could pay off in more sales, and more personal satisfaction. What could be sweeter than approving a commercial you're in?

Final Typing Test

Okay, you're ready to go for it. You've read over the chapter and you have some idea of your type. Now it's time to commit yourself. The following quiz is designed to help you firm up your decision. Check boxes "yes" or "no" carefully.

ARE YOU:

The Housewife Type:	Yes	No
Are you between 18 and 40?	☐	☐
Are you average attractive-looking?	☐	☐
Do you have a warm, natural personality?	☐	☐
Are you average height and weight?	☐	☐

The Young Husband or Father Type:

	Yes	No
Are you between 25 and 35?	☐	☐
Are you vulnerable-appearing?	☐	☐
Are you nice-looking but with some character or comic quality?	☐	☐
Are you average height and weight?	☐	☐

Young Woman-Next-Door Type:

	Yes	No
Do you appear to be between 18 and 25?	☐	☐
Are you pretty in a natural way?	☐	☐
Do you have a bright, warm, enthusiastic quality?	☐	☐

The Cosmetic Model Type (Female):

	Yes	No
Do you have a flawless complexion?	☐	☐
Do you have large, well-fringed eyes?	☐	☐
Do people describe you as beautiful?	☐	☐
Do you have a small, perfect nose?	☐	☐

The Cosmetic Model Type (Male):

	Yes	No
Are you ruggedly handsome?	☐	☐
Do you have a strong jaw?	☐	☐
Do you have a good head of hair?	☐	☐
Do you have a good complexion?	☐	☐

The Fashion Model Type (Female):

	Yes	No
Are you at least 5'7"?	☐	☐
Can you fit perfectly into a size 8?	☐	☐
Do you have long, good legs?	☐	☐

The Fashion Model Type (Male):

Are you 6'–6'3"? □ □
Are you a perfect 40 R? □ □
Are you good-looking? □ □

The Glamour Type:

Are you at least 5'7"? □ □
Do you have a good figure and long legs? □ □
Do you have good, full hair? □ □
Do you draw wows or whistles from men? □ □

The Handsome Man Type:

Are you 6'? □ □
Are you a perfect 40 R? □ □
Are you described as handsome by your friends? □ □
Do you have a good hairline? □ □

The Young Mother Type:

Are you between 20 and 30? □ □
Do people describe you as lovely, soft, gentle? □ □
Do you have a good complexion? □ □
Do you have a slim figure? □ □

The "Real People" Type:

Are you average-looking? □ □
Are you verbal (willing to talk)? □ □
Are you convincing? Do people believe
what you say? □ □

The Character Type (Male):

Do people see you in a particular job or profession,
such as truck driver or doctor? □ □
Do you stand out in a crowd? □ □
Are you a good actor? □ □

Do you have a "great face"?   □   □

The Character Type (Female):

Do people see you in a particular job or profession,
such as waitress or stockbroker?   □   □
Are you a good actress?   □   □
Do people say you have an "interesting face"?   □   □

The Executive Type (Male):

Do you have a businesslike, attractive appearance?   □   □
Do you exude energy and serious intent?   □   □
Are you at least 5'9"?   □   □
Do you speak with a warm authority?   □   □

The Executive Type (Female):

Are you attractive in a businesslike way?   □   □
Do you have authority when you speak?   □   □
Are you between the ages of 28 and 60?   □   □
Are you well put together and well groomed?   □   □

The Spokesperson Type:

Do you have an executive look about you?   □   □
Can you convert people to your point of view?   □   □
Do you have a good speaking voice and diction?   □   □

The Celebrity Type:

Have you received publicity?   □   □
Are you outgoing?   □   □
Are you articulate?   □   □

An Expert:

Do you have skill or experience in a field?   □   □
Are you articulate?   □   □
Do you have proof of your expertise?   □   □

Have you won awards or do you have a title (e.g., Beekeeper of the Year)? ☐ ☐

Owner of Your Own Business:

Are you able to be yourself on camera without being self-conscious? ☐ ☐
Are you articulate? ☐ ☐
Do you have a definite personality? ☐ ☐

Celebrity Look-Alike:

Can you act exactly like the celebrity? ☐ ☐
Can you look precisely like the celebrity? ☐ ☐
Is the celebrity you look like well known or current? ☐ ☐

Note: Under each type, you must have checked "yes" to all questions to qualify. If you have any hesitation, any possible noes, any maybes, forget it, this category is not for you. If you are a candidate for more than one category, I advise that in the beginning you narrow it down to one type. As you gain experience, you can broaden your range.

3

Let's Take a Long Look

Hurray, another red-letter day, and just when I needed it.

That's what I thought recently when an actress walked into my office for a general interview. I had just received a rush call for her type, and here she was—a good career type: attractive, hair, skin, figure, everything perfect; and according to her résumé, she had a good acting background. It was as though the Big Casting Director in the Sky had sent her. True, she was a little bit too businesslike in her dress, but that could be easily fixed. I couldn't help smiling at my good fortune. She must have picked up my enthusiasm, for she smiled back—just as broadly. Let me tell you, my heart sank, for her smile left everything to be desired.

I'm afraid my disappointment was written all over my face, for the actress immediately confided, "The reason I would like to do commercials is because I have a big dentist bill coming up. I need to have my caps replaced. I was hoping I could do a commercial that didn't call for a real close-up."

As it happened, this commercial did call for a close-up. But even if it didn't, no one would have her on a set with that restriction.

Now, I would have loved to help her pay her dentist bill, but I couldn't even call her in on an audition. She was doing what many people who want to get into commercials do—jumping the gun. I think of the established actress who came in on a call for a cute young housewife—perfect, but ten pounds overweight. I think of the talented actor who came in for a clean-cut handsome-man role sporting a beard. They simply were not prepared. Result—they blew their chances.

I don't want that to happen to you. Making sure that it doesn't is what this chapter is about.

Wasting Your Chips

You have just so many chances—so many favors from people who know a casting director or agent, so many agencies with products that call for your type, so many connections that may lead to a job. A wasted interview or audition is just that. There are few second chances. Although an agent or casting director may see possibilities in you, there's always a little prejudice that lurks behind. There's too much competition in the business for second chances.

If I seem to be drumming it in, I am. If you're a housewife type who must lose ten pounds, lose them. If you need a better toupee, your hair styled, your makeup corrected, do it. If you're the middle-aged father type, but you prefer to sport long hair, a moustache and a beard, make a choice between your individuality and your career. If you're a beautiful teen-ager but you have bad skin, improve your complexion. Whatever improvements you need to make, start making them now.

More drumming in. Even after you're established, be sure you keep at the ready. First impressions count, but so does the next one—and the next one.

If it sounds demanding, it is. In the end you'll be contending with the hardest critic—the TV camera; nothing slips by it.

You're Not Alone

For the past several years, I've been teaching TV-commercial acting classes in New York City. It provides me with a personal view into the TV performer. I discover things I could never learn in a general interview or even working with performers. For one thing, I get an impression of how lonely the business can be. I also see how hard and demanding it is to look at yourself objectively. (For most people, looking at themselves in the way the TV camera demands, is—well—ego-deflating.) If you're inclined to put yourself down, you're in double trouble. From my side of the desk, I see many attractive, talented people give away their low self-esteem by a gesture, a mannerism, a remark.

So if you have qualms about studying yourself, be comforted. Most performers find it hard. I can only give you the same advice I give my students. Realize you're in a very personal profession. Try to stand outside yourself. Whether you're working in a play or doing a commercial, you're your own instrument, your own tool. Love the challenge. And above all, in trying to come up to standard, be gentle on yourself.

Keeping a Notebook—Here's Looking at You

By the time they come to my class, most performers have an idea of their types. Their main questions are: How do I perfect my type? How do I put myself together? What would I have to do for you to put me in a commercial?

The first thing I recommend is a notebook—a catchall, some sort of organizer to pull all endeavors together. Notebooks that are sectioned off with celluloid tabs are an orderly way to keep tabs on yourself.

Generally, I would recommend a section for Physical Analyses, one for Psychological Analyses, one for Regimens and Progress, one for Wardrobe, School, etc. You may also use your notebook to keep track of business expenses, appointments, etc. But for the purpose of this chapter, let's stick to the self-evaluation section. Following is a suggested way of setting it up, plus things to put in and paste in. One bit of advice: Don't go about it gung-ho. Fill in things as you go along. Make it fun as well as insightful.

UNDER PHYSICAL ANALYSES

Paste in an instant photo of yourself.

Write in physical data—height, weight, color of hair, eyes, etc.

Write in comments people make about you—e.g., "If I had your figure, I could wear rags."

Write in areas you need to work on—thighs, tummy, skin, legs.

Paste in magazine ads of people who are your type.

Write in any action that needs to be taken—weight loss, posture improvement, etc.

UNDER REGIMENS AND PROGRESS

Write in or paste in beauty programs.

Write in or paste in exercise programs.

Write in or paste in skin-care treatments.

Write in or paste in diets.

Write in or paste in facial exercises.

Write in or paste in makeup hints.

Paste in pictures of you wearing makeup.

Write in *under each program* a place to check if you did exercises, etc.

Write in areas where you need to take action.

UNDER PSYCHOLOGICAL ANALYSES

Write in how other people describe you—e.g., "You're so convincing, you could sell a kid artichokes."

Write a 100-word description of your personality as you see it.

Write in attitudes and fears.

Write in assets—optimism, warmth, outgoingness, initiative.

Write in liabilities—timidity, touchiness, procrastination, low self-esteem.

Write in ways to take action; express yourself more with people; catch "down" moods.

Write in dialogues with people you meet and know—it's a good way to get in touch with your feelings.

UNDER WARDROBE

Write in clothes you will need for your type.

Paste in pictures of people who are your type—emphasis on clothes.

Write in acquisitions as you make them.

Paste in pictures of yourself in various clothes; include the rear view.

UNDER SCHOOLS AND CRAFT

Write in classes you need to take.

Paste in articles about people with whom you may want to study.

Write in lessons that are pertinent to you—e.g., speech tips, acting-class notes.

Write in actions you need to take.

Note: Chapter 4, "Playing Pygmalion to Yourself," tells where and how to find specific beauty, wardrobe, and school information.

Mirrors, Mirrors, Everywhere

Most of us use just a few mirrors around the house—the bathroom mirror, the dressing-table mirror, and possibly a full-length mirror. When we look at them we tend to pose (it's only human). We compose our faces, straighten our posture. By doing this, we get a very limited and static view of ourselves.

That may be okay for others, but not for you. That's why I suggest that you, as a TV performer or would-be one, put mirrors around the house. It can really be a constant course in self-awareness. You get to see how you appear to others, in interviews, in auditions. And most important, you get to see how the TV camera will pick you up. You get to see yourself in motion.

WHERE TO PLACE YOUR MIRRORS

First of all, place a mirror near your phone so you can observe yourself as you talk and laugh and commiserate with your friends. Observe how you act and react. When you laugh, do your teeth hang out too much or do your gums show? No one ever tells us these things (except our kids), so we don't usually know.

As so many commercials are for food, place another mirror in a spot where you can study your eating style; notice if you slump over or chew in an unattractive manner.

Place a mirror in a spot where you can watch yourself as you stand up, sit down, walk—the living room, maybe.

If you don't have a full-length mirror, invest in one. Place it on the inside of your front door so you can check your entire appearance when you go out.

Set up two mirrors to check your rear view. Place one in front, one behind. Your rear view, after all, is the way you are observed leaving offices and audition rooms.

The Initial Appraisal

You'll need just one full-length mirror for this first and most important self-observation. But before you start, be sure to take an unprepared look at yourself—that is, wear the clothes you usually wear, stay with your usual hairstyle, etc.

Once in front of the mirror, view yourself with as much candidness and objectivity as you can. Take in your entire physical person, up and down, sideways and back. Ask yourself such questions as, Do I slouch? Am I stiff? Is my hair attractively styled? Do my ears protrude? Try to look at yourself as though you were facing another person in the mirror.

When you're finished, sit down and write a 100-word description of yourself. Please don't forget to mention good points.

Involving Others

In the classes I teach, I am often amazed at how people do not see themselves. I hear comments like "I didn't know I scowled when I thought." "You're right, I do purse my lips." Actually, probably better than any mirror are the eyes of honest friends. That's why I'm all for involving others in your self-discovery and -improvement program. For instance, when you finish your essay on yourself, read it to friends, ask their opinions.

If you have a friend who is a photographer, work with him or her. You'll both benefit. Go to a local park for outdoor, full-length shots and work indoors for beauty and close-up shots. If you don't know a photographer, ask your family and friends to act as your photographer. When the pictures are developed, study them together. Ask for criticism. Stick pictures on appropriate mirrors so you can check your progress.

If you have videotape equipment, study your performances with your friends and ask advice. If you have a friend who's in the business, all the better. The same goes for voice taping. Ask a friend to listen objectively to your recordings and to help you evaluate your speech. Of course, professional advice is better. In the next chapter, under "Schools," I will go into the advantages of having trained critics, as well as where to find them.

"I Don't Need It—I've Made It"

Most of the above are first steps designed to help you realize your type and eventually to get you an interview, an audition, and finally a commercial. But such self-analysis, believe me, is not just for beginners. I find many established people grow sloppy with success.

Many actors and actresses come for auditions wearing jeans and a T-shirt. I have seen top models and actresses come in with curlers, or with their hair pulled back with a rubber band, or with no makeup. They feel that the interviewers know they can act, are aware of film technique, and can envision them with correct makeup, hair, and wardrobe. Some actors and actresses actually feel a certain pride and prestige in coming in as if they just threw themselves together. It's a theatrical concept that has traveled to commercials. The trouble is, it doesn't work in commercials.

What They See Is What They Buy

As a candidate for a commercial, you will be dealing with people who are not from the theater, people who do not have a photographer's eye. Account people and clients are business people. They often do not have the imagination and training to envision you as a type. Many are men, and they don't understand what makeup and hair and wardrobe can do. You can't hope that they'll say, "Oh, with a little eyeliner ... "

I'll go through the trouble of fluffing out actresses' and models' hair, or I'll ask them to go to the ladies' room and comb their hair or put on makeup. I've done this frantically, at the last minute, for I've seen them on other commercials, in theater, over a period and know their possibilities. But you can't count on a casting director to run out to the elevator as I've sometimes done, drag you into the ladies' room, and have you do your hair or makeup.

> REFRAIN: In TV commercials, you simply have to look the part at all times—at the general interview, at the audition, on the set.

Remember, commercials deal in types, and the people who judge you are looking for performers to represent a type. I've had account men come to me at a shooting and say, "Gee, she didn't look like that at the audition. We saw her as a housewife. We didn't expect her to be that glamorous."

Repeat Refrain.

A Taste of My Own Advice

While writing this chapter, I happened to catch a look at myself in the mirror. "Look at you, Vangie," I said to myself, "you, so full of preachy advice. You could do with some shaping up yourself."

I agreed with myself and went to work. And I actually followed my own advice. I put a few extra mirrors around the house to check my mannerisms and posture. I listened carefully to my voice in the tapes I made writing this chapter.

One notebook for self-appraisal, dozens of beauty and dieting books, and several containers of makeup later, I discovered that self-evaluation is only half the battle. Finding the right diet, makeup, and Yoga classes is both time- and money-consuming. But all my effort has been worth it, I believe. If nothing else, it prepared me to write the next chapter.

4

Playing Pygmalion to Yourself

Last seen (in the previous chapter), you were looking in mirrors, observing and analyzing yourself—your face, your figure, your posture, your mannerisms. Now you're ready to take the image that looked back at you and transform it into an attractive version of your commercial type.

In this chapter, you'll find the hairstyles, makeup, and wardrobe appropriate for your type, and hints on how to individualize them. If you need spurring on to diet and exercise (who doesn't?), I've included reasons why you should keep at the ready for interviews and auditions at all times—why you should look like you just walked out of a commercial even when picking up your mail.

Fortunately, for actors, our culture today does not have taboos about men using hair and skin-care products. The market is replete with cosmetic lines for men only. Hairstylists have taken over what was once the barber's domain.

Now, before I go into specific ways to prepare, let's talk money.

Investing in Yourself

There's no question you'll have to untie the purse strings; getting your act together takes bucks. But that doesn't mean you have to go broke. Not if you follow my one rule: Stint wherever you can.

A paperback beauty book these days can cost as much as $12.95. Use the library. Browse in bookstores (see the list of beauty books at end of chapter). Get free beauty consultations at department stores. Look up low-cost dental work. Check the yellow pages for beauty schools that do hair inexpensively (see section on hair). Shop for clothes at low-cost name-brand stores. Look for mirror sales or go to auctions. These are just a few suggestions. Now, let's search out the classic look for your type.

Styles for Women

Is your hairstyle right for your type? Although it's common sense that a housewife doesn't go around with hair so long she could mop the floor with it, you'd be surprised how an actress uncertain of her type can throw the desired look off.

To start with, I suggest you look at TV and magazine ads for hairstyles worn by your type. Find the one that most flatters your face and features and go with it.

If you're a model or a comedienne, you'll abide by a different set of rules, but the general rules for hairstyles worn in commercials are the same.

The hairstyle must be in fashion, but on the conservative side. An easy wash-and-wear style that's ready to go on interviews and auditions at the drop of your phone receiver is ideal.

Unless you're under twenty or a model, your hair should not fall much below your shoulders. From tip of earlobe to shoulder is the rule. It is better to err slightly on the longer side, because if it's a good commercial, you'll be willing to cut it. Besides, you can vary your style—pull it back, wear it up, or let it hang loose.

In sum, no matter which hairstyle you choose, a good hair stylist is a must. He has the scissor wizardry to cut your hair to type and to cut it so it keeps its style washing after washing. Do bring magazine pictures of styles worn by your commercial type to your appointment with him.

Money-saving tip: If you can't afford a stylist, there are beauty schools that will work with you.

Caution: Be sure operator will listen to your needs and not just thrust a hairstyle on you. Be doubly sure to bring along pictures so you can guide him or her. Manufacturers of hair products, Clairol for one, have beauty clinics. That's not a bad way in. They just may send you on to their advertising agency.

If you have fine, thin hair that tends to go limp, get a body perm. Don't get into the hands of someone who'll give you a tight, stand-up-on-end perm. Remember, you want something soft that will hold your style from first audition in the morning to end of day.

SHOULD YOU OR SHOULDN'T YOU?

Only a TV camera knows for sure what kind of hair coloring you should use for commercials.

On the whole, a natural shade of medium blond to light brown photographs best. Also, TV cameras have no prejudice about gray; it photographs as well as does a dark blond. But if you decide to cover your gray, stick as close to your natural shade as possible or go lighter.

As a rule, you'll do well to stay away from extremes, especially very light platinum or black black. Jet-black hair is plain unphotogenic. It abhors light, and without highlighting, it can look like a dark blob.

Leslie Blanchard, author of *The Hair Coloring Book,* suggests frosting or streaking to give your hair an overall lighter look without having to do the whole head. But whatever hair coloring or method you choose, avoid dark roots—the camera will spot them quicker than another woman.

Hairstyles for Men

The same goes for men's hair as it does for women—a good hair stylist is as important as a good agent.

I know one actor who went from bartender extra to leading man merely by having his hair lightened and straightened. He resigned himself to having a standing appointment for this rather expensive process, but it paid off.

Even if you have great hair, don't bypass a hair stylist. He or she can teach you how to use a dryer, blower, how to brush your hair, how to give your hair height. When you go, do bring along pictures of hairstyles appropriate for you and your type. In general, spokesmen or mature men wear their hair shorter. Check *GQ*, *Esquire*, the *New York Times*, fashion magazines.

One more thing: If you shampoo every time you shower, macho man or not, be sure your shampoo is gentle.

HAIRPIECES

If you need a hairpiece, you should invest in a good one that matches your own hair. In bright sunlight, a poor match is instantly detected by the camera. I speak from experience. We recently nearly had to scrap a commercial because the camera told the tale. Unfortunately, we had to edit out some otherwise excellent close-ups.

BEARDS

While a beard may flatter you, it definitely limits the roles you can play. Bearded scientists, lumbermen, professors are usual, but as yet I haven't had a call for a bearded young father.

MOUSTACHES

Model types and sometimes young father/husband types can sport a moustache. However, as moustaches tend to go in and out of style, make sure you're "with it."

Hair Conditioning for Men and Women

Keep your hair just-shampooed clean at all times. As most commercials are shot in the city, you'll have to cope with oily dirt that may require daily washing. Luckily, today, gentle shampoos line store shelves. Use conditioners once a week to keep your hair looking alive and lustrous.

Maintenance is extremely important. Beverly Ballard, who I've had in on hundreds of commercials, has never once appeared at an audition with her hair less than perfectly groomed.

Cosmetics—The Tools of Your Trade

Of course your skin should be in good condition for interviews. A bump or blemish calls attention to itself—and even if it doesn't, you think it does.

Your skin should also be in good condition for auditions and shoots. True, clever lighting can wash out lines and skin blemishes, but raised bumps cause uncorrectable shadows. The client does not want to suggest in any way that using his product may make your skin break out.

Pure and simple, bad skin can eliminate you from the whole show and shebang. So make friends with a dermatologist. Any sudden skin problems, he's there to advise and treat you.

On your own, be as ritualistic as possible in keeping your skin in good condition. Develop a cleansing and conditioning routine and stick to it. This may involve a daily routine as well as a weekly facial. Naturally, if facials tend to make your skin break out, you'll avoid them before photography sessions, interviews, auditions, and shoots.

One more rule—and for some of you the one most difficult to keep: When you go on location or holiday, avoid the sun. A tan or burn presents all sorts of makeup and camera problems.

Note: If you're a cosmetic model, your skin must be flawless—

no enlarged pores, no broken blood vessels; even coloring over the entire face.

Makeup for Women

I never see such a look of terror on a face as when an actress (sans makeup) comes in on an interview and I say, "Okay, let's go next door and I'll put you on tape." "On tape!" she usually screeches. "I don't have my makeup on!"

Please save yourself the trauma and me the time (if indeed I have the time) while you go off to the ladies' room to put your face on—wear your makeup to all interviews and auditions. (Shoots are exceptions. There will be a professional makeup person on the set.)

That settled, you'll want to know what makeup to use and how to make up for the camera. Quite simply, wear makeup that's flattering yet natural-looking. Let me emphasize *natural-looking.* The camera exaggerates. You'll want to highlight, but not too much.

Chances are your present dressed-up daytime makeup does the trick, but let me give you some precise guidelines so you'll be sure. Let's take eye makeup. Use just enough to take you to your natural best look. Be especially careful of eyeliner on the lower lid. It can give you a hard look, especially if it's a dark solid line. Use your blusher timidly to give yourself just a touch of glow. Use a base that will even out your skin, cover blemishes, sallowness, and discolorations, but shun corrective makeup that's visible.

If you have any doubts, read every makeup book you can get your hands on. And do take advantage of every free makeup consultation at department and cosmetic stores. Don't be afraid to ask questions. "You mean I should shade here under the jawline?"

Once you've got a consensus (important before you buy one item) and from it developed a makeup for yourself, become adept at applying it smoothly. Practice retouching without ruining the initial effect. Interviews and auditions are anxiety-causing enough without having to redo your whole face. Practice contouring so that with a few deft strokes of the magic blusher you can do such things as accent your good bones and brighten your eyes.

When you've mastered the art, put together a makeup kit. Look over those items you might want to carry with you to freshen up before interviews and auditions—e.g., blusher, eye shadow, creams, and powder. Buy duplicates (small-size bottles and tubes) and pack them in a waterproof makeup kit.

Facial Care for Actors

As a TV performer, you'll need more than your lone bath bar to take care of your skin.

Cleansing lotions are an economical buy. They serve a dual purpose: They gently cleanse your skin (unlike soap, they do not disturb skin's natural acidity) and, because they contain toners (astringent), they tighten and freshen your skin.

Facial scrubs thoroughly clean your skin and are also good for dislodging ingrown hairs.

Use a moisturizer daily. They contain emollients to keep your skin soft and smooth.

An item to avoid: too much sun.

Your Basic Professional Wardrobe, Men and Women

You'll wear the clothes you select for your professional wardrobe when you have your picture taken. You'll wear them for general interviews. You'll wear them for auditions. Sometimes you'll wear your own clothes in commercials. There's no doubt your wardrobe is a key part of your investment. You must rely on it to get your type across.

I suggest you start your shopping by looking at TV commercials. Look for the clothes your commercial type wears. You'll notice that housewives usually wear skirts or slacks, blouses, sometimes sweaters. Young husbands usually wear plaid shirts and slacks or jeans. (See list below.)

Newspaper and magazine ads are another good source of ideas.

Cut out the fashions worn by your type and paste them in your notebook.

START WITH WHAT'S AT HAND

Chances are you already dress as your type. So open your closet and pull out those clothes you wear the most. Avoid the ones in the back—you've probably already rejected them.

Try on your favorites in front of a full-length mirror. If you've rigged up a two-sided mirror, all the better. Put aside those clothes that fill the bill. When you go shopping (chances are you'll have to do some extra buying), see if you can find duplicates.

Elaine Mangel, stylist for Bean-Kahn, top commercial film house, is very happy (why not, it's less work) when the director or producer says, "What he wore at the audition is just fine for the shoot."

For auditions she suggests the following basic wardrobe you will need for your type:

Housewife	Skirts; slacks; jeans; blouses; shirts; sweaters; jackets.
Young Husband or Father Type	Plaid shirts; slacks; jeans; sweaters; sports jacket; casual jacket.
Model (Female) Fashion and Glamour Types	Trendy casual clothes; while avoiding extremes, they should have a fashion flair.
Model (Male) Fashion or Handsome Man Types	Casual slacks, shirts, sweaters, sports jacket, but with a definite fashion look. If you have black tie, it can definitely help, although you don't have to wear it to the audition.
Young Mother Type	Same as housewife. In addition, a soft-looking cotton dress or blouse with perhaps a ruffle near neck.
Real People Type	You're probably wearing it. Check the type you fit into.

Character Type (Male)	Generally same as young husband, with the addition of a denim work shirt. For audition, call ahead to find part you're auditioning for—blue-collar worker, store clerk, etc.
Character Type (Female)	Generally same as housewife. Call ahead and try to get some detailed information and modify your audition outfit accordingly.
Executive Type (Female)	A suit with blouses; or classic skirt, blouses, and jacket. Minimum jewelry. An overall neat, tailored look.
Executive Type (Male)	Business suit, shirt, tie. Definitely on the conservative side.
Spokesperson	Well-fitted blazer or sports jacket, gray slacks. Conservative business suit, shirt, and tie.
Celebrities and Experts	You'll need your "meet the public" outfits. Don't suddenly dress differently than you would for such occasions.

A UNIFORM THAT'S NOT A UNIFORM

Of course, there are thousands of variations within a type. Even if you're a spokesman, the shirt and tie, blazer, and gray pants you choose will have the stamp of your individual taste. Following are some simple rules to follow in making your selections.

Style	Clothes should be simple. For women, no fussy bows around the neck.
Color	Unless you're a high-fashion model, your best bet is conservative colors, medium to light—not too dark, not too light. For men, beiges, brown, blues are best. For women, light blues and beiges. Avoid camera-hogging plaid, polka dots, reds, strong whites, or blacks. Men, watch your ties; on camera, some designs attract attention away from your face.
Fit	Clothes should be comfortable to move in, and not too revealing. If you keep pulling your skirt down

because you're afraid too much leg is showing, or keep your hands folded over a button threatening to pop, it's bound to distract your interviewer's attention as well as yours.

Quantity

Once you find a style that becomes you and is your type, be sure to buy a similar one. You'll need at least two appropriate outfits for interviews. If one is at the cleaners, or you spill something at the last minute, you have a reserve.

Maintenance

Once you've selected your outfit, always keep it cleaned, pressed, and at the ready. Remember, you may have just one hour's notice to go on an audition. If you can't afford to wear these articles of clothing on an everyday basis, keep them hanging in your wardrobe where they're easily accessible. You'll probably get plenty of wear out of them simply making the rounds and, hopefully, going on auditions and shootings.

Diet and Exercise

The TV camera is fattening. It flattens your image out and adds at least eight pounds. It's also prone to exaggerating bulges, tension lines, poor posture.

I don't particularly care how you go about dieting as long as you get your daily requirements. The only thing I would love is that if you lose any weight, you stay at that weight. It's very difficult when I call someone three months after an interview and discover he's gained or lost twenty pounds. People do it. I went out to the Coast one time for a shoot and found that the gal I'd interviewed six weeks earlier had gained about ten pounds. It ruined the whole shoot; instead of being a young mother, she looked more like a middle-aged housewife.

KEEPING FIT

I plead with you to keep fit. Being a TV performer requires a lot of stamina. Some days you have to run all over town on auditions. Sometimes on a shoot you have to stand the entire day from 8:30 to 5:30 (particularly if you're a spokesperson). Sometimes in a commercial you're required to do some jogging or dancing. Even on an ordinary shoot you'll hear, "Take twenty-five. Can we get up from the table and walk to the right of the stove once more, please." A little tiring! Even without the extra stresses and the business demands, you need to exercise to look your best—eyes and skin clear; body firm and straight. Now, God knows, there are enough regimens. Follow the one that suits you. And remember to get regular checkups.

You're a Public Person Now

Once you've got your act together and you're ready to go, you'll find that outside your front door you're not a private person anymore. So even if you still need an American Express card to identify you, don't leave home without your best look. "But," you say, "who sees me around the neighborhood?" People in the business, that's who. Don't expect they won't recognize you under your headful of curlers or, if you're a guy, under your day's growth.

If you're in midtown New York particularly, look neat. You're almost certain to encounter people in the business. If you're in L.A., don't go shopping looking like the cat dragged you out. Eventually, you're bound to run into a director, cameraman, art director, etc., who might someday be in a position to hire you. In case you think I'm being extreme, let this true story bear me out.

While flying out to the Coast recently, I was going through my *Academy Players Directory,* doing some preliminary casting, when I discovered I was not alone in my search. When I first wrote down a name, the man seated next to me said, "Oh, he didn't look so good the other day. Of course, he wasn't shaved and was wearing a bathrobe." As I wrote down more names, he would make comments in like manner. "Yeah, I saw him on a 'Magnum P.I.' the other night. He has improved."

Intrigued by his comments, I began to ask him various questions about people. What about so-and-so? "I haven't seen him for a while," he would say, or "The residual checks are coming in pretty good."

From the comments he made, I thought he must be an agent. No, maybe a manager, I thought, recalling the actor with the bathrobe. It is not unusual on the Coast to have breakfast meetings, and maybe he was with his client.

When he commented that one of my entries had moved to Beverly Hills, I figured whoever this man was, he knew the intimate details of a lot of actors' lives, so he must be very close to them.

Finally, at the end of the trip, my curiosity at a peak, I asked him if he was an agent. "No," he answered, "I'm just flying back from Arizona. I'm with the postal service." But of course, I realized, he was a mailman.

The commercial, in the end, was cast by a mailman. Incidentally, it turned out first-class.

You don't know how many times I've been at the Beverly Hills Hotel Beauty Shop and heard gossip about various people. This one's hair is overdyed and falling out—the other one's beginning to show her age.

Moral: Always look your best—you're on even when you're not.

BOOKS

Avon. *Looking Good, Feeling Beautiful: The Avon Book of Beauty.* New York: Simon & Schuster, 1982.

Arpel, Adrien, and Ebenstein, Ronnie S. *Adrien Arpel 3-Week Makeover Shapeover Beauty Book.* New York: Simon & Schuster, 1979.

Bandy, Way. *Styling Your Face.* New York: Random House, 1981.

Blanchard, Leslie, with Zack Hanle. *Leslie Blanchard's Hair-Coloring Book.* New York: Doubleday, 1982.

Clark, Linda A. *Secrets of Health and Beauty: How to Make Yourself Over.* Old Greenwich, Conn.: Devin-Adair, 1969.

Fonda, Jane. *Jane Fonda's Workout Book.* New York: Simon & Schuster, 1981.

Ford, Eileen. *A More Beautiful You in 21 Days.* New York: Simon & Schuster, 1972.

Glamour Magazine. *Glamour Beauty Book.* New York: Simon & Schuster, 1972.

Gross, Joy. *30 Days to a Born-Again Body.* New York: Berkley, 1978.

Jackson, Carole. *Color Me Beautiful.* New York: Ballantine, 1981.

Klein, Arnold W. *The Skin Book: Looking and Feeling Your Best Through Proper Skin Care.* New York: Macmillan, 1981.

Manzoni, Pablo. *Instant Beauty.* New York: Simon & Schuster, 1979.

Millkie, Ron, and Carlson, Rey. *You Don't Have to Be Beautiful to Be a Model.* New York: Pilot Books, 1978.

Rose, Linda. *Hands.* New York: Simon & Schuster, 1980.

Sassoon, Beverly. *Beauty for Always.* New York: Avon, 1982.

Scavullo, Francesco. *Women.* New York: Harper & Row, 1982.

Queenly, Sharon. *Revlon Art of Beauty.* New York: Doubleday, 1982.

Shorell, Irma, and David, Julie. *A Lifetime of Skin Beauty.* New York: Simon & Schuster, 1982.

Struthers, Sally et al. *Sally Struthers' Natural Beauty Book.* New York: Doubleday, 1979.

Tiegs, Cheryl. *The Way to Natural Beauty.* New York: Simon & Schuster, 1980.

Traynor, Mark. *Mark Traynor's Guide to Professional Makeup Techniques.* New York: Keystone, 1974.

Von Furstenberg, Diane. *Von Furstenberg's Book of Beauty.* New York: Simon & Schuster, 1979.

Zebroff, Kareen. *Beauty Through Yoga.* New York: Arco, 1980.

Stevens, Mark. *Model.* New York: Harper & Row, 1981.

Powlis, LaVerne. *The Black Woman's Beautv Book: A Complete Guide to Great Looks.* New York: Doubleday, 1979.

Since you're interested in doing commercials, you probably have a head start on all of the above. But there's one more area you must work on (if you're not doing it already): It's the subject of the next chapter—"Learning Your Craft."

5

Learning Your Craft

"A commercial," you say. "Who has to learn how to do one of those?"

You do.

"Okay, maybe," you say, "but certainly anyone who's performed in the theater doesn't have to learn anything."

Not so.

The fact is, no matter where you're coming from, if you want to do commercials, you're going to have to learn how to act on camera and how to deliver lines. And you're going to have to learn to do both within definite confines. For simple as it may seem, doing a commercial is a craft quite apart from any other form of acting. There's a special technique to delivering a compelling sales message that will come across on a small screen in thirty seconds.

If you're thinking, There she goes again, being a perfectionist, let me tell you the good part. Anyone can do it; it's not that hard.

A Way for Everyone

As I see it, people who are interested in doing commercials fall into three categories:

1. Professional theater, TV, and movie actors and actresses
2. Aspiring TV-commercial performers
3. People who want to do just one commercial

People in different categories need different advice. But let's start out with advice that's important to you no matter what stage you're in.

Stand Up and Say, "I Am a TV-Commercial Performer"

Come a new semester, I go around the room and ask my students about themselves. It's one of my first class exercises and I consider it their first performance.

I listen especially for how they identify themselves, how they talk about their goals. It's amazing but I've gone through a room of forty people and only one person said, "I'm an actor."

I would understand such modesty if I taught beginners, but most of my students have experience; some a great deal of experience. Still, they not only are hesitant about saying they're actors or actresses, but when we discuss goals, they say, "I *think* I would like to go into commercials." (My emphasis.)

It's true you must earn your right to say you're a TV performer. But even if you're a beginner, you should be able to say, "I want to get into commercials" or "I want to do a commercial." You earned your right to make the statement the moment you took steps to identify your type. Gail Sheehy, in her recent book, *Pathfinders,* writes: "People who set goals get there faster." I concur. So before you do anything else, I suggest you start on your first performance and say loud and clear, "I am a TV-commercial performer." Write it down and put it on your mirror.

Becoming Aware of Commercials

The first step for anyone interested in doing commercials is to plant yourself in front of the tube and watch critically:

Notice the different kinds of commercials:

The Spokesperson	(actor is the representative of the manufacturer)
Slice of Life	(realistic minidrama with a beginning, middle, and end)
Testimonials	(real people telling of their experiences using products)
Vignettes	(usually made up of quick scenes, different types of people each saying one line)

Notice also the commercials that use your type. For instance, if you're a housewife type, you'll fit into the slice-of-life commercial. If you're a certain character type, you'll probably be in one of the vignettes.

Notice how the commercials are set up. Do they have problems and solutions? Who presents the problem? Who presents the solution? Notice how quickly the solver recognizes, sympathizes with, and then solves the problem.

Notice the degrees of enthusiasm in different commercials. Fast foods lead the way in hyperenthusiasm. Notice the low-key tone of a corporate commercial for an oil company.

Notice how much actors look into the lens or look at each other. In taping auditions, casting directors will help you with where to look, but if you make their jobs easy for them by already knowing, they will have to be impressed.

How to Make Up Commercials

After you've watched hundreds of commercials, you'll want to make up commercials and practice them.

To start with, recall the times you told a girlfriend about a lipstick, or, if you're a guy, the time you told a friend about a beer or whatever interests you. Recall the points you made, how you tried to get them across, how you showed your enthusiasm. Become aware of everyday commercial situations—how a salesperson sells a product to you, how you react when someone starts raving about a product. Notice what your feelings are, what your attitude is toward the person.

If you can find friends or family to do situation commercials with you, good. If not, deliver commercials before a mirror. Mark off a four-inch circle to represent the camera lens and keep your eyes on it so you will get used to looking at a camera lens.

If you can't make up commercials yourself, use the sample commercials included on pages 157–66. Tape-record commercials from your radio and television set, type them up, and record them yourself. This will give you a basis for comparing your version with the "on-air" version.

Schooling for Beginners

Developing a character is not a task for the beginner. Learning to be yourself is. For that reason I recommend you start with an improvisational class.

As you've probably observed in watching commercials, the basis of all acting in commercials is naturalness. The ambience of commercials is one of intimacy.

An improvisational class will teach you to get in touch with your feelings and express your spontaneous attitudes—the hardest thing in the world for an actor or actress to do. You'll learn how to act in a situation and how to react. You'll begin to study the rudiments of relationships, begin to learn how to take an action, how to affect the other person, what your objective is in a scene. These are all essential in the thirty-second minidrama you will appear in. I'd go so far as to say that even if you've had schooling, it's incomplete without a course in improvisational acting.

TV-Commercial Classes

TV-commercial classes are ideal once you've got your basic acting technique. This is the type of class I teach, as do many other professional casting directors. I personally feel that classes taught by people in the field are better than those given at universities.

In these classes you'll learn TV and film techniques. In my opinion, the best part of the class is seeing yourself on camera. By observing your mannerisms—how you move and how you sound—you'll learn how you come across. You'll also learn the subtleties of working with a camera, and how to work within its confines. One thing you must learn is that while the same basic acting skills are employed in theater and film, there are big differences in techniques. In TV, actions and reactions are compressed into a few seconds. The camera magnifies movements and emotional responses. You cannot get away with the broad gestures that work in the theater.

CLASSES AS PLACES FOR CONTACTS

Many actors and actresses come to this kind of class solely to meet casting directors. This is especially good for professional actors and actresses coming from one city to another.

All in all, I'd say if you don't have some acting background, stay away. Too frequently, people come into my class who have no training whatsoever. They have basic speech defects or they're overly self-conscious. I can't do anything for them. If you're not ready, the casting director may think of you as being unqualified—and that's a hard impression to turn about. So if you need work, start with the basics.

Special Advice for Real People, or People Who Want to Do Just One Commercial

You certainly don't need to go to the Royal Academy to deliver a testimonial for an arthritis pain-killer, nor for that matter do you have to take speech lessons or even worry particularly about how you sound. After all, the reason you're valuable to a sponsor is your naturalness. But you do want to show up at your best when your chance to do a commercial comes around. Therefore, I suggest you do everything you can to see yourself on camera. Get on game shows. Seek out friends with videotape or home movie cameras.

Opportunities abound. Recently Yoplait yogurt set up taping equipment in malls and other public places around the country. As part of their promotion, they put ads in local newspapers inviting people to taste their yogurt and comment on it in French or a reasonable facsimile. This is only one example of your chances to do a commercial or at least to see yourself on videotape.

If you're like many people, once you get the bug, once you're selected for a commercial, you may like the experience so much, you'll want to do more. You'll want to learn your craft.

More Classes

Most professional actors or actresses constantly work at self-improvement. They take classes to develop their physical awareness and to broaden their physical ability.

As you cannot take all the classes that might benefit you, I recommend you concentrate on the simple, basic ones. Either a good dance or exercise class will help make you conscious of your posture, help strengthen your muscles, help you to move easily. Later you can go on to more exotic things like karate, fencing, or mime. Happily, improving yourself is a lifelong project, and every step can be rewarding.

SOME RULES BEFORE YOU SIGN UP
- Keep away from any school that won't allow you to audit classes.
- Be sure the school's methods are contemporary.
- Beware of any acting school that believes in imitation rather than working from yourself.

- Don't take any television-commercial class that doesn't have color videotape equipment.
- Find out if the teachers have worked in casting, acting, and make sure they are successful in their fields.
- Talk to people who have taken the class.
- Be sure the school is licensed and accredited. (The schools in the Los Angeles area are now being accredited by the state to ensure their validity and effectiveness.)
- Be sure the school does not involve too much of a sacrifice. Check into how payments are made—you should not have to pay the entire amount up front if it's a very large sum.

How to Find the Best School Near You

It would be impossible for me to list all the schools throughout the country, and even if I did, I believe there's no better advertisement for them than word of mouth. Ask fellow actors and actresses where they studied and which classes seemed to do them the most good. Inquire with the Screen Actors Guild in your area for recommendations.

If you have any questions about a school, either call the Better Business Bureau in your area or call the state attorney general's office and ask for the consumer-fraud division.

6

You and Your Photograph

Every day about fifty photographs come across my desk. That's a lot to get through and so I can only look for one thing. I look for winners.

As I riffle through the pile, many thoughts go through my mind. I wonder at the surprising spectrum of people who want to do commercials. A typical day's mail brings photos from housewives, from stuntmen, from schoolteachers, from pet owners, from children, from a girlfriend of someone in the mailroom, even from astronauts. Of course, most come from professional actors and actresses.

Mostly, though, I think about the photos competing with the other photos. Actually, the photographs are people to me. I'm delighted with the one that flags my attention—that says, "Hello, I'm the one"—and I feel a little mean about the ones I reject. I can't help thinking of my graduation picture—my frozen smile, my faraway look at the future, how the girl in it won a diploma, I don't know. Something in me tells me that maybe this actor, this housewife I've put on hold forever, simply hasn't been photographed to best advantage. I want to be generous, but, realistically speaking, I can't afford to be.

So you see, I have an ulterior motive in writing this chapter. I hope that by telling you what you need to know about your photograph, I will also be salving my conscience. Better yet, I may be helping a new talent get discovered.

In this chapter I will attempt to clue you in on what casting directors and agents look for in a picture, alert you to their common complaints, inform you of standard picture requirements, and help you decide what works best for you, head shot or composites. I will also discuss the many ways you will use your pictures. But first, let's clear up one often asked question—

Will My Picture Really Get Looked At?

Yes. Yes. Yes.

Casting directors and agents scout talent from pictures.

When Ann Wright, a top New York casting agent, called me recently to make a lunch date, she told me she couldn't meet me till 1:00 as she made it a practice to see new people from 12:00 to 12:30 and 5:00 to 5:30. (I usually try to see people on a general interview early in the morning.)

"Who are these new people?" I asked her during lunch. "Do you get them from recommendations or what?" I wasn't surprised at her answer. "I know actors never believe we see them from their pictures," she said, "but we do."

Most agents review pictures at least twice a week, if not every day. It's not uncommon for me to call an agent on a specific job and have him or her say, "I just got a picture in the mail of an actress who looks just like the person you're describing. If she's as good as her picture, I'll send her over to you."

Many casting directors and agents keep your picture in a folder or loose-leaf book under types: "Housewives 25–35," "Character Men over 45," etc. When they have a call for someone in your category, if you're right for the part, you can bank on it—you'll be called in.

I would like to point out that in most cases it does not matter whether a picture comes in the interoffice mail, from a housewife in Knoxville, Tennessee, or from an actor—all have an equal chance.

The Picture that Jumps Out of the Pile

Let's get back to me at my desk looking through that pile of pictures, and get down to specifics. What will make a photo catch my eye? What will make me hand it to my assistant and ask her to set up a general interview with you?

I've examined the kind of picture that I act on, I've checked out my criteria with other casting directors and agents, and I have come up with the three characteristics that impress me the most.

A FRESH, OPEN QUALITY

In the best of all worlds—and that's what the television-commercial world is supposed to be—moving men are tough but sweet; wives are warm and tender; husbands, witty and dear; children, plain and adorable. We like them. We want them as family, neighbors, and friends. They could sell us the moon and the Kraft cheese it's made of.

These are the kinds of people casting directors and agents look for. Your picture should say you're the best of your type. Your expression should be warm, optimistic, enthusiastic. Your eyes bright, clear. Your smile true, sincere.

Above all, you should look natural. Therefore your photograph should avoid dramatic, moody poses. If your friends look at your picture and say, "Interesting," your picture is probably not commercial. Watch out for ecstatic expressions, frozen smiles, or too much teeth. They work against you.

BEING TRUE TO TYPE

Imagine you are a typical housewife or businessman in a TV commercial. Imagine the camera has zoomed in on a close-up of you. Now imagine the frame is frozen. That's exactly how your picture should look. Everything about it should register your type on sight—your hairstyle, your expression, your clothes. Remember, as an actor on a TV commercial, you will be on screen close up for just a few seconds. The viewer must instantly recognize you as a housewife, a bank president, or whatever role you're playing.

BEING TRUE TO YOU

Your picture should be a part of you that you leave behind—sort of like a lingering essence. It should work for you after you leave a casting director's or agent's office. In a sense, it should bring you to life. When a job for your type comes in and I spot it in my files, it should restate your image. I should be able to recall you sitting in the chair opposite me; imagine you the moment after the smile in your photograph.

In other words, your picture should go beyond the commercial requirements of having a fresh, open quality and being true to type. It should capture you animated. The casting director should be able to see you as you would appear on the TV screen.

Your Picture Should Look Like You, and You Should Look Like Your Picture

This may sound impossible, but if you are true to yourself, it will happen. Not looking like you is the most common complaint against photographs. You have no idea how disappointed I feel when I spot a photo of an actor perfect for a part, call him in, and he shows up looking ten years older than his photograph.

If a casting director asks you, "When did you have this picture taken?" that's your tip that you need new photographs. I've rejected photographs because I could see they had been greatly retouched. I've also seen old pictures work against people in a different way. I've had directors look at some old pictures and say, "She's too young for the part." All my saying "She's really older than this picture" falls on skeptical ears. I admit I'm so disappointed when this happens, my negative feelings may be revived the next time I hear that person's name.

Pictures that are prettier or handsomer than you are also cause problems. Avoid anything that makes your picture not you. Avoid special lighting and retouching. If you have made any major changes in appearance—changed your hairstyle, grown a moustache, gained weight—have another set of pictures taken. If you have any doubts, compare your picture with what you see in the mirror. Ask your friends if your picture looks like you.

The Standard Professional Picture

If you are in the business of acting in commercials, your picture should say, "I'm a professional." That means it must meet standard requirements. Snaps or instant pictures might get looked at, but, except for children, I've never seen one land an interview.

There are two basic kinds of professional pictures: the head shot with a résumé on the back and the head shot with a composite on the back. I've classified them this way to stress that in both cases you will need a head shot.

Your geographic area, your type, or your purpose will determine what kind of pictures you use. The whys and whens of each are fraught with exceptions, so do read the following carefully.

THE HEAD SHOT WITH RÉSUMÉ ON BACK

The head shot is an 8×10 picture of the face and neck. It is usually cropped just below the shoulders. The résumé is stapled on the back. This kind of shot is sometimes called a "glossy" (a holdover from the days when professional pictures were used exclusively for newspaper theater publicity and a glossy surface was required). Today, for the most part, the head shot is printed on photographic paper called semimatte or dry matte. This is a less reflective surface than the true "glossy," but it does have a certain luster.

Recently, there's been a trend toward the color photograph. It is more expensive, to be sure, but if you can afford it, it is usually worth it. First of all, it stands out among all the black-and-white pictures. Second, it tells the casting director or agent your physical characteristics in a way your résumé never can. How else can an agent know the exact color of your eyes, their quality, or the color tones of your hair without your being there?

THE HEAD SHOT WITH COMPOSITE ON BACK

This format measures 8½ × 11 and has a head shot on the front and four pictures of the actor on the reverse side. It is usually printed on thin nonphotographic paper that tends to flatten out the quality. They often look like they've been lying around for a while.

Composites are especially valuable in showing a range of expressions and roles. But getting the four or five poses can be tricky business. Many actors, I find, tend to ham them up. Ideally the results should look like "stills" from a commercial. A good way to practice for your shots is to pose before your mirror as though it were a TV screen. Instant photos are ideal for testing various poses.

There are two kinds of composites: one for non–character types—which requires a change of wardrobe; and one for character types—which requires a change of wardrobe and makeup. For an example of the latter, see the photo of Will Hussung.

Below are some poses for non–character types.

AVERAGE YOUNG MAN IN 27–35 BRACKET

- Wearing a business suit sipping coffee and reading the *Wall Street Journal*
- Wearing a plaid shirt playing trains with his little son
- Wearing a work shirt and hard hat
- Having dinner with a lovely woman in a chic restaurant or in front of a fireplace

AVERAGE ATTRACTIVE YOUNG WOMAN 25–35

- Wearing a business suit and glasses at a desk looking over some papers
- Wearing a shirt and pants polishing a window
- Holding a baby or playing with a young child

- Wearing party clothes, perhaps dancing with an attractive man

Character-type composites usually show occupation and role. Typical occupational composites are of people dressed as chefs, bank presidents, coal miners, cops, etc.; typical role composites are of people made up to look like Dracula, magicians, clowns, historical figures, etc.

Note: Extras, especially character types, are often chosen from composites without an interview. A picture of an actor dressed in a costume is all a casting director or agent needs. An actor quite well known for his character photographs is Jan Leighton, who has pictures of himself as George Washington, Ben Franklin, and literally dozens of other historical figures.

Head Shot or Composite?

The 8 × 10 head shot with a résumé on the back has been standard in New York. The 8½ × 11 head shot with composite has been standard in California, Chicago, and Florida. However, since more and more actors and directors are dividing their time between New York and the West Coast, both kinds of pictures can be found throughout the country. In fact, most West Coast agents I've talked to recently say the two kinds of pictures are now equally popular.

Except for certain character types, I personally don't care for the composite. I find that expressions are often strained and people tend to mug mercilessly. I prefer to look through a résumé on the back and learn about their acting experience. But then, I do believe that when in Rome . . . So if your West Coast agent cries for a composite, by all means get one.

Regardless of where you live, if you're just starting out, I suggest you go with the head shot. If you're doing print work (modeling for newspapers and magazines), you will need a composite. I will discuss cosmetic or modeling pictures and portfolios in chapter 16 on models.

The Many Ways a Picture Works for You

Your picture is your door opener. It is your advertisement. It is your attention getter. It is your calling card. You will send it to casting directors, agents, producers, commercial directors, art directors, copywriters, creative directors, and casting services. You will send it to business people, who will send it on to friends and to friends of friends. You will leave it behind after auditions, give it out on the set, send it out as a reminder, and carry it with you all the time. Your picture will speak for you, promote you, sell for you again, again, and again.

The Final Decision Maker

I've seen a picture decide the winner again and again—even when an audition was taped. If you could stay behind after a taping and watch the selection process, you would witness a scenario something like this:

The producer, writer, director, casting director, account man, product manager, and art director are all gathered in the viewing room watching audition tapes. Everybody is giving his opinion.

"I don't think her hair is long enough," says the art director.

"She looks like a good housewife type," says the product manager.

"He's too macho," says the copywriter.

"She looks too sexy," says the producer.

After several viewings, the field is finally narrowed down. The process of matching people begins: He makes a good husband for her. . . .That child goes with those parents. . . .That actor plays well against the other.

It's at this point that someone usually pipes up: "Rather than go through the tapes again, let's just look at the pictures." This is when a role-perfect picture will get you the commercial. If the audition has not been taped, your picture, of course, is paramount.

Which all brings us to the subject of the next chapter—the person who can really make the difference in getting you a winning picture, your photographer.

The Whys, Wheres, and What-to-Knows About Getting a Winning Picture

"I could cry, Vangie," an actress told me recently as she handed me her pictures. "I just got these especially for commercials, and they turned out awful. If only I hadn't been in such a hurry to get them. I just took the first photographer that came along."

I took one look at her, one at her pictures, and I thought, You could cry? What about me! There she was, a highly talented theatrical actress ready to break into commercials. And there I was with a rush call for her type. And there she was, made for the part. And there her pictures were, doing her in.

What could I do? There wasn't time to put her on tape. How could I go about convincing others she was terrific for the part? I just couldn't send her to the client with her picture saying, "See, here is how she really looks."

Which brings me to the point of this chapter: Your picture is only as good as your photographer. Finding the right one, and knowing how to work with him or her, knowing the details of getting pictures down to the technicalities—contacts and duplicates, etc.—is as important as your face and talent.

I suggest you use the information in this chapter as you would a handy reference. It can help you avoid costly and time-consuming mistakes, and serve as a positive selling statement for you all along the way. But first, let's go in search of the one person who can assure you of the right picture—the right photographer.

How to Find Him or Her

Ask.

Ask everybody you know. People love to be asked for recommendations.

Ask people you know in the business.

Ask friends to ask people they know.

Ask anyone associated with theater, dance, the arts.

If you're an actor, *ask* to see other actors' pictures.

Ask agents or casting directors. (If you need to have pictures retaken, they can often lead you to a good photographer.)

If you live in a small area, ask and check out local photographers. *A word of caution!* While a photographer may do an excellent portrait, or take a picture that will win the Photographer's Annual Award, remember you're looking for someone who knows how to take a professional picture for *commercials*. Don't make a hasty decision.

LET YOUR FINGERS DO THE TALKING

If, after all your asking around, you still don't come up with a lead, get on the phone—*earnestly*. As a rule, don't bother with letters of inquiry—dialing is faster and easier on your fingers. Please make your inquiry brief. I can really empathize with the person on the other end of the line. I have received long-distance calls from people as far away as Omaha, Nebraska, starting with a long story and ending with a request for information on how to get into television commercials. Believe me, simply stating, "I'm interested in acting in commercials. Could you recommend a photographer who takes good professional pictures?" is all you need to say. If your contact can't recommend someone, ask if he or she knows someone who could.

If you live in a small area and have exhausted all the possibilities, you may have to travel to the nearest big city. Do it. A photographer who can give you a winning picture is worth the trip.

OTHER POSSIBLE SOURCES OF INFORMATION

- Your local advertising agency—ask for the art department.
- Your local theater group—ask for the publicist.
- Your local newspaper—ask for the photography department.
- Classifieds—look under "Photographers" and "Acting Schools."
- Your local library—ask the librarian for book listings of local photographers, advertising agencies. Ask for photography books.

Publications

The following publications list names of photographers in the Northeast, Midwest, South, and West, and include samples of some of the photographers' work. If the library does not have a copy, write:

The Creative Black Book
    Friendly Publications, Inc.,
    401 Park Avenue South
    New York, New York 10016
    Phone: (212) 228-9750

Backstage
    165 West 46th St.
    New York, New York 10036
    Phone: (212) 581-1080
    West Coast and Chicago Version

ASMP Book
   The American Society of Magazine Photographers, Inc.
   205 Lexington Avenue
   New York, New York 10016
   Phone: (212) 889-9144

Whitmark Directory
   Whitmark Associates
   4120 Main Street
   Suite 100
   Dallas, Texas 75226
   Phone: (214) 826-9400

Portrait of the Ideal Photographer

How do you know him when you find him?

Excuse the pun, but you click.

It takes two to make the picture that will get you into commercials. You must present yourself in a way that you want to be photographed, and the photographer must elicit and capture that.

The most important factor is rapport. Most of the top photographers agree that there should be a short meeting, a mutual interview, before a commitment is made. Your initial meeting with your photographer is the time and place for it. Tell him or her everything you hope to get out of your picture. Remember, you're shopping for the commodity that will get you into commercials. Don't be afraid to be assertive—charmingly so, of course. Ask questions and then ask some more. Be sure to iron out all business details. Above all, listen to what he or she has to say. Later I'll go into how to recognize the right answers.

The Photographer's Workplace

A photographer usually works in a studio or apartment, but don't let where sway you. Don't be overly impressed with a huge studio and loads of equipment. Often the photographer who works in the relaxed atmosphere of his or her apartment gets as good or better pictures.

Sometimes the whole outdoors is the photographer's studio. Some feel that the natural light makes the subject look more natural. (Van Williams, a very successful photographer, likes to work in locations like Central Park.) They find it works especially well with children, young people, and outdoorsy types such as athletes, hardhats, etc.

Although "the outdoor school" has its points, it has one big drawback: The photographer obviously has no control over nature's lighting, and so the result can be less than flattering. If you're an aging beauty, you may wisely prefer the control of studio light. Besides, unless the commercial is shot outdoors, studio photography has the added advantage of being closer to the lighting used in a commercial film house.

In any event, talk over location pros and cons with your photographer.

How to Present Yourself at Your First Meeting

Rule number one: Go to your preliminary meeting in the makeup, hairstyle, and clothing that you plan to wear for your audition. (See chapter 4.) You'll probably have to make some adjustments for the shoot, but it's a good starting point.

Hair. Again, it's better to err on the long side here. Most photographers have a good knowledge of hairstyling and are able to help you decide whether to cut or not to cut. If you plan to have several pictures taken, longer hair gives you more style possibilities.

If you use a rinse or color, be sure it's a shade you want to stay with (especially true for color photos). If your hair is very dark, ask your photographer whether it will show up against the background he plans to use or whether it needs lightening. You should be able to come to an agreement you can live with.

Note: Your photographer will probably ask you to come to the photo session with your hair clean, dry, and on rollers (if you use them).

Makeup. It's especially important that you wear the exact makeup that you plan to wear for your photo session. (See chapter 4.) Ask your photographer if he or she thinks you're wearing too much of it or if you should use something heavier to camouflage or highlight.

If you have a photogenic problem such as freckles or a too full face, bring it up at your first session. Your photographer is in a position to advise whether to cover all your freckles or not (some are nice) or whether you should shade to slim a full face.

Most photographers advise no makeup for men unless there are special skin problems.

Clothes. Look through your closets before your interview so that you can discuss what you have to wear with your photographer. For head shots, you will be concerned only with tops. Take along a couple of alternate shirts or blouses to check out. Most photographers ask for a light solid top, a dark solid top, and something with a small print or plaid. The pattern should not distract from your face. If you're wearing a layered look, be sure there is not too much contrast between the layers—e.g., a black sweater over a white blouse.

If you're developing a series of pictures, you will need complete outfits that show your figure. Pin down exactly how many different garments (including jeans) you will need for all your pictures. As a rule, your clothes should be simple and you should wear as little jewelry as possible. Most photographers comment that turtlenecks are not flattering without a jacket. *Big no's* are frills, fad clothes (they date a picture), turtlenecks, clothes that are too tight, and clunky jewelry.

If you're posing for character pictures, you will have to supply all the tops and hats. Occasionally a photographer will have a hard hat lying around, but don't count on it.

BRINGING ALONG PICTURES

I admit I've loaded you down with enough things to carry, but how your photographer sees you is the most important subject the two of you will discuss. It's absolutely necessary that you be in agreement on this point. If your photographer sees you as a "housewife type" and you're aiming to be a glamorous "spokeswoman," there's a problem. I suggest you bring along any magazine pictures that have the look you want. These will serve as a point of reference and more clearly define what you're aiming for and what your photographer thinks he or she can give you.

Also bring to the interview photos or snapshots of yourself that you don't like. Your photographer will know what to stay away from.

Judging a Photographer's Work

Don't make a commitment until you've seen shots of the photographer's work. Even if you don't have a trained eye, there are ways you can judge whether the photographer takes the kind of professional pictures you want. Here are some questions to ask yourself?

Do they look like the kind of professional pictures other actors have?

Are they in focus, *not* blurry-looking?

Is there too much contrast—hair a dark blob, skin pasty white?

Do they have a crisp, bright quality, or do you feel that you're seeing the person through heavy gauze?

Is the lighting tricky? Is half the subject's face in shadow?

Can you tell the shape of the head or does the hair blend into the background?

Does the subject stand out from the background? A number of agents have mentioned to me that they feel most actors seem to look better against a light background.

Does the subject appear alive, happy, natural?

All the photos in this book are samples of good professional pictures.

What's the Fee and What Does It Include?

With so much riding on it, it's worth being a good consumer. Shop for your photographer as you would for a new car. Do not pinch pennies, however. Like many actors starting out, you probably don't have a lot of spare cash and you may be tempted to try and save a few dollars on pictures. Wrong! One very successful on-camera actor told me that when he first embarked on his career, he found a bargain photographer who would charge him only $25 for his head shot. The cash was demanded in advance. The photographer then posed him in a Park Avenue doorway, asking him to smile as he clicked away. That done, he handed the actor the roll of film, told him to have it printed up, and disappeared. Needless to say, the pictures were less than great.

Minimally, a photographer should include in his or her fee:

- A general interview
- A photo session
- Contact sheets and help in choosing your pictures
- One or two 10 × 12 or 11 × 14 original prints
- Any necessary retouching

For this, your photographer will charge anywhere from $75 to $200. Obviously, the fees of very popular photographers in large cities will be at the top of the spectrum.

Additional original prints will range from $5 to $15. Be sure you know the exact number of original prints included in the price. Check on how much any additional ones will cost.

Color head shots cost at least twice as much as black-and-white. The price of the film is, of course, one reason. The photographer's advice on color-coordinating your makeup, hair, and wardrobe is another.

You do have to pay extra for every roll of film taken. (Thirty-six pictures to a roll). As a matter of interest, most photographers say they usually get the "winners" within the first roll and a half. If you're having pictures taken for a composite or portfolio, your photographer should shoot several more rolls to get the four or five pictures you'll need.

Get-a-Winning-Picture Checklist

Do you like the photographer's work? Have all your questions been answered (within reason)? Is the price reasonable? Do you think you can work together well?

If you've answered "yes" to the above four questions, then you'll probably want to hire the photographer on the spot. If you have doubts, don't settle for less than the best. Interview other photographers. When you do decide to hire "the one," you will probably be asked to leave a deposit. This is usually 50% of the total fee.

Preparing for Your Photo Session

After you've decided on your photographer and scheduled your photo session, you should have at least a week or two to prepare. So that you make the most of your session, let's go over the important elements.

IN THE WEEK BEFORE YOUR SESSION

• Maintain a healthy, light diet. You don't want to do a lot of partying and food bingeing. That goes for professionally fat character people, too.

• Maintain your exercise program. Photographer Tony Mauro asks his clients to jog or exercise within a couple of hours of the session. He feels the exercise puts a glow into the person's face and takes puffiness away from around the eyes.

• Get plenty of rest.

• Get your wardrobe together. If you don't have what you and your photographer discussed, you'll have to buy or borrow. Try on all clothes to be sure they fit. Check your mirror and see how they look in different poses. Be sure they're cleaned and pressed.

• If, after talking to your photographer, you plan to have your hair cut, have it done immediately. Give yourself time to get used to it before the photo session; otherwise, you may feel a little self-conscious.

• If you're having your hair lightened, streaked, or rinsed, allow time to study the results. You may need additional touch-ups.

• If you've already lightened your hair, don't spend money on pictures to find out you have dark roots.

• If you're a woman, you may wish to have some pictures taken with your hair down, and others with it pulled back. Practice arranging both styles.

• If you're planning on a facial, have it done well before the photo session. Don't eat anything that will make your skin break out.

• If your photographer has made any makeup suggestions, experiment with them. Reread the makeup advice in chapter 4.

• If you're into meditation or other calming exercises, this is the week to practice them. If you need suggestions, you might read chapter 12, "Going on an Audition."

THE NIGHT BEFORE
• Get your clothes and makeup together and ready to go.
• Get a good night's sleep.

Most important: Prepare to enjoy yourself. Have faith in your photographer. He will guide you through. Concentrate on the session and on getting the pictures you want.

The Day of the Photo Session

You have met your photographer and are familiar with his setup, the ambience of his studio, and his modus operandi. You have made all your last-minute preparations. You have brought along the wardrobe you will wear on an audition. You have arrived on time feeling good about yourself.

Before shooting, your photographer will probably chat with

you and help you relax. This is a good time to refresh his memory: who recommended you, what you are looking for in your picture. Remember, it's up to you to get the picture you want. *Take responsibility for it from the beginning.*

HOW LONG WILL THE SESSION LAST?

According to most photographers, you should allow a minimum of two hours for head shots. A variety of pictures taken for your composite or portfolio will, of course, take longer. Often these are done in a couple of different locations on different days. If any shots are done outdoors, the weather is a factor. A rainy day may call for a postponement.

THE SHOOT

Of course, you're nervous. Just about everyone who gets in front of a camera for a professional picture is. Even some actors who come alive when performing a scene go stone cold in front of a camera. A good photographer knows this, and he knows that the camera's better-than-20-20 vision will pick up your stress. He will help you relax. Various photographers use different methods.

Elizabeth Meads, an actress, recently described to me her photo session with Larry Lapidus.

"Think of something you're proud of," he said.

"Feel it a little more. . . ."

"Add a little love in your eyes."

Elizabeth found his method directive even to placing her chin exactly at the needed angle. Incidentally, it was the thought of her cat that finally got her the winning picture. And it was Larry's method of getting her to communicate how she felt about her cat that did it.

Kathy Lapone finds the act of concentration makes actors relax. She gives very specific directions—to move in a certain way, to say certain words that create a pleasant expression. Her pictures show it works.

Another photographer, Brian Haviland, goes right into shooting. He believes the very process gets the actor to relax. He often shoots several rolls of film hoping for "the one." He gets it.

Bert Torchia, who does mostly character pictures, works as though each picture were the final shot. After a few shots, he makes changes in lighting and poses. Usually he takes just one roll. That's all he needs.

Nick Leviton, who also does character work, doesn't believe that you simply put on a hat and you're that—a magician, a cop, a nurse. He develops an entire ambience using different locations, wardrobe, and lighting. The results are outstanding. Each shot looks as if it came from a different movie.

These are just a few examples of how photographers work. Your photographer may have you do an acting exercise, he may play music, etc. If you know of something that helps you relax, tell him. If he asks you to do something that makes you uneasy, don't. For instance, if your photographer offers you a glass of champagne to loosen you up and you know that champagne makes you more silly than relaxed, ask for a Coke.

Whatever, speak up. If you feel your photographer has not taken the pose, the expression, that will give you a successful picture, ask him to do a few "just for you." Above all, don't leave the session without getting the picture you want. I have had actors come in and say, "I knew he was asking me to smile too broadly." "I felt I wasn't getting the right look and pose." "I knew I didn't have a smiling shot." Don't be intimidated.

Contacts

After a photo session, your photographer has the film developed. It is printed on 8 × 10 sheets called "contact sheets" or "contacts." Each sheet contains one roll of film set in rows of passport-size pictures. From among those, you will make your picture choice.

How Do I Select My Picture(s)?

Your photographer will grease-mark his selections and discuss them with you. I would advise you not to make your final decision there and then. Take your contacts home and study them. If you have the time, show them to some experienced people in the field. It's a good excuse to get your agent(s) or casting directors more involved. Be sure to bring along a magnifying glass (contacts are pretty small) and a grease pencil for them to mark their favorites.

After you've made your selection(s), your photographer will advise you on how your final choices will look enlarged, and what can be easily retouched. Often, pictures that appear too dark or too light on the contact sheet can be corrected for your original print. Discuss the way the picture is to be cropped. Be sure it includes your full head and your hair.

How Do I Get Original Prints?

Your photographer will give you one or two enlarged 10 × 12 or 11 × 14 prints. These are called "original prints." You will have your duplicate prints made from their negatives. Any necessary retouching will be done on these original prints.

Once you've received these, your association with your photographer may end. Still, I strongly recommend that you keep the door open. You may want to show him your duplicate prints (see below).

What About Retouching?

Like most casting directors, I prefer as little retouching as possible. I believe your picture should look like you on your best day.

As part of your package, your photographer will take care of all necessary retouching, such as spots that occur in developing, or stray hairs the sensitive camera eye picks up.

If you require heavy retouching, I would advise you to choose another picture. If the fault is with the photographer, ask for a reshoot. It, after conferences with friends and advisers, you realize that your nose is indeed that large, don't retouch. Either live with it or get a nose job.

Duplicate Prints

Ask your photographer for advice on where to go for duplicate prints. Be sure to see samples in advance and ask to see the reprint paper to be used.

Once you get them back, show the prints to your photographer and ask for his opinion. If they need to be redone, your photographer will usually have more clout with a reproduction house.

How Many Visits Will Be Involved?

How many times you see your photographer really depends on the individual photographer. In asking around, I found most see their clients six times. I'd count on the following visits:

1. General interview
2. Photo session
3. Review of contact sheets
4. Choice of pictures to be enlarged and discussion of retouching and cropping
5. Review of original prints
6. Review of duplicates received from the lab

How Long Will It All Take?

Once you decide on your photographer, work out a time schedule together. Base it on:

Photo Session	Leave plenty of time to make preparations for hair, wardrobe, and makeup before photo session. Don't plan anything else for this day.
Contacts	You'll usually receive these within two to three days after the photo session.
Original Prints	Once your photographer receives your final decision on which contacts you want printed up, this

should not take more than a week, including mini-
mal retouching.

Duplicate Prints   Allow another five days from the time you give
your original prints to the duplicating service.

Once you receive your duplicate prints, leave time to check
them with your photographer. The entire process, from finding a
photographer to getting duplicate prints, can take as long as eight
weeks or more. While you're doing this is a good time to work on
your résumé, the subject of the next chapter.

Putting Together a Winning Résumé

I'm usually the last one out of a movie. I usually find my friends in the lobby stretching their necks and searching the crowd for me, "Where's Vangie?" written all over their faces. If they were to fetch me, they would find me in the back of an empty theater watching the list of credits roll up the screen (I look at the bit parts, too). Unlike most people who head for the exit the second the movie's over and music's up, I'm interested in who played what. After all, that's a casting director's job.

Credits Shown to an Empty House

When I see a movie or play, I'm of course in an ideal position to judge each performer's ability and type. But just imagine I didn't see the movie or play, that all I had before me was a cold list of credits: name of performer, part played.

Unfortunately, that's what most résumés remind me of. They are the (ho-hum) standard, all-purpose résumé most actors and

actresses use. Essentially, they list vital statistics, physical characteristics, theater background, a lot of plays performed in community theater—the prescribed number of Shakespeare, "Mooney's
Kids Don't Cry," Garcia Lorca, etc.; a rundown of training and
skills, and that's it.

Even though the photo may be terrific, when I flip it over, as I
always do, and ask my usual question, "But can she act?" I have
no clue. I'm expected to translate the skimpy data, apply it to
commercials, and come up with some sort of answer. Even less
enlightening is the composite (*sans* résumé): All I have to go on is
a group of pictures.

As you can see, I'm not for either of these approaches. I do
prefer to see a résumé, but it must tell me about the candidate's
ability to do commercials.

The Commercial-Oriented Résumé (A New Concept in Getting You a Job in Commercials)

First of all, let's examine what you want your résumé to do for
you.

> You want your résumé to get you an interview with a casting
>   director who casts commercials.
> You want your résumé to make your interview work and get
>   you a job in commercials.

I have to admit that today a good picture and a standard résumé
will often get you an interview. That's a fact. It's standard practice, and it works. But am I wrong to believe your résumé should
jump out of the pile and demand an interview? A résumé that
sells you not as an off-Broadway actor, or a model, or an expert,
but as a television performer, can do just that.

A résumé also should nail down the interview or job. If you've
ever watched a talk show, you've noticed how the interviewer
cleverly touches on highlights of the guest's career and personality. This information is usually gathered from a fact sheet. It's

what makes the interview alive, interesting, provocative. That's what your résumé should do. It should point up the landmarks, signs, clues, and information that will allow me to learn about you; give me a handle to break the ice, draw you out; reveal you as a creative, likable personality, a perfect commercial type.

Taking Inventory

Many books on résumés advise that before you write your résumé, you take inventory—put down on paper all of your occupational and personal history. I'm 100 percent for it, especially for the television-commercial performer. In the long run, you will not be looking for one job, but many. The pieces of information about yourself you gather and put down will serve you again and again, for different reasons and at different times.

Case in point: You might once have supported your acting career by demonstrating hair products in a department store. Not one of your more impressive credits, you may think, not for your résumé. And unless you're just starting out, you're probably right. But think what a strong selling point such experience would make if you were going out for a Clairol commercial. By all means include it and any credit like it in your inventory.

You'll find that whatever you put down helps give you a better sense of yourself; it reveals your strengths and brings up forgotten achievements.

Two recommendations: Although in the end your résumé will be one page long, use all the space you want in preparing it. Be honest in listing your credits. If you claim to be a champion skier, make sure your are. Lies have a way of catching up with you.

Gathering Material

Here's where your personal notebook will come in handy. You've already put down information you can refer to—vital statistics, physical characteristics, your impressions of yourself, etc. For your preparation material, I recommend you set aside a special section—one you can easily refer to when you want to bone up for an interview, one you can add information to as you grow in acting credits, training, etc.

To help jog your memory, pull out everything about you that you have in the house: high-school yearbooks, scrapbooks, reviews, awards, publicity, old résumés, even the family album (there's the photo dad took of you receiving the high-school basketball award).

What to Put Down

Once you've got it all together, you're ready to start. But don't just list things—give them color with impressions, stories, incidents, even embarrassing ones. Use the winning résumé on page 97 as a guide to categories. Include:

All your physical characteristics: color of hair, eyes; height; weight; etc.

Everything about your acting experience: film, TV, theater, nightclubs, etc. Go back to your high-school play if you must.

The plays you've appeared in and the parts you played in them.

The stars you've worked with.

Reviews, awards, publicity.

Allied experience. If you've worked in nightclubs, put down what you did. Did you sing? Did you improvise? Was there anything about your performance that could help the casting director use your background?

All your training. Any impressions, insights about it, teachers, etc. (Any improvisational experience or training is very valuable.)

All your skills: languages you speak, sports you play, areas of expertise.

Physical, athletic abilities, indicating degree of expertise.

Key thoughts to jog your memory about anecdotes.

Your personal feelings about acting, commercials; your likes, dislikes.

What If You're a Beginner?

Some experts suggest that if you have no professional credits, you should use the composite. As you've probably guessed, I don't agree.

It's true that, as a beginner, your résumé must be more imaginative than the more experienced candidate, but you'd be surprised at the power of a fresh approach.

If you have good theatrical training, make it count. Emphasize all the classes and lessons you've taken in drama, voice, dance, etc.—the most impressive ones first.

If you've been a homemaker or a salesman and now want to get into commercials, there's most likely something about you that loves to perform. Search it out. Maybe you have worked in a department store, demonstrating products. Have you helped set up the Tupperware program in your neighborhood? Have you as a consumer convinced a local store to stock up on a product? Someone interested in products usually can sell them.

You probably can think up a number of other accomplishments. I personally believe if you are a good type, have done everything to get your act together, you have as good a chance as anyone to get into commercials.

Selecting and Culling

I know what you're thinking: How do I get pages of information on a one-page résumé? Of course, you don't. Once you've got everything together, you have to cut and pare and edit it all down to manageable length. It can be a very creative though frustrating task. Remember, think commercials. Think your type. Pull out only those things that will work in getting you into commercials.

Now You're Ready to Do Your Résumé

Before you start, look at the winning résumé on page 97. Better yet, clip the page so you can easily refer to it. You will notice that it breaks down into six categories:

1. Vital Statistics
2. Type
3. Physical Characteristics and Measurements
4. Experience and Union Memberships
5. Training
6. Skills and Assets

VITAL STATISTICS

This is your personal data material. It goes at the top of your résumé and is important. Above all, information should be accurate—a wrong number can cost you a commercial. Here are the general points to be covered:

Your name:	Put it in **BOLD PRINT**.
Phone numbers:	Put down home phone, note pickup, answering service opposite your name.
Time you can be reached:	Make it as easy as possible for casting directors and agents to track you down at all times. Next to home numbers, specify days, evenings, time. Very often calls come in at the end of a day. The 5:00–8:00 period is especially busy.
Agent's number:	If you're signed to an agent, put down his/her name and phone number. If you're free-lancing, write in, clip on, or stick on your résumé the name and number of the agent *who sent you.* This is vital as another agent may have introduced you to the same casting director and when the casting director tries to contact you—lo, wrong number.
	Note: At the end of the audition, be sure to check that vital information is correct and that all your numbers are "working" numbers.

TYPE

I'm for selling your type on top—big and IN CAPS. The center of the page, under the vital statistics, is an ideal spot to catch attention. If you're a character/comedy type, specify roles: bar-maid, bank clerk, truck driver, etc.

PHYSICAL CHARACTERISTICS AND MEASUREMENTS

This section has the information that people will refer back to most often. It will be used in selecting you for an audition. It will be used in matching you with other talent. For instance, would you make an appropriate wife for that husband, an appropriate father for that son? Casting decisions are often made after 5:00, and the stylist must use this information to immediately get ward-robe together.

So put on top, where it will be seen, height, weight, hair color, color of eyes, age range (this refers to the age you appear on film), suit and dress sizes. Unless you're a model, this is optional: Women should list bust, waist, hip measurements; men should list collar, sleeve length, waist, and inseam.

Of course, all the information you put down should be current and correct. Alas for casting directors, it often isn't. Temptations abound to shave off or add on. This is especially true when it comes to putting down age range. People tend to claim they can play younger. Weight and height (men are especially guilty in adding on inches) come a close second. Believe me, fabrications seldom, if ever, work. When you show up for the fitting, the truth will out.

UNIONS

If you belong to a union—SAG, AFTRA, SEG, etc.—be sure to put it at the top. Most important, SAG. Although there are ways around it (see pp. 265–66), being a member greatly enhances your chances.

EXPERIENCE

You're familiar with the blurbs that advertise hit shows. You read them and you want to see the shows. To me that's the kind of punch your acting credits should have. Every word should be concise, convincing, designed to hook the casting director, producer, director; get you an interview and make that interview so vital that you will get the job.

Of course, you may not have had big parts or great raves, but still you can make whatever you have work for you. I admit, it takes skill and hard work to sell yourself in such a limited amount of space, but you've got to do it.

The Setting Up
Here is where the commercial-oriented résumé really deviates from the usual one:

You do not necessarily put your heaviest experience first.
You do not necessarily start with your last performance and go back chronologically.
You do not necessarily put the most prestigious area first.

Set up the categories with commercials in mind. Put experience closest to it first. All credits should go under respective headings:

Industrials	Film
	Live
TV	Soap Operas
	Series
	Specials
	Cable
	Local
Film	Feature—Theatrical Release Made for TV
	College—Experimental
Theater	Broadway
	Regional Road Tours
	Off-Broadway
	Community Workshops, Readings, etc.
Commercials	Upon Request

What to List and How to List It

Productions. Choose productions that the person reading your résumé is most likely to know or at least to have heard of. The supporting role in the "Milliken Breakfast Show," a very popular industrial, or a small part in "General Hospital" would both be known in the industry.

In theater, stick to contemporary plays. Everyone knows *Same Time Next Year* but not *The Ion.*

Describe the role. Casting directors see a lot of plays and watch a lot of television. But we can't see them all. Major Frank in *Cloud 9* means nothing to me unless I've seen the play. Describe your part.

PLAY	ROLE	
They're Playing Our Song	John Fletcher:	young, romantic lead, lovable, witty guy.
TELEVISION SOAP		
"As the World Turns"	Helen Rogers:	warm, understanding, mother type, early forties.

Walk-on or lead. You may prefer to mention your leads in community theater than your bit part on Broadway, but the latter in the end is more impressive: You are more likely to have been seen, and it shows you're a pro.

Raves. Excerpt any glowing reviews from newspapers or television about the part you played.

The Result

If you've followed the above rules, you should come up with jam-packed credits that read like these:

Played Martha in Long Wharf performance of *Who's Afraid of Virginia Woolf.* "A brilliant performance"—John Jones, *New Haven Times.*

Played Dr. Walker, a warm, concerned psychiatrist, in "One Life to Live." Won *TV Guide* Award for best featured actor.

Compare this with the standard credit:

After the Fall, A. Miller	Maggie
"Pursuit of Happiness"	Prudence
"As the World Turns"	Nurse

See what I mean?

THE COMMERCIAL RÉSUMÉ WITHOUT COMMERCIAL CREDITS

You've noticed in our sample résumé that next to "Commercials" we have stated "Upon Request." There's a good reason for this: A list of your commercials might well throw off an advertiser. For instance, a car manufacturer might see that you've appeared in a competitive car commercial. Even though it might have been five years ago, believe me, he'll be influenced negatively by it. According to SAG rules, you have to mention only those commercials in direct conflict with the product you're auditioning for.

The old bane, overexposure, is another reason you should omit your commercial credits. A long list of credits is impressive, but important people might feel your face is becoming too familiar to viewers.

There is, however, no taboo about listing the kinds of parts you've played in commercials—something standard résumés seldom do. If you've played character types, I recommend you list the various roles you've played—bank teller, moving man, switchboard operator, etc.

TRAINING

Under "Experience," I've suggested you list TV credits first, then film, then theater, etc. The reverse is true in listing your training. I would arrange this as follows:

Theater
Film
Soap Opera
TV Commercials
Voice
Dance
Speech
Etc.

You'll notice that theater is first. Theater training suggests you have knowledge of improvisation. As noted in chapter 5, "Learning Your Craft," it is the basis of commercial naturalness.

TV-commercial classes or training schools follow a close second. They show you have on-camera experience. Also, they suggest you have a grasp of the limitations of thirty seconds, that you know how to compress your actions and reactions.

Other classes—voice, dance, speech, etc.—show you have an interest in developing your craft. Do list them. I also recommend you list people you've worked with, especially if they have a name in the industry. It's impressive and a good conversation starter. But be sure you don't borrow names. Be truthful. The person interviewing you may be his/her best friend. Besides, people in the business will know who is head of the Goodman Theatre or Carnegie-Mellon, etc.

SKILLS AND ASSETS

This is the catchall area of your résumé. It includes everything—language, sports expertise, special skills, special physical assets (good hands or feet, for example), and even negative assets, such as removable bridges (perfect for a denture commercial). Just because it's at the bottom of your résumé, don't give it short shrift. These assets lead to jobs. One actress I know calls every agent in town when she gets a cold, just in case there's a cold-remedy commercial casting.

Of course, if I'm looking for an actor who knows judo, I'll go through résumés with this skill in mind, and call in only those people with the skill for an audition. But you'd be surprised how often a minor skill can give a performer an edge. One thing the people involved in selecting talent (the director, producer, product manager) do after an audition is flip the pictures over and read the résumés. It's then that the fact you can dance or "move well" can make a difference. The commercial may call for someone who whirls his wife around in the ecstasy of having the ring around his collar removed—and you're it.

Please, if you have a skill such as playing the piano, don't just put down "plays piano." List whom you studied with. I was just looking for a piano player for a hand lotion commercial, and the fact that you studied at Juilliard with Rosina Lhevinne would make you that much more interesting. You can't very well fake the keyboard in a closeup.

Because of the variety of assets in this category, I recommend you list them as follows:

Languages	Indicate if you speak fluently. Indicate if you can translate.
Sports	List all sports and indicate your degree of expertise.
	List any awards or medals you have received.
Skills	List mechanical skills such as drives truck or operates word processor.
	List degrees or licenses you may have.
Other	Indicate if you're a home-economics major, fashion expert, teach, work with children, etc.
Physical Assets	Indicate if you have good hands, feet, or legs. (See chapter 19, "Other Doors.")

This is optional: Indicate removable bridges, teeth, chronic sinusitis, or bronchitis. If you don't put these attributes on your résumé, be sure to mention them in your interviews.

Music
: Indicate whether you read music. Indicate instruments you play. Indicate degree of professionalism. Indicate with whom you studied. Indicate voice type—soprano, tenor, contralto, etc.

A Word About Your Résumé's Appearance

It's up to you to marshal the material for your résumé—to put down your credits in compact and convincing language. But what if you have no talent for making up a résumé or whipping one into shape? You go to people who specialize in professional résumés. The professional result, believe me, is worth the money. You come out with a well-written, polished, well-laid out, typed-up and printed résumé.

A few hints if you make up your own résumé. After, and only after, you're absolutely happy with its contents, go to a good printer. Make certain you specify 8 × 10 size. Check out the quality of the paper. Use color if you like; it's a good flagger and signature. Avoid copying machines in drugstores, libraries, etc.; they're not designed for professional copies. If you go to a copier, ask to see samples first. Look over your copies before you leave. Be sure each one is sharp and well inked.

Department of Minor but Important Details

Be sure when you come to an interview that your résumé is attached to your picture. People sometimes hand them to me separately and ask if I have a stapler. Perhaps I do. Perhaps I don't. In any event, it's not a very good show. But I will forgive you if you have a great résumé.

Now you're ready to go to press. Almost. Before you have your résumé printed, answer the following questions:

DID YOU:

Put your name in capital letters?

Put your current telephone numbers at the top?

Make sure your physical characteristics and measurements are correct?

Include your union memberships?

Put your "type" toward the top?

Gear all credits to commercials?

Include under "experience" the roles you played? Include contemporary plays? Indicate nature of roles—lead, walk-on? Tell where you performed—TV, Broadway, summer stock? Include great reviews? Indicate if you played with a star?

List training pertinent to commercials? List them in proper order? List people you studied with?

List all your special skills and assets? Gear them to commercials? Indicate pertinent information about them? List them properly?

Make the most of all your credits?

Weed out any information you can't substantiate?

Use language that's telegraphic, hard-hitting?

Note that you do extra work?

Okay? You *did?* Then you're ready for the next big step: how to get those interviews.

AGATHA ACTRESS
403 East Houston Street
New York, N.Y. 10002
Arnold Agent: 943-2113

937-4306 24-hour answering service
321-6703 7 P.M. to 8 A.M.

SAG AFTRA AEA
AVAILABLE FOR EXTRA WORK

Height: 5'7"   Weight: 118 pounds
Hair: Light brown   Eyes: Blue
Age range: 18-25
Size 8 dress

TYPE: YOUNG MOTHER, STEWARDESS, WIFE, OFFICE WORKER, BANK TELLER, COLLEGE SENIOR

EXPERIENCE (Among Credits)

INDUSTRIAL	AT&T	Played featured sales representative	Director: Jo Frederick
	CHEMSTRAND	Played young lab technician—Lead	Director: Ann Thomas
FILM	*Rocky VI*	Played Rocky's (Sylvester Stallone) married daughter—warm, lovable type. "A talent to watch," *L.A. Times,* Johnson	
EXTRA BITS	*Manhattan*—Woody Allen; *The World According to Garp, Death Wish*		
TV SOAP	"General Clinic"	Played Betty Young, new mother Award for best newcomer, *TV Guide*	

Continued

THEATRE Lead or Featured Parts

Crimes of the Heart	Babe Botelle, kookie young sister	Cleveland Playhouse
The Cherry Orchard	Anya, poetic young girl	Williamstown Theatre
Moonchildren	Sally, young hippie	Off-B'way Playwrights Horizons

TV COMMERCIALS Upon request

TRAINING

B.A., Northwestern University	Drama major—won drama award
Herbert Berghof Studio	Uta Hagen professional classes Pete Miner
TV Course, Video Association	
Soap Course	Betty Olo
Dance Interpretation, Jazz	David Berger
Voice and Speech	Sandy French
Singing—Soprano	Claude Senje—advanced classes
Mime	

SPECIAL ABILITIES

Speak French fluently; move well; ride horseback—English and Western saddle; drive stick-shift cars, motorcyle; ski-slalom; ice skate and roller skate.

Worked 2 years as director of Children's Theatre while at Northwestern. I feel I am especially good working with children.

9

Starting Out and Stirring Up Contacts

I just saw an old movie on TV where an elevator operator picked up a passenger, burst into song, and was immediately signed for a movie by his passenger, who turned out to be a big-time producer. Such things don't happen anymore? Especially in the competitive field of TV commercials? Just the other day an elevator starter at our JWT Atrium Building asked if I would see his niece, and of course I did.

I'm always amazed at how people get interviews with me. An old school friend sends a pupil of hers; a client sends his son-in-law; someone has gotten my name from the *Ross Reports* (a publication with lists of agents and casting directors).

I realize, if you're just starting out in commercials, you may be at a loss as to where and how to make initial contacts. Even if you're on your way and have an agent, there comes a dry time when you need to drum up business. This chapter is addressed to both beginners and pros stumped for contacts. In it I hope to set your fingers to dialing phones and set your feet to making the rounds.

Starting Out Where You Are

You don't have to go to the Big Apple or L.A. to find work. In fact, if you're a beginner, you're better off starting out on your own turf. Even if you live in a one-TV-station area, you'll be surprised at the opportunities there are to do commercials. In a one-store town, there are probably nearby opportunities that can lead to jobs in commercials; when you're ready to hit the bigger cities, you'll have some impressive credits to put on your résumé.

Contacts and More Contacts

Start by contacting talent and/or model agents, film companies, advertising agencies, and casting services. You will find them listed in the yellow pages of your local phone book or in the source publications listed below. (Refer also to chapter 11 on agents.)

If your local area happens to be a big city, don't overlook the small advertising agencies, film companies, and radio stations. They have plenty of work and as most agents don't have time to contact them, the competition is not so overwhelming.

Advertising Agencies. Since their business is to write and produce commercials for advertisers, they are a prime source. If there is no casting director listed, send your picture to the creative director. His office will forward it to the appropriate person.

Film Companies. Investigate feature-film and industrial-film companies as well as commercial-production houses. Many produce a wide variety of film material.

Public-Relations Agencies. They are often involved in catalog work and/or local ads.

Screen Actors Guild (SAG). If there's a local office in your area, they may have a personnel list of the local advertising agencies and film companies, names of people to contact.

Here are some other sources that I hope will sprout viable contacts:

Television Stations. They're often involved in the production of local ads and local news shows. Good places to look if you need a job to support yourself—even if you get a job typing, you're there where it's happening and have a chance to promote yourself.

Radio Stations. Ideal starting places if you have a particularly good speaking voice or a character voice. Possible opening to do lead-ins to regular commercials.

Department Stores. They often have modeling jobs for people of all sizes and ages. It's a way to meet people, learn how to wear clothes, and get into the discipline of good grooming. Usually they have their own advertising department. You can talk to them about their local TV advertising.

Cable TV Stations. An especially promising field. Most local areas do all sorts of programming. Maybe you could read the weather or do the news. In any event, people could clue you in on what shows are coming up, who the local advertisers will be, and who may need someone to do commercials.

Advertising Departments of Manufacturers or Service Organizations. Many don't use advertising agencies; they do their own commercials and so will hire you directly.

GET INTO TALENT DIRECTORIES

Be sure you send your picture and contact to your regional talent directory. These guides are routinely thumbed through by producers, directors, and casting people when looking for talent.

Players Guide	1500 Broadway, New York, N.Y. 10036
Academy Players Directory	Academy of Motion Picture Arts and Sciences, 8949 Wilshire Blvd., Beverly Hills, Calif. 90211
Chicago Unlimited Directory	203 N. Wabash, Suite 1020, Chicago, Ill. 60607
Whitmark Directory	4120 Main, Suite 100, Dallas, Texas 75226

If you work on both coasts, it would be a good investment to have your pictures in both the *Players Guide* and the *Academy Directory*.

PERSONAL CONTACTS—FRIENDS OF FRIENDS OF FRIENDS

Put it out there. Let every single person you know or come in contact with know you're an actor looking to meet the right people. Ask your super, your mailman, your analyst, your cleaner, your cousin-in-law—even your IRS man.

Include anyone who works in the field in your lists. If you know some top brass, great, but don't overlook stagehands, secretaries, and people in the mailroom. They are often catalysts for an interview. I personally suspect my mailroom of running a casting department of its own. I need a favor—a package delivered on a Friday night—they come through. They need a favor—"Will you see a friend of mine who wants to get into commercials?"—I come through.

Other actors, actresses, and models are almost certain to be generous in helping you; they know the struggle. Don't forget the headwaiter at the local restaurant who appears in community theater, or the friend who models for a local department store.

Friends who work for manufacturers or services are a great source. They might ask the internal advertising manager to ask an ad agency to see you. I know this works. I always see people who are recommended to me through a client. And above all, don't overlook friends of friends and relatives. Everybody knows somebody. Your favorite aunt's best friend may have a son who works as a TV stagehand. There's a good chance that if he asks the casting director or producer to see a friend, he or she will.

RESEARCH SOURCES—SOME GREAT CONTACT IDEAS

Madison Avenue Handbook, Backstage (East and West versions), *The Creative Black Book, Motion Picture Directory, Whitmark Directory of the Southwest*—all list film companies, advertising agencies, talent agents, and casting services.

The *Standard Directory of Advertising Agencies* (the "Red Book")—lists all the products advertised on television, plus their manufacturers and advertising agencies. Use it to find manufacturers and agencies active in your local area who advertise products calling for your type. Among other things, it can save you time by pinpointing leads.

Weekly *Advertising Age, Backstage, Anny, Variety,* and the *Hollywood Reporter*—known as "the trades"—will help keep you informed on personnel and account changes, who and what are going where. Read regularly for hot-off-the-press tips. Cut out items on agencies that use your type and put them in your notebook. This information can come in handy when you go on interviews.

Note: It's better to catch people after they've been on a job a week or two.

The *Wall Street Journal* and business sections of newspapers in general, although not as inclusive or detailed as the trades, will help keep you abreast of what companies have changed advertising agencies. This almost always means that the new agency will launch a major new campaign—a particularly good time to make your availability known.

Also, the *Wall Street Journal* carries stories about new products that are being test-marketed, most often outside the major metropolitan area. This can be an opportunity to form a relationship with a major advertiser.

PROCEDURE FOR MAKING CONTACTS

This step is as simple as stuffing your picture and résumé into an envelope or lifting a phone, but it's one of the most dramatic steps you will take. Now you're really putting yourself on the line.

What comes first: mailing or calling? If you have close contacts, of course, phone directly. Cold calls are shots in the dark. It's true, you might just hit at the moment an agency is casting your type, but you'll generally be asked to just send in your picture. Better to send the picture first. I recommend you affix a note telling what you are currently doing. It might be something like the one I received recently: "Shouldn't you be interested in meeting this actress who just won an off-off-Broadway award as well as rave reviews for her performance in . . ." Don't send videotapes; they have a way of getting set aside.

If your research has not turned up the name of the person you should address, call the company and ask who is in charge of advertising. In the case of an advertising agency, ask who is in charge of casting.

Using the Telephone as a Business Medium

You're on stage. The mouthpiece of your telephone is your microphone, the person on the other end your audience. How do you use the telephone to win interviews? You're an actor—for goodness' sake, call upon your acting skills. Think of it all as doing a commercial—you're the product. Remember, the action of your scene is to get a positive response, to get the person to say, "Yes I will see you." If you're not verbal, write down what you plan to say, or keep target points in front of you. Be direct and concise. Use simple declarative sentences. And do psych yourself up. Do have a smile in your voice. Remember, the phone is a sensitive instrument. It transmits more than the message. It transmits the attitude behind the voice—tensions, moods.

Okay, you've got your "script" ready—don't forget the specific details of your interview. Say, "I'd like to have an appointment on Wednesday at nine o'clock. Ask where and when the interview is to take place and write it down.

Above all, don't take no for an answer. Offer alternative possibilities. If the response is "We're not interviewing at this moment," don't say "Thank you" and hang up—ask when you can call. Answer "He just stepped away from his desk"—"She's at a meeting"—"She's taping now"—with "When do you think he [or she] will be back?" May I add, it helps to be friendly with secretaries. They carry a lot of weight. I can't say no to mine when she comes in and says, "He sounds so nice, couldn't you see him?"

Finally make a minimum of ten calls a day. It's easier than making one. Being rejected by ten people seems less personal and more the state of the business. Don't stop because you already have five appointments. Make calls if possible on days you're going on interviews or auditions or shooting.

Remember the law of averages. Even if you follow all these pointers, there are days when you'll just simply be put on hold. Hang in there.

WINNING-AN-INTERVIEW APPROACHES

The I'm-New-in-Town Approach

"Hello, I'm Jim Winston, an actor. I've been doing commercials successfully in Washington, and since I'll be living in Chicago and plan to continue my career here, I'd like to come in to see you."

The I-Have-Something-to-Show-You Approach

"Good morning, I'm Joan Fuller. I've been modeling locally for Bamberger's. I have a fashion-oriented book to show you, and since you handle the Jantzen account, I felt it would benefit us both to meet."

The I'm-Your-Type Approach

"Hello, I'm Paul Lopez. I've noticed your Close-up toothpaste commercials on TV and as I'm the type you use in your commercials and have perfect teeth, I believe you would be interested in seeing me."

The Flattery-Will-Get-You-Everywhere Approach

"Hello, I'm David Bradley, an actor. I've read your article in *Ad Age*, 'An Actor's Approach to Commercials,' and I found it very informative. I really would like the opportunity to meet you."

The I-Met-You-at-the-Theater Approach

"Hello, I'm Shirley Brown, an actress. I met you at the opening of *My Fair Lady* recently. Rita Moriarity introduced us. She suggested I call you," etc.

The New-Account Approach

"I just read in *Ad Age* that you got the Burger King account. I know you'll probably soon be casting for commercials and I believe I'd be an ideal type for you."

The "Red Book" Approach

"Hello, I'm Jan Ballard, an actress, and I've been going through the list of accounts your agency handles. I notice they are mostly household products, and as I'm a typical housewife type, I thought we should meet."

The Come-See-Me Approach

"Hello, I'm Alan Wilson. I have a monologue that I am doing at the Under the Bridge Workshop and I would like to invite you to come see me." *Note:* Follow this up with a flyer.

The Catch-Me-Before-I-Become-a-Big-Star Approach

"Hello, I'm Tony Emmet. I wonder when you're seeing people. I'd like to come in later this week as I'll soon be going into rehearsal for a terrific new show downtown."

The I-Have-a-Scene-for-You Approach

"Hello, I'm Pat Sloan and I have a three-minute scene I'd like to do for you. Could I come in sometime next week?"

SOME "PUT-OFF" APPROACHES TO AVOID

If any of the following approaches sound like yours, reread this chapter.

The Vaguest-Yearning Approach

"Hello, I'm Virginia Schwartz and I'd like to be in television commercials."
Answer: "Who wouldn't?"

The On-the-Run Approach

"Hello, I'm Brenda Dawson, an actress. I'm in Chicago for a few days and I was hoping to pick up a commercial while I was here."
Answer: "Try turning on your set."

The Defeated-Before-You-Start Approach

"Hello, I'm Hank Lowe. I've only done modeling. You probably don't see people like me."
Answer: "Not with that attitude."

The Dumb-Question Approach

"Hello, I'm Teresa Lumpkin. Do you see people?"
Answer: "No, I live in isolation."

The Long-Story Approach

"Hello, I'm Mary Batsell, and my aunt, who works as a receptionist for the Flim Flam Film Company in Florida—they do industrials mostly, or maybe features, I'm not sure—anyway, she was talking to one of the cameramen about how I wanted to get into commercials—you probably don't know him, Fred Thompson?—anyway, he suggested . . ." and on and on.
Answer: "The number you have reached . . ."

The You-Mean-You-Didn't-Get-My-Picture Approach

"Hello, I sent my picture to you three weeks ago and I haven't heard from you. Didn't you receive it? My name is Sara Threat."

Answer: "Who?"

Note: Of course, you can say you sent your picture, but don't put people on the spot. Especially in a big casting office, your picture may not always be remembered or instantly reviewed.

The Joke-Call Approach

"Hello, I'm Bill Cosby [it's not even a good imitation] and I would like to do a commercial for you. Ha ha."

Answer: "Ha."

The Worst Approach of All

"Hi, I'm Joe Mills. Why haven't you called me?"

Nobody Home

If every time you go out you worry that you'll miss *the* career-launching phone call, you're right, you just might. For the sake of your sanity, get an answering service. You have three choices: a machine, a pickup service, or a central message exchange. Each has its advantages and disadvantages.

A *machine* will answer your call and take messages. You can also call the machine to get messages. The cost is a little steep, but once you install it there are no other charges.

With a pickup service, your call is received by switchboard. A person answers and takes messages. You can keep in touch by calling the switchboard. Some services have electronic beepers you can carry with you. The disadvantages: Unlike machines, people are sometimes rude. Some services can't pick up regularly. There is an installation fee and a monthly service charge.

A *central message exchange* is not connected with your phone. This is a place for your contacts to call. There is no installation fee, and the cost per month is less than that of a pickup service. The major disadvantage is that if any prospective employers call your home first, they have to make another phone call.

When It's Better Not to Use the Telephone (Using the Mail to Get Interviews)

If you decide to set your sights beyond your hometown, you may find yourself bowled over by Ma Bell's long-distance phone bills. The cheaper alternative and in some cases the more effective is an "I-would-like-to-meet-you-next-time-I'm-in-L.A. letter." It goes something like this:

> Dear Casting Director:
>
> In watching TV commercials, I noticed that in the No-Nerves Coffee commercials, an account handled by your agency, you use my type.
>
> I plan to relocate to L.A. next month. I am currently doing local TV and radio commercials. Attached is my picture and résumé. May I please have an interview with you on January 14, 15, or 16. Anytime in the morning is fine. I'll call on the 13th to verify.

LETTERS TO MANUFACTURERS

A letter that lets an advertiser know you like his product is a possible way to get an interview that will lead to a job. Your letter may be turned over to a research department in charge of scouting "real people" for commercials. You could be interviewed for the next batch of commercials the company makes.

A typical letter might read:

> *Recently at a dinner party, I spilled wine on my expensive new dress. Believe me, I was upset. One of the guests told me about your product, Spots-Off Pre-Wash. I was skeptical but I thought what do I have to lose, so I gave it a try. Was I surprised when my dress came out looking like new! I just had to write and tell you what a great product you have. I would welcome any opportunity to tell the world about it.*

Note: You must actually have had a positive experience with the product and sincerely want to give a testimonial. Manufacturers also forward your pictures and résumés to their advertising agencies, who will usually respond.

Thank-Yous and Reminders

I know you're going to get that interview, so let's talk about what comes next. A thank-you, of course. Send a note a few days after the interview saying how much you enjoyed talking with your interviewer and that you hope he or she will keep you in mind for future projects. Include your picture and phone number. A check-in call, say once a month, is perfectly permissible. In any event, keep sending pictures, postcards, flyers. Keep your name and picture in people's consciousness so that when you call and mention your name, you ring two bells. Eventually, the big day will come and you'll be called for an interview—the subject of the next chapter.

10

How and How Not to Handle an Interview

ME: Hi. You're Sally Silent?
SALLY: (*Already seated*) Yes.
ME: How are you?
SALLY: Fine.

(*A series of amenities initiated by me and answered monosyllabically by Sally follows.*)

ME: Do you have your picture?
SALLY: I sent it to you three weeks ago.

(*I buzz my secretary and ask if she could please look up Sally Silent's picture.*)
ME: While we're waiting, tell me a little about yourself.
SALLY: (*Eyes down*) Not much to tell. I've done some modeling.
ME: Where?

SALLY: A department store. Doylestown, Pennsylvania.

ME: How do you see yourself?

SALLY: I don't know where I fit in.

ME: Have you done any acting?

SALLY: Some.

ME: Where?

SALLY: Community theater.

ME: What parts did you play?

SALLY: Mostly small parts. You wouldn't know them.

ME: I go to a lot of theater. Tell me about one.

SALLY: (*Eyes up, at last*) *Barefoot in the Park*.

ME: What part did you play?

SALLY: Connie.

ME: That's the lead, isn't it?

SALLY: (*Eyes down again*) Yes—but it's amateur theater.

ME: (*To myself*) If she'd only look at me. (*Aloud*) Was it successful?

SALLY: All right, I guess.

(*My secretary enters.*)

SECRETARY: Here's Miss Silent's picture, Vangie.

ME: (*To myself*) Thank God, something to talk from. (*I look at the picture.*) Very nice. I think you could make a good housewife type.

SALLY: I liked another picture I had better.

ME: (*Frantically searching for something positive to talk about*) You studied soap-opera acting with Peter Miner, I see.

SALLY: Yes.

ME: Did he put you on tape?

SALLY: Yes.

ME: Have you brought something to read?

SALLY: No.

ME: Would you mind reading something cold?

SALLY: Oh, I couldn't do that.

ME: Well, thank you for coming in.

SALLY: Okay.

(Sally, thank God, exits.)

The above interview, in case you did not guess, is the how-not-to-handle-an-interview kind. If you think it's exaggerated, it's not. I could actually write several such scenarios all equally disastrous: the Brash-Salesman kind; the Above-It-All-Struggling-Actor kind; the How-Come-You're-Not-Offering-Me-a-Million-Dollar-Contract kind. . . .

Now, ignoring Sally's lack of response, you'll notice some special things about the above interview. I, the interviewer was trying to get acquainted with her, trying to get a feel for her as a person, what she was like. You'll notice also that there was no concrete job discussion or offer. That was not because Sally sat like a lump of clay but because job offers rarely occur during a general interview. That's what separates it from an audition or "call" where you're being asked directly to compete with other actors or actresses for a specific part.

What Is a General Interview?

Quite simply, a general interview is a meeting set up so that the casting director, agent, or producer can get a look at you, find out something about your skills and abilities, and consider how you might fit into any future commercial project he or she might be working on. It's a talent search really.

For me, as a casting director, the general interview is one of the most exciting parts of casting. I wonder who will come through the door. Will it be another comedienne with the selling power of a Madge the Manicurist, or a model with the provocative individuality of a Brooke Shields? I want the person to succeed; all talent people do—it's our business.

So please don't undervalue this meeting. *This is the break you've been waiting for and working toward.* You're going to see someone who is in a position to use you when the right part comes along or to send you to someone who can. Naturally you want to make the best impression you possibly can. In my view it's worth investing as much energy and thoughtfulness in preparing for a general interview as you would in getting ready for an actual audition.

Getting a Read on Your Interviewer

Meeting someone cold puts you at a disadvantage. So if you know someone who knows your interviewer, or someone who's had an interview with him or her, call that person and see what you can find out. (*Word of caution:* We don't all experience people the same way, so if the person says the interviewer is an ogre, take it with a grain of salt—you might love the person.)

If you don't know anyone who knows your interviewer, try calling his secretary or assistant. Most producers and casting directors have one or the other or both. Ask in a polite way what accounts the person you're seeing handles, what his title and responsibilities are. If you're shy about doing this, you could invent a little pretext for calling: You're coming in on an interview tomorrow and you were just wondering if the casting director would like you to bring something to read. Whatever, don't ask a secretary or assistant for a personal judgment; it will get to the boss.

Keeping up with the trades can sometimes help you find out about people. You might find the person interviewing you is giving a seminar, has received an honor, etc. Such bits of information dropped discreetly in an interview are good ways to make points.

Finding Out About the Agency Interviewing You

Do research before you go on an interview. Go to the library and get the *Standard Directory of Advertising Agencies.* See what accounts the advertising agency handles, what kinds of commercials they have been doing over the past year. Look specifically for those commercials that match your type.

For example, you might find that the agency handles Tide.

You're familiar with their commercials and think you're perfect for them. When the casting director asks you what kinds of parts you're looking for, you can say, "Well, I think I could do those terrific ones you made for Tide." If the question doesn't come up in the interview, find a casual way to drop your thought into the conversation.

Don't be afraid to volunteer information. It tells the casting director that you're intelligent (after all, you liked his agency's commercial), that you've taken the trouble to bone up on the agency, and that you're interested in the advertising business. We people in advertising need to be appreciated just like people in all other walks of life.

Preparing for Your Interview

Ultimately you want a job in a commercial that uses your type. Although this seems obvious, it's important that before you go on an interview you underline this specific goal in your mind. Everything that happens in the interview itself depends on it. The way you look, what you say, what you do. It is the touchstone for all the preparations I have touched upon below.

BE PREPARED TO TALK ABOUT YOURSELF

Don't be a Sally Silent. Don't let the interviewer do all the work. Go in prepared to say something. Look over your résumé and select pertinent information.

Prepare to elaborate on your credits—any unusual experiences, anecdotes; your feelings about schools or acting classes. Think of things that express you as your type: your hobbies, parts you've played. (You'll probably find that many of the things you do are things your commercial type would do.)

More, review the kinds of jobs you've had, even those that have nothing to do with show business. Define why you want to get into commercials, your plans for the future. Crystallize a strong impression of you as your type. After all, that's why you're there—to get a job in a commercial using your type.

ROLE PLAYING

Find friends or family members who will playact the interview with you. New ideas might come up. Besides, it will help put you at ease.

Note: Once you're at the interview, you can forget your script; some of the things may never come up—your best stories, etc. Never mind, they may at another time.

BE PREPARED TO LOOK YOUR TYPE

The call is to come in for an interview tomorrow morning at ten o'clock. At last! After you've come down from the clouds, the first thing to do is take one of your pictures, stand before the mirror, hold the picture up to your face, and compare. Do you have the same hairdo? Are the clothes you wore for your picture (or similar clothes) at the ready? Are they clean and ironed? Do they fit? If you haven't worn them for a while, try them on to make sure. Is your makeup bag fully equipped? Are you set to be put on videotape? A clear yes to all these questions, believe me, will enhance your chances of having a successful interview. There's no question that how we look affects our confidence. Any doubts, reread chapter 4 "Playing Pygmalion to Yourself."

BE PREPARED TO PUT YOUR BEST SELF FORWARD

The tube is your best tutor here. The moment you start making contacts (even before), watch interviews on TV. Notice how people conduct themselves, their poise (or lack of it), their posture. Notice the way they talk about themselves. How loud showoff replies repel. How articulate answers impress. Notice how the person interviewed picks up on questions. These interviews are often gone over before air time. You can prepare to do the same by anticipating questions. Notice the value of a little humor. How specific answers and anecdotes give color and interest to the person.

I'm not suggesting you adopt other people's mannerisms. But what you *can* adopt is that which primarily makes these inter-

views successful: being oneself and not taking oneself too seriously.

BE PREPARED TO READ SOMETHING OR TO BE TAPED

Your interviewer naturally would like to get an idea of how you
handle lines, what your voice quality is, how easily you can slip
into a role. More than likely, he will ask you to read a piece of
material. It's better to prepare something you can read in advance—a commercial, a poem, a small dramatic scene. That way
you won't have to read cold.

If you're not asked, make it a point to tell your interviewer that
you have something prepared. Let him decide if he wants to hear
it or not. Again, this shows that you're really interested and have
taken the time to make a presentation. I suggest you make whatever you select upbeat. Most casting directors find *Medea* a little
heavy. Besides, there are not many calls for child-slayer types.

Tape

The interviewer may want to put you on videotape—either in
his office or in a nearby office or studio. Chapter 12 discusses this
in relation to auditions; the difference may be that in this interview on tape you may not be given a script but just asked to talk
about yourself. They'll be less interested in precise information
than in the quality of your personality. Be warm, pleasant, and
outgoing. Practice a little to yourself.

PREPARE YOURSELF EMOTIONALLY

If this is your first interview, you're going to be nervous.
There's no getting around it. It's normal and healthy and nothing
to be ashamed of. Most good actors or athletes are nervous before
a performance. It's what gives them extra energy.

I honestly can't tell you how to overcome extreme nervousness
in one easy lesson. It takes practice and meditation. An actress
told me of a simple breathing exercise that might help: Just follow
your natural breathing, count each exhalation up to ten, then
start over again. If you breathe slowly, as though very relaxed,

you can't help but become relaxed.

As in a general interview, there will be no specific job offer, so you don't have to be anxious about being turned down. You can't lose what you never had. Your life is not riding on it. You are simply meeting with another human being.

In my eyes, concentration is the best antidote for nervousness. If you've ever watched a tennis match or golf tournament on TV, you have heard the announcer say of a player who is losing ground, "He has lost his concentration." In other words, the player has become scattered, nervous.

It is simply impossible to be concentrated and nervous at the same time.

How can you achieve concentration? Three ways: (1) by being prepared, using all the aids we've been talking about; (2) by staying alert—looking at the interviewer and really listening to what he is saying; and (3) by having a clear idea of what you specifically want from the interview. Do you want an honest evaluation? Do you want contacts? Do you want encouragement? Do you want a job for a specific commercial? Do you want information? Do you want to be called in for an interview? It's amazing but once you bring vague expectations down to a realistic goal, butterflies disappear.

Remember, the person you are seeing wants you to succeed as much as you do. In the advertising business, there is no greater thrill for those of us on the production side than finding someone with talent.

The Interview Itself: A Summing Up

You'll find some of the following suggestions, repeats of the preceding material. No matter. They bear repeating. Please don't be bogged down by their number or content. Just remember what you've learned about preparing and, above all, be yourself. Okay. Ready?

Get pertinent information over first—e.g., you see yourself as a he-man and you're interested in doing commercials for the agency's beer account. Exception: If you're bursting with excitement over a new show you're doing, bring the excitement in with you. It's always good to indicate you're busy.

Be enthusiastic. Energy is life and, wherever it is, it brings life. Don't conserve on this kind of energy.

Volunteer any information that may suggest a job. "I see you have the Pond's account. I use it and my mother, grandmother, and great-grandmother do, too."

Elaborate. Choose topics you can spin off on—a funny or moving experience in the theater or in one of your classes. Get into gossip if you want. It's always interesting.

If you're still nervous once you get into the casting director's office, simply say so. Quite often you'll find that simply acknowledging tension releases it.

Use the experience as a fun and interesting one. Find something you genuinely like in the person interviewing you. Make it easy for the person you're seeing to like you.

Look at the interviewer. That way you're in position to watch his reactions and can judge which way the interview is going. If you feel you're falling flat or coming on too strong, you can correct it.

Even if ashtrays are present, request permission to smoke. Some people are very touchy about smoking.

Sell yourself at whatever stage you're in, beginner or old pro. If you're good at selling yourself, you're going to be good at selling products.

If you're asked a question, pick up on it. If he says, "I see you're into karate," pick up on it. "Yes, I am. I'm working toward a brown belt. Not only does it help me defend myself, it helps me maintain my concentration in acting. . . . "

Don't interview the interviewer. The casting director has his own routine—go with it. Don't take over. Leave it to his direction. On the other hand, don't make him work too hard.

Don't be afraid to speak up on your own behalf, short of obnoxious bragging.

Don't tell sad stories, show bitterness or defeatism.

The interviewer will generally indicate when the interview is over. Watch for it and make the first move to rise.

If you can, at the end of the interview, ask where you could get other contacts. But don't ask to see someone else in the same agency.

Ask the interviewer how you may keep in touch: phone calls, postcards, etc.

Above all, keep focused on the reason you're there—to sell yourself as a specific commercial type, etc.

Be honest.

11

Getting an Agent

An actress friend of mine recently told me a story that illustrated how much ingenuity, hard work, and anxiety can go into getting an interview with an agent.

As she tells it, she was just dying to get an interview with a very important agent in town. Now, usually agents will not grant you an interview until they've seen your work, so when my friend finally got a showcase, the first thing she did was phone the agent and invite her to the performance.

The agent agreed to come, but my friend wanted to make certain she'd be there. To assure her presence, she got an actor friend, who supported his acting by working for a limousine service, to drive the agent to the performance.

Still worried that there would be some mix-up, my friend tried to spot the agent in the audience during the performance, but her role did not allow for much looking around. Even if it had, she wouldn't have been able to pick her out; she had never met her.

After the performance, the green room (reception area) quivered with hugs and handshakes and effusive compliments. My friend was so busy looking for the agent, she hardly noticed the people. Mechanically, she acknowledged a woman her acting coach seemed to be pushing on her. Another actress, she figured. It wasn't until the woman was at the door wiggling her fingers and calling out "Loved it, thank you for sending the limousine" that she realized who she was.

Incidentally, mistaken identity and all, she got a profitable interview.

Although you'll probably not have to go through all my friend went through, getting an agent is one of the biggest challenges you'll meet in becoming a TV-commercial performer. But really, it's nothing to get uptight about. Agents are usually quite nice people. They're as anxious to find a talented commercial type as you are to find an agent.

What Is an Agent?—Your Point of View

An agent is the mediator between you and those who will employ you—in most cases, casting directors. The agent is your representative, your job source, your promoter, your adviser, your protector, your booster, your business manager. Your agent's role can develop into almost that of a private manager. Sometimes an agent is a handholder; some agents in L.A. still accompany talent to auditions, old-fashioned-style. Sometimes an agent acts as part psychiatrist, part Dear Abby. I will go into their many other functions more specifically later under "23 Things a Good Agent Will Do for You." But first, as I'm the person who buys the talent that agents sell, let's look at how I see them.

What Is an Agent?—My Point of View

I rely heavily on agents; I like it if you have one. Sure, I keep files and lists of people, but the faster way is to screen through agents. I'd say these are the two most important things I look for in agents:

1. Someone who knows the worth of the talent he suggests, and helps me evaluate if they're right for the part.

2. Someone I can rely on to manage your business, and most important to check out your availability and your conflicts—that is, whether you are already contracted to be in a commercial advertising a competitive product or service.

When it comes down to it, you and I want the same thing from an agent: someone who will take responsibility.

From Where I Sit . . .

From what I hear on the other end of the line when I make calls to agents for talent, I'd advise you first and foremost to search out agents who'll take time to know you and your work.

Every day I hear agents try to sell talent. Take it from me, there's a vast difference between an agent who will sarcastically remark, "Well, I've gotten her in at other agencies," and the one who will say, "I saw her in the Open Stages Workshop Tuesday night and she played exactly that kind of role and was very funny."

Recently I had an actress come in on a call. As she was leaving, she told me she was going to stop off at her agent's office; he had sent her to me on her picture alone; she had never met him. She didn't have to tell me that; it was apparent. She was completely wrong for the part. Her audition was a waste of time.

How Do You Decide Which Agent(s) Are Best for You?

If you live in a city with any commercial activity, you will most likely have a choice of at least a half-dozen talent agents. You should be able to find several that are right for you. Before you contact any of them, I recommend that you look into their credentials:

- Are they franchised with SAG and AFTRA?
- Do they have offices or an association in more than one place—e.g., Chicago–New York, Houston-Dallas, Miami–Ft. Lauderdale, L.A.–San Francisco?
- Do they have someone who works full-time on commercials, or is it handled part-time by a secretary or assistant?

Once you've checked out their reputations, you'll want to zero in on those who are best for you. Your choice will greatly depend on where you are in your career.

STARTING OUT

You have no contacts and few meaningful credits. You're looking over a list of agents. Which one do you pick? Your answer may be "Are you kidding? Anyone who'll take me." Okay, let's go with that.

Your best bets are the newer agents. They are open to finding new people and are sometimes as eager as you. But don't worry, it's not a case of the blind leading the blind. In order to get a SAG franchise, they have had to work as agents or the equivalent for at least two years. Sometimes they've worked for bigger agencies and are now branching out on their own. They have contacts and clients. You will want to free-lance with them at the beginning to see what they can do for you.

IT'S EARLY IN YOUR CAREER AND SEVERAL AGENTS ARE PRESSURING YOU TO SIGN EXCLUSIVELY

Although the recognition is flattering, this is not the time to sign. Only if a big agent asks you, one of those who get the majority of the casting calls, should you consider signing. Casting directors will call them first to set up the nucleus of their audition before calling the smaller agents, who might have only a couple of available people. You probably won't be able to, but nevertheless see if you can't free-lance with the big agent for at least three months. This will give you time to determine if there is too much competition for you within the agency—in other words, too many people of your type—and to see if the chemistry is right. In any event, you won't go too far wrong in signing for a short time.

YOU ALREADY HAVE A THEATRICAL AGENT

Your agent has helped you get some wonderful regional theater assignments, important showcases, and even a small feature-film role, but he's sent you up on only one commercial. You're signed with him for theater and feature film; now he wants you to sign for commercials as well. His commercial division is small. He does not get the bulk of the calls. But after all, a casting director did see you in one of the off-off-Broadway shows he sent you up on, and through it you got a commercial. What is the fair thing to do?

You should free-lance. You can be registered with other agents and still allow your agent a crack at getting in on a commercial call. It sometimes happens that one of the other commercial agents starts doing well for you and, although he's not heavy in theater, demands that you sign in all areas. At that point you'll have to decide.

YOU'VE MADE IT

You've been free-lancing and you're getting more calls than you can handle. What to do!

This is probably the best time to sign. Look over what the various agents you've worked with have done for you. You'll no longer need the agent who will sell you and promote you; you'll want the agent who will be more selective in the type of commercials that you do.

Moreover, you'll want an agent who's good at negotiating. At this point, you may want to ask for more than the scale rates. You want to make sure you're not overexposed on a commercial that may not pay well. You may want to do only network commercials (they pay better) or only those that run in certain regional areas (to prevent overexposure in L.A., for instance). Choose carefully.

The Advantages of Signing with a Medium-Size or Small Agent

Signing with a medium-size or smaller agent has its special advantages. They'll probably give you more attention than a big agent will. They'll promote you more, and in the long run be as effective. As a signed client, you get preference, although at the beginning you may want a trial nonsigned period.

Do Certain Agents Specialize?

Definitely. Some agents tend to specialize in housewife types, others in character types, and still others in voice-overs. They may cover the other categories, but because of a roster of good people of one type, they usually get calls for their specialty. If you're a beginner, there's an extra bonus. When their "winners" aren't available or want too much money, you have a good chance of being sent up as the "new" face or voice.

MOST IMPORTANT OF ALL

Choose the agent who strongly believes in you and your abilities. Big or little, they can perform miracles for you.

Note: In some areas—e.g., L.A.—you have no choice whether to sign or not sign. You choose an agent, you sign with that agent.

23 THINGS A GOOD AGENT WILL DO FOR YOU

An agent will act as your PROMOTER:

- Advise you about pictures and send them out for you
- Help you put a composite together
- Set up general interviews for you
- Push you in on auditions
- Check out conflicts
- Get you preaudition scripts and information from casting directors that may help you get the part
- Apprise casting directors of other talents you have—e.g., that you really can sing and dance or have a comedic side
- Sell you to a not-quite-sure casting director

- Work out your schedule for shooting
- Arrange for booking information

An agent will act as your BUSINESS MANAGER:

- Negotiate terms and conditions of your contract
- Check contracts to see if they conform to agreement
- Advise you on special contract provisions involving areas of exclusivity and releases
- Keep records of usage and residual payments
- Bargain separately for services or rights not noted in the original contract
- Keep track of late payments and penalties
- Get you releases when commercials are withdrawn from use

An agent will act as your FRIEND:

- Boost you
- Advise you on people's responses to you in general and after auditions in particular
- Act as middleman, make calls for you that you may be hesitant about
- Serve as a buffer to your rejections
- See your workshop or off-off-Broadway productions
- Act as mother, father, and psychiatrist

Finding an Agent

Fifi Oscard, a well-known New York agent, told me that she gets most of her people through recommendations. Casting directors recommend them; directors recommend them. This is true with most agents. Fine. But the catch is that the recommendations come from people who have worked with the actor or actress. What if you're just starting out? What if you've not worked with anyone who can recommend you to a good agent?

The same thing that holds for other contacts holds for agents.

Start with friends, and friends of friends. Ask an actor or actress you know to introduce you to his or her agent. Ask everyone you know if they know an agent or have a friend or a friend of a friend who can arrange an interview for you. As I mentioned before, this is a business of favors. I know recommendations work (see chapter 9 on contacts).

OTHER SOURCES

First of all, look at my agent list at the end of this chapter.

For lists in your particular area, call SAG and AFTRA and get their lists of franchised agents. Get the *Madison Avenue Handbook,* the *Ross Reports,* or the *Creative Black Book,* all of which list agents. Read the trades religiously. You can also call ad agencies and ask what agents they use, but I can't guarantee you'll get an answer.

Some agents hold open interviews. Call and ask if and when they do.

OVER THE TRANSOM AND UNDER HIS OR HER NOSE

Here's where a good picture can break barriers. If your timing is right, you may just luck in. The agent may be looking for your type, you've just sent or dropped off your picture, and, lo, there it is crying, "Me, me!"

BLOW YOUR OWN HORN

Remember, an agent is interested in 10 percent of your TV-commercial income. In trying to sell yourself to agents, it's up to you to show how they can sell you to casting directors.

Attach a hard-hitting sales message to your picture. List anything that will make you a good salable client—e.g., a housewife who can do both straight and character parts. Spotlight any recent professional experience, anything that will convince the agent that you can make money for both of you. In other words, sell yourself to agents the way you do to casting directors, producers, etc.

SHOWCASES

In show-biz lingo, a showcase is a "platform" for actors and actresses to display their talents. Essentially, it goes like this: Performers get together, do scenes, and invite casting directors and agents to watch them perform. I get notices every week. I've attended many and I can say that everybody benefits. Actors who might not belong to a theater group have a chance to be discovered, and agents and casting directors have a chance to do the discovering.

As a captive but interested audience, I have a few suggestions. Scenes from a well-known play are best. Most agents and casting directors will know the play and you can get right into it without explanations. Also, people can concentrate on individual performances. It certainly beats being in an off-off-Broadway play that's so dreadful that anyone in it is colored by it.

I must admit I like the fact that these showcases are short and can be done in the late afternoon in town. After a hard day's work, I don't always relish going way downtown to some loft or cellar to see a performance, but like most casting directors and agents, I go regardless.

Advertising Your Performance

By all means, spread the word. Send notices of your performance to every agent in town, or at least to the agents with whom you would like to work. Send a flyer. Send a picture. To nail it down, call the agents and say, "I'm going to be in such and such. Can you arrange to come and see it?" Even if they can't, they know you're working.

Come the performance, be sure that your picture and résumé are given out or easily available to the people who attend. You'll find agents will usually go backstage after the performance (I know I see many familiar faces). They will also usually call you. Above all, make certain to follow up—call and say thanks or write a note.

Other Ways to Get Your Performance Seen

Some of the union offices have auditions and open interviews.
AFTRA, for example has an open house where agents and casting directors are invited to see new people.

If nothing's going on, organize something yourself. If you're not
an organizer, prepare a monologue or scene with another actor.
When you call agents, say, "It will only take three minutes." A
time limit is a little harder to resist.

A LITTLE HUMOR, IMAGINATION, AND CHARM GO A LONG WAY

As a casting director, I'm the recipient of all sorts of ploys to
get an interview or audition. For instance, during the recent holiday season, an actor called me and said, "Hey, listen, I want you
to catch my act—I'm Santa Claus on Forty-sixth and Fifth Avenue." Someone else called and said, "This is your last chance to
hire me before New Year's." (Maybe the yuletide brings it out.)

The sincere approach usually gets me. People call and genuinely
say, "Look, I know you're busy. I'd really like to meet you." A
straightforward approach—"Can I come in and see you next
Wednesday at ten o'clock? I have a scene I'd like to do for you"—
does the trick, too. My point is that since agents are as interested
in talent as I am, they should be as open to your inventiveness.

What Do Agents Look For

You're a good commercial type. You have talent. You'll get an
agent.

Maybe.

From my talks with agents, there's more than enough qualified
talent around. When it comes down to taking on people, they can
afford to look for something more. Summed up, that "something"
is a winning attitude.

I thought a garnering of their criteria might help you win over
one or two or three agents, so I've sorted them out and here's
generally how it goes:

Agents look for people who show they really want to work—who seem honest, whose appearance indicates they've taken time to put their type together.

They look for people with energy and enthusiasm, people who are truly committed (take classes, make contacts, etc.) and are willing to work on their own.

Agents don't want people who feel the world owes them a living and that they should be discovered overnight. Agents are bearish on people who think commercials are a quick way to make bucks or something to do instead of playing bridge.

Before you look for an agent, I suggest you check yourself against the above. To get an agent, it helps to be just what he or she is looking for, wouldn't you agree?

It's a Two-Way Road

You've read agents' criteria. But if you have an agent, you may think, Huh—they should talk. From the complaints I hear from actors and actresses, the perfect actor-agent marriage seems to occur as often as the perfect husband-wife marriage. Performers complain their agents don't get the calls. They don't really work for them. They don't call on time. They don't hustle up business. They don't keep track of conflicts. They don't ask for enough money. They don't send them around. They see their performers in only one way; they don't realize all the types they can play, all the things they can do.

Okay, there are some bad agents. But before you judge yours, consider this.

Agents hate it as much as you do when they have to say, "Sorry, it's slow right now." Agents can cover just so much and make some money. Agents often keep busy just filling calls. (You just may not be right for any of the parts). Agents do a lot of unremunerative work. No job, no fee. Agents only get 10 percent whether a commercial runs in a test market or nationally.

Working with Agents

Whether free-lancing or signed, it's essential you make contacts on your own. That means you contact casting directors at agencies, independent casting directors, film-production houses. If your agent knows you're working for yourself, he or she will work harder for you. Here are some suggestions:

Feed your agent any leads you can. Keep him or her informed of people you meet, any connections you make.

Keep your agent abreast of all your activities. Invite him or her to anything you're in—workshops, showcases, etc.

Keep yourself in front of your agent's eyes. When you're feeling especially up, looking good, stop by, say hello, refresh his or her memory of what a wonderful actor you are.

Do your own bookkeeping. If you're free-lancing, know your conflicts; know when you received your last payment; etc. This is known as being a smart business person.

Changing Agents

Finally, I'd say be sure you know what your agent does for you. Every so often, an actor will come in complaining that he wants to change his agent. "He doesn't do anything for me!" I know that the only reason the actor's there is because his agent pressured me to see him. Some gratitude.

If the "marriage" is over and you're justifiably unhappy with your agent, better change. And do it soon. Don't be gullible. If you want out and your agent doesn't, don't fall for promises of future jobs. It's unethical for an agent to suggest any future jobs that are not firm offers.

Do You Absolutely Need an Agent?

No, you don't.

It's quite possible to land your first job without an agent. For example, you could be recommended by a client. You could be picked up in a supermarket as a "real person" possibility. You could do your own commercial or be an employee or family participating in it. The casting director could have called you from seeing your picture.

You could do any of the above without an agent, but why should you? It's risky. In the end, most people call on an agent to negotiate for them, and I think they're wise. It's simply a good investment to put a job that you get on your own (especially if it's your first one) through an agent. After all, the agent is a source of future jobs.

I'd like to close this chapter by underlining one rule in working with your agent: *Do your share of making contacts.*

12

Going on an Audition

Your telephone rings. You answer it. It's a call from one of your TV-commercial agents.

"Hi, this is Eileen at the Marje Fields Agency. You've got an audition tomorrow afternoon at two o'clock. Are you free?"

"Yes, of course," you answer, trying to keep the excitement from your voice and, at the same time, desperately searching for a pencil.

Eileen then tells you what the product is (if you're free-lancing, she'll check to see if you have conflicts), what the role involves, and where you're to go. She concludes with "Do you have any questions?"

"No, I can't think of any. I'll be there," you say aloud, and under your breath mutter, "Where's that pencil?"

After you cradle the phone, you jump into the air, "Yippee! I've got an audition!" On the way down, you get an awful feeling. Did she say 2:00 or 2:30? You go through tortures. You hate to call back and seem like a dope. All sorts of other questions arise. What floor is it on? Are there any lines? Could you get a script before? It will all work out, you comfort yourself.

Believe me, that's not always the case. Actors have shown up a day late or have gone to the wrong agency.

Questions You Should Ask

First of all, don't let the lack of a pad and pencil get you messed up. Keep both by your phone, ready to record information. For extra insurance, have a list of questions before you. Leave space for answers. If you don't understand the information, ask again. Below are some to-the-point questions:

What's the product?

What products or services are competitive to the product's claim? (see chapter 22.)

What's the shooting date?

Where do I go? Place, address, floor, room, directions, if needed.

Date, day, time?

Whom do I ask for?

What's the part?

Anything special: Should I dress or wear my hair in any particular way? (If it's a character role, find out which kind, because that will make a difference in how you wear your hair and what you wear.)

Is it a "look"?

Do I have any lines?

Can I get a script ahead of time?

Will I be put on tape?

The Audition Begins

The audition begins the moment you put the phone down. You know the product and you have an idea of the role. Now is the time to prepare.

Familiarize yourself with the product's sales message. If you can't get a script in advance, look for ads in magazines. Once you find the ad, look for the main selling line. Repeat the line over and over again until it rolls off your tongue. If the product is Worcestershire sauce and the line is "You'll worship Worcestershire sauce," roll it off your tongue a few extra times.

Familiarize yourself with the product itself. Provided it's small and inexpensive, buy the product. Use it. Get a sense of what it's about. If it's a shampoo, consciously feel the cap of suds on your head; experience your fingers massaging through it; notice how it feels rinsed and wet, with a comb running through it, dry and fluffed out. Housewife types who make $150,000 a year put this kind of work into each job. Before they sell a tea, they've practiced sipping it, smelling its aroma. Of course you can't purchase a computer, but you can visit a store that sells them, and ask questions.

Familiarize yourself with the character. Your ability to do this depends entirely on your knowledge or intuition of what your character will be like. If you know little about your character, study the magazine ads and TV commercials that include your type. Think of people you know who are like your character. If, on the other hand, you know exactly whom or what you'll be playing, you can prepare yourself at length. One thing you can do, especially if you've been called for a particular character part, is check to see if you have any appropriate photos of yourself and bring them along.

What to Do When You Get to the Audition

Let me suggest that if you have any doubts about the exact location of your audition, you go there a day—or a week—before. You'll only be unnecessarily nervous if you don't know the location for sure. If you can pick up a script at the same time, you'll clear up two doubts with one trip.

Try to arrive at your audition a half-hour early. You'll probably be kept waiting, but you should be able to use the time well.

The first thing to do is to go to the reception desk and ask for a script or a storyboard. The receptionist will indicate a time sheet on her desk; if not, look for it. But unless you're ready to go in and audition immediately, don't sign in. Wait until your appointment time. Once you're signed in, you can be called in, and you don't want to be called in until you're ready.

If the script is a slice of life and you're to play with a partner, look around for an actor or actress with whom you work well. If you don't see anyone you know, ask a likely partner if he or she will go over the script with you. Once you both agree to work together, sign in at the same time. As people are usually called in order of sign-ins (rather than audition time), you're almost sure to be called in together.

LET ME EXPLAIN ABOUT TIME

Primarily, the sign-in sheet (see p. 138) is used to determine how much you will be paid—if anything—for the call-backs (the second and third auditions). You are not paid for the audition.

Time starts from the moment of your appointment time. Early does not count. Late does count. For example, if your appointment time is 10:00 and you sign in at 10:15, that's when your time starts. If your appointment is at 10:00 and you sign in at 9:45, your time starts at 10:00.

Note: Be sure to sign out after you leave the audition.

The Audition Room

If you've never been on an audition before, not knowing what an audition room or taping room is like could add to any stage fright you may have.

They come in all sizes and shapes. Mine is 9 × 12 and, like most, has a camera, two lights, a monitor, and an elevated stage area.

When you audition, you will see two or three highly visible cue cards on which your lines are written. They're there to prompt

COMMERCIAL PLAYERS
1. Print your name.
2. Print agent's name
3. Circle applicable interview

EXHIBIT E
SCREEN ACTORS GUILD
COMMERCIAL AUDITION REPORT FORM

AUDITION DATE _____

CASTING REP. _____ COMMERCIAL TITLE _____
ADVERTISER _____ PRODUCT _____ JOB # _____
ADV. AGENCY _____ CITY _____ PRODUCTION CO. _____

PLAYER'S NAME	(PRINT)	SOCIAL SECURITY #	(PRINT) AGENT	PLAYER'S ACTUAL CALL	PLAYER'S TIME IN	PLAYER'S TIME OUT	PLAYER'S INITIALS	CIRCLE INTERVIEW #
								1st 2nd 3rd 4th
								1st 2nd 3rd 4th
								1st 2nd 3rd 4th
								1st 2nd 3rd 4th
								1st 2nd 3rd 4th
								1st 2nd 3rd 4th
								1st 2nd 3rd 4th
								1st 2nd 3rd 4th
								1st 2nd 3rd 4th
								1st 2nd 3rd 4th
								1st 2nd 3rd 4th
								1st 2nd 3rd 4th
								1st 2nd 3rd 4th
								1st 2nd 3rd 4th
								1st 2nd 3rd 4th
								1st 2nd 3rd 4th
								1st 2nd 3rd 4th
								1st 2nd 3rd 4th
								1st 2nd 3rd 4th
								1st 2nd 3rd 4th
								1st 2nd 3rd 4th
								1st 2nd 3rd 4th
								1st 2nd 3rd 4th
								1st 2nd 3rd 4th
								1st 2nd 3rd 4th
								1st 2nd 3rd 4th
								1st 2nd 3rd 4th
								1st 2nd 3rd 4th

PRODUCER
1. Complete top half of form.
2. Sign your name.
3. Mail white copy to SAG on 1st and 15th of each month.
4. Designate person to whom correspondence concerning this form shall be sent _____

SIGNATURE OF AUTHORIZED REPRESENTATIVE

you. All in all, audition rooms are not scary places. They're somewhat like the place where you had your graduation picture taken.

There You Are in the Reception Room and There I Am in the Audition Room

Usually only one person, the casting director (me), does the taping. Sometimes another person operates the camera. Sometimes a producer is present. Sometimes a writer is there to help you with the reading. But for our purposes, let's have me run the whole show.

Picture me in the room. I've been taping for three hours and it's hot (the lights always heat up the room no matter how good the air conditioning). There's pressure on me to find Mrs. Right Housewife and so far no luck. It's a tough script and I didn't get it until the morning. The product's name is tricky and the selling line could qualify as an acting-school tongue twister.

In breezes Joan Drake. As she tosses her bag on the chair, I think, Good, it's Joan. I know she can act.

"Oh, Vangie," she says, "it's so good to see you. You know, I ran into George out there and we've just been chatting and I haven't had a chance to look at the script. So let me just look at it for a second." Oh dear, I think, let's see how "You'll just worship Worcestershire sauce" comes out.

Joan begins to read. Stops. "Oh, my God, my voice," she says. "George was the first person I've talked to—no wonder it sounds so awful. I probably should have done my scales."

She then proceeds to go through a stumbling audition, making hash out of the Worcestershire sauce. I'm glad to see her leave. By not using her waiting time advantageously, she ruined her chances and wasted my time as well as hers.

"A Funny Thing Happened to Me"

Some comedians are the worst disappointments. They spend their waiting-room time doing stand-up routines; trading jokes or anecdotes with colleagues; acting out all the parts. George Burns types or the older vaudevillian actors often turn the receptionist room into a Friars' roast. They're big hits with the receptionist, who at day's end is limp from laughing, but come the audition, they too often bomb. Their minds are not on the audition; they really want to get back to their previous audience and tell another joke they just remembered.

To me, it's no joke. Hanging over most auditions is a sense of rush. The "suits" (account executives) pressuring. There's a need to get through the day; to get the winner.

I tell you this to show that audition tension isn't one-sided. And the better you're prepared, the better you spend your waiting time, the much, much better your chances of endearing yourself to the casting director and winning the commercial.

How in That Crowded Reception Room Can One Rehearse?

It can be very tough—or impossible—to rehearse in a crowded reception room. You definitely need quieter space. Look for designated rehearsal rooms; if there are none, try the ladies' or men's room. In my agency it's not unusual to see actresses standing before the mirror delivering lines. No one thinks they're crazy. The people who work on that floor are used to it, so you can emote away. And while you're at it, you can check your hair and makeup.

Alcoves, exits, and corners of halls can also serve as makeshift rehearsal space. But be careful you don't get locked in a "no reentry" fire exit and miss the entire audition. It happens. I remember the time Diane Keaton got locked in a phone booth. She called her agent—pretty smart!

Wherever you hang out, be sure you can say your lines out loud. You must hear how you sound, and how the script sounds.

"Hi!"

. . . I say from behind the camera.

"Hi," you say putting your things on a chair or on the floor (that's where most people put theirs). You hand me your picture. If we've never met, a one-line "I'm Jane Doe—I play Sally Rogers on 'One Life to Live'" is all you need to say. As much as I'd like to chat if we know one another, I just can't afford to at this time.

You step in front of the camera, and it's like going on stage. You're on. Rehearsals are over. You must perform.

This is the time to let go. Here's the fun part. This is the time to get into the scene and really enjoy it.

"Now Just Relax"

Telling you to relax is a favorite directive of mine. Some people tense up when told to relax, but you don't—you take the good advice. While the casting director is getting set, you use the few moments to find the lens. It's your friend, the person you'll be talking to. You feel your feet firmly planted on the floor and you take a deep breath. The more you can focus on physical things, the better. But if you're prepared, if you've brought the character with you, you might not even have to use any crutch. You're concentrating and you're relaxed.

But Not Too Much

Some people who have auditioned a lot become jaded (a neat though obvious defense mechanism). They come in and say in a blasé way, "Okay, what do I do?" and proceed to give a resigned performance. It comes across as defeat. Resignation is not relaxation. Better to have a little tension and know how to use it. That said . . . Tape's rolling. Action.

The Importance of Slating a Commercial

To slate a commercial, you simply give your name and the take number. "Hi, I'm Felice Sherlock. This is take one." Sometimes the person taping will keep track of the slate, but usually you will do your own slating.

Slating your name on each take can tip the scale in your favor.

Omitting it can cost you the audition. Say you're one of the final-
ists. Your best take has been edited out and spliced onto one tape.
This tape also includes the best takes of the other contenders. It is
shown to as many as five or six decision-making groups of people.
Now supposing you omitted your name on your take. It's between
you and two or three other actors. People ask, "Who's that?"
Nobody knows, and the casting person is not present to tell them.
I know it's crazy, but in the rush of last-minute deciding, people
will simply go with the person whose name they know. So please
don't get lost in anonymity.

Usually you'll be told if you should slate any other information.
Be alert for any question asked you. If it's asked, it must have
some meaning. Say you're asked whether you can ski. Be sure to
include information on each take. "Hi, I'm Felice Sherlock. I'm an
expert skier. Take one."

A CHANCE TO SELL YOURSELF

Slating is your chance to say hello to the people who will view
the tape, to show your warmth. Remember, warmth is one of the
biggest requirements in commercials. If you're doing four takes,
you might add a little humor. "Hi again, I'm Felice Sherlock. I'm
still an expert skier. Take four."

Believe me, in this business any little extra something you can
give influences decisions. Use every opportunity to stand out.

You're on Your Own

Nancy Fields over at Ted Bates is one casting director who likes
to do her own taping and directing. She feels she knows the people she is bringing in and what she can get out of them. But
chances are you will not always be so lucky as to get a casting
director like her.

The purpose of the taping is to decide if you're the right type
and if you can act. (*Important:* See the next chapter on breaking
down script.) However, often a casting director may not be running the tape. He or she may be putting out calls for other com-

mercials or tied up in some way. The person taping may be a substitute. It's up to you.

Get What You Want

The person taping indicates that time's up, but you don't feel your reading did you justice. Don't settle for it. Speak up. "Let me just try it once more." If you have another idea as to how to do it, say, "Gee, I have a terrific idea that I think might work—let me try it. I'll do it very quickly." Usually, no one, even under pressure, will refuse you.

Can You Ask to See Your Tape?

Sometimes you'll be allowed to see your tape, sometimes not. Very often the person taping doesn't want to take the time to rewind and rerun the tape. There may be a good reason: the call is big, time's short. Still, there's no harm in asking. Seeing yourself on tape can help you adjust your performance. But if the person is reluctant, accept the refusal gracefully.

Goodbyes

Leave briskly. You might ask, "Shall I leave the script outside?" If you're in a play or up for an important part, you might mention it as you're leaving. Next day, if you were there, you'd hear me tell a writer as I screened the tape, "He's up for a new TV series," or "She's in an off-Broadway play right now." I'll appreciate anything I can use to sell you.

"THANK YOU VERY MUCH"

The people outside the reception room—the secretary, the tech person—everybody is auditioning you. It's a good practice to treat everyone along the way courteously. Everybody influences the decision. They'll either say nice things or not very nice things about you.

Thank the casting director for the audition: "Thank you very much." Thank the receptionist: "Thank you very much." Thank the secretary: "Thank you very much."

Call-Backs

THE FIRST CALL-BACK

Any audition after the first one is known as a "call-back." The first call-back means they've narrowed down the choices. A number of people have seen your tape; they've liked it, and you're a "possible."

Sometimes the locale of the second audition is changed to the director's office or film studio or even to the client's office. Usually, however, it will be at the same place you had the first audition.

At the first call-back, you will again be put on tape, but this time there will be more people present—probably the producer, writer, art director, often an account person, and maybe the client. Everyone loves to have the director there, too, if possible.

Your performance will be directed more. Perhaps the performance you gave before was not quite right and you will be asked to go in a different direction. Don't hang on to your first performance. Be prepared for script changes throughout this and subsequent call-backs.

THE SECOND CALL-BACK

This means that they've narrowed the field down even more. There may be only one other contender. At this point it's worth all your efforts. Call the casting director (by now you should feel some rapport) and see if you can get any more information. Ask if there's anything you can do about your hair or wardrobe.

Remember, all the talent in on a second call-back is highly capable. At this point the decision usually hinges on many subjective viewpoints, with the final yea or nay coming from the client.

THE THIRD CALL-BACK

This usually means you've all but got it. Have your agent call to see if there are any other contenders. The agency may want to check to see if you can perform a certain action such as smile as you take a bite of pizza. Perhaps they just want to get a perfect take that they can use to sell you to the client. The director may appear to meet you in person to see if your chemistry is okay. By this time you will know the script and, with the extra direction, your performance will be near shoot-day perfect.

Sometimes You May Wait and Wait

Sometimes your part may call for very little preparation. There are no lines, not much to do except wait. And to make matters worse, sometimes there's a jam-up or backup. Sometimes the camera has broken and you have to wait longer. There you are. You've scheduled another audition. It's getting close to the time you should go to the other audition. What do you do?

Don't get yourself all steamed up. You should say when you first arrive, "Look, I can only wait twenty minutes. Could I change my appointment and come back in an hour?" It's better than sitting there, working yourself up, and ruining both auditions.

Even if you have nowhere else to go, the wait at an audition can be long and frustrating. I recommend you bring along reading material and use the time to study or work on a play you're doing; the diversion may help your audition performance.

First Refusal

BETWEEN FIRST AUDITION AND SHOOTING DAY

Let's say you're auditioning for one of our accounts. The shooting date has been set for next Tuesday. A decision has not yet been made. The part is still between you and another actor.

It's at this juncture that I, the casting director, would call your agent and tell him or her that I want a first refusal—that is, I want first choice on you for that day. Your agent will probably say, "Okay, I will let you know if someone else wants to book that day."

The next day you win the final call-back; the agency calls and gives your agent a definite booking. Everything is great.

Or it could work another way. My agency has first refusal on you for next Tuesday. A second agency comes along with a booking for the same Tuesday. Your agent tries to have this other agency move their shooting date back one day. They can't. Your agent now calls my agency and says put up or shut up. We do just that. We want you. Your agent then calls the second agency with regrets; it's all settled.

If only it were all that simple. This area is knotted with complications. For example, an agency has a first refusal on you but can't give an immediate answer. A second agency comes along with an offer. Time passes. Technically you're free to go with your second offer. However, the first agency pleads for more time. The client is due in from Arizona that afternoon. They'll give an answer by the close of the business day. Your agent doesn't want you to lose both jobs and tries to keep the second job on the hook while giving the first agency the required time. Will he succeed? Maybe.

Still another complication. While you're waiting for an agency that has first refusal on you to decide, a second job comes in that is better than the first one. In this case, your agent will probably demand an immediate yes or no from the first agency.

Free-lancing can make things even more complicated. You may have one first refusal through one agent and another through another agent. To avoid such imbroglios, be sure when you're sent on an audition to inform all the people involved of any first-refusal dates.

You can see from the above how important it is to have a good agent, how important it is to keep your records straight, and how important it is to know probable shooting dates before you even go up on an audition.

The Booking

You just heard. It's set. You're it and there's no question about it. This one's been right up to the wire. (It's not uncommon; you often don't get booked until a day or two before the shoot.)

Instead of pulling your hair between the first refusal and booking, I suggest you have it done. The same goes for the whole area of preparation and maintenance. Twenty-four hours' notice is too short a time to make an appointment to get your roots or your nails done. Even if you could get an appointment, you'd be too busy between booking and time of shoot to keep it.

THERE'LL BE MEETINGS AND THINGS TO DO

You will talk with the stylist and discuss what you should wear. You may have to go shopping with the stylist. (You will be paid for this.)

You may meet with the director. Either you'll meet on another set where he's shooting that day or you'll meet at the agency and go over the script with him. (You will be paid for this.)

You may also be required to go to a rehearsal. In my view, this happens too infrequently. It's usually done only if the commercial is complicated.

You will be given the product to use (sometimes for legal reasons).

You will get the latest script to memorize.

You may have to run to your union office to join the appropriate union or to pay up back dues.

But it's worth it. After all this, the big moment. The shoot is just hours away.

SOME AUDITION DO'S AND DONT'S

- Do come in dressed and looking your type.
- Do have your picture and résumé ready.
- Do bring a feeling of warmth, energy, aliveness to the commercial. Jump up and down if you need a little energy to start.
- Don't waste time in chitchat.
- Do come in prepared with ideas on the script.
- Don't go in and criticize the script.
- If you choose to read from the script, hold it parallel to the floor so as not to cover your face.

- Don't criticize or belittle coactors.
- If you're working with a partner, relate to him or her. However, keep your face toward the camera rather than in direct profile. This is called "cheating to the camera."
- Do not be oversensitive to the pressure of the person taping. Do not come in, throw your performance at the camera and race out. It's not the time you take to do your performance that annoys casting directors, but the time you waste.
- Do listen to directions. One of a casting director's pet peeves is giving directions to an actor or actress who, because of nervousness, is inattentive and does the complete opposite.
- Establish where the camera is, where you should stand.
- Don't critique your own work. After a take, don't say, "Oh, that was awful."

13

Approaching the Acting Part of Commercials

THE SCRIPT AND STORYBOARD

Let's imagine you in the reception room of an advertising agency. You're at the reception desk and the receptionist hands you a script. (If you have only one line, you may not be given a script, but let's assume you do need a script.) You might say, "Thank you very much," turn around, and look for a place to study. Don't. Not yet. First ask to borrow a storyboard—you'll need it for your study. Although storyboards are not necessarily given out at an audition, there is usually one copy around. The receptionist will show you where.

Okay, there you are in a nice almost-quiet spot, script and storyboard in hand, ready to start studying. You may have been given a complete script. Or you may have been given only the scene you're in. Or you may have been given just your line. Whatever the case, you'll find your storyboard invaluable in giving you the total picture. Let's look at it first (see pp. 164–65). A storyboard has small boxes of pictures, called "frames," that depict what is happening throughout the commercial. Underneath or next to each frame is the narration or dialogue, or the audio portion of the commercial. The video directions are given in caps.

Okay, you're ready to work. First of all, look at each frame. Notice how the scene is established, how it moves into the product demonstration and to the tag. Now give the storyboard a few glance-throughs, asking yourself these questions:

First glance: What are they selling? How does my character help sell the product or service?

Second glance: What's the overall mood? Realistic, charming, broad comedy? The style of the storyboard drawings will give you the feel of the commercial and your attitude in it.

Third glance: What does my character look like?

If you look like the cute young mother in the storyboard except that she has her hair pulled back, pull your hair back. If you look like the young husband and he's wearing an open-collar shirt, open your collar. Everything helps.

You'd be surprised, when we're viewing the tapes, how many times a pleased voice rings out, "Why, she looks just like the character in the storyboard!" If your acting lives up to the physical likeness, you almost have the commercial clinched—especially if the client has already approved the storyboard.

Fourth glance: Where does the action take place? In an office? An airport? A kitchen? If all you've been given is a segment of script, this will help fight your feeling of being in limbo.

Now Let's Look at the Script

Quickly look the script over and check to see if you understand it without the storyboard. First read the script out loud twice. Don't act, just read it aloud. To be sure you understand it, try putting it in your own words. Say the product name out loud several times. If there's a special campaign or selling line, repeat that several times until it sounds natural.

Now down to the serious study. A commercial often is a mini-drama. It has a beginning, a middle, and an end. It usually sets up a problem and solves the problem, and everyone lives happily ever after. Keep this in mind as you study the following pages. I am going to take you through the script breakdown process in detail. You should find that after going through this process a few times, it will become second nature to you.

Knowing Your Role

Are you the person giving the advice? Are you the person receiving the advice? Knowing your position (stance) is the first clue as to how you'll play your role.

As the adviser, you are usually caring, concerned, mindful of the person to whom you are talking. Some examples: You are a representative of the manufacturer; a friendly neighbor; young mother; older relative; the sexy-beautiful person everybody wants to be; the hip young expert who knows all about cars.

As the person taking the advice, you are a stand-in for the television viewer. As such, you are not an idiot but an attractively vulnerable person who just needs advice with a particular problem. Some examples: You are a husband with a cold; a neighbor with spotty glasses; a teen-ager with acne; a new bride who can't cook.

DESCRIBING YOUR CHARACTER

You've decided whether you're an adviser or advisee. Now, to bring your character more sharply into focus, describe yourself as the character in one sentence.

I'm a nosy, well-meaning neighbor about 55 who loves to solve everybody's problems.

I'm a 22-year-old mother with a brand-new baby, and I'm a little frightened that I may be using the wrong product and may give my baby a rash.

I'm the youngest bank VP Chase has ever had and I'd like to tell everyone about the wonderful features our bank has to offer.

After you have defined the character, call up three qualities that you as a person have in common with the character you play.

You both are warm, soft, excitable.
You both are enthusiastic, assertive, knowledgeable.
You both have a helpful, taking-over but generous quality.
You both are doubting, teasing, gentle.

Think of the Character in Physical Terms

Take on the character's physical posture. If you're a spokesperson for a large corporation, stand with authority. If you're a humorous, lovable young husband, you may assume a relaxed, thumbs-in-pockets slouch.

IF YOU CAN'T FIND THE CHARACTER IN YOU...

...make up one that will work for you. If you're a spokesperson, think of a political figure or a movie star. If your character is a mother with a lot of children and you have none, think of your relationship with your nieces or nephews or children of friends. If your character is a professor, think of an old teacher you admired.

WHAT'S YOUR OBJECTIVE?

I first heard the word "objective" when I was studying drama at Bennington. I discovered that, as used in the Stanislavki method, it meant *what the character wants in the scene.* Subsequently, in the Cassavetes Workshop and studying with other acting groups, I found people used the word "objective" interchangeably with "action" and "goal." However used, I saw time and again how knowing one's objective/action/goal made a scene from *The Cherry Orchard* or *A Streetcar Named Desire* come alive.

When I went into casting I thought, Why not use the concept in commercials? So I did. And I still do. Come in for an audition with me, and if the scene's flat, you'll hear me question you:

Joan McMonagle.
Type: housewife.

Beverly Place.
Type: housewife.

Nancy Dutiel. Type: cosmetic model.

Willie Carpenter.
Type: young husband.

Susan Spilker. Type: young
woman-next-door.

James Gillis.
Type: handsome man.

Erin Gray.
Type: glamour girl.
PHOTO: Betsy Cameron

Nancy Daniels.
Type: young mother.

Will Hussung. Type: character.

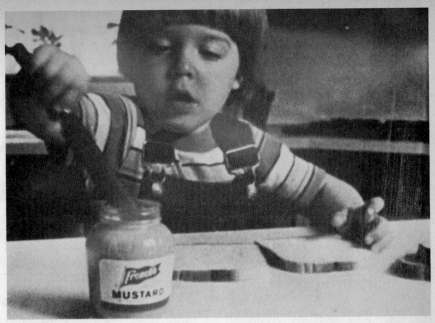

Ryan Janis

Beverly Ballard. Type: spokesperson.

Jan Leighton as Ben Franklin, Einstein, Teddy Roosevelt, and F.D.R.

"What's your objective? What kind of reaction do you want from the other person?" And you'll discover I won't take an "I want him to like me" for an answer. Asking for a physical response—a smile or a scowl—makes you concentrate harder and think in more specific terms. When you get the reaction you have worked for, your own counterreaction is vital, natural, spontaneous. And, lo, it's proven again that knowing your objective works as well in a cherry Jell-O commercial as it does in *The Cherry Orchard.*

Every Line Calls for an Objective. Of course, the overall objective of all commercials is to sell a product or service. But there are many smaller objectives in arriving at it, each growing toward the overall objective. You'll find an objective underlying each of your lines.

Examples of Objectives. If you're the convincer, you'll probably come up with some goals like the ones below. Keep in mind that you want a physical reaction.

I want my husband to smile at me after eating this soup.

I want my neighbor to feel the softness of this towel I just washed with my detergent.

I want my boss to shake my hand for my suggestion that he purchase a computer.

Hyping Up Your Objective. If your objective seems too weak in itself to get the response you want, make it stronger. For example, if your husband in the script has a minor cough and you're trying to get him to take the cough medicine you have in your hand, imagine he has pneumonia and you're trying to get him to take the cure for it.

I am ever amazed at how a strong and clear concept of an objective can make reactions come through true—can make a phony storyboard smile unselfconscious and right.

WHOM ARE YOU TALKING TO AND WHAT IS YOUR RELATIONSHIP?

You may be talking to the viewer. You may be talking to another character in the scene. You may be talking to the product. In each case, you must have a relationship with him or her or it. Look at your script and storyboard for what the relationship is. Your character-and-objective studies should have given you strong clues. If there's nothing in the script, invent some background for the relationship just as you did for your character.

If you're talking to the lens (viewer), you might do as Andy Duncan, a frequent principal in commercials, does: visualize the audience you're addressing. If it's a muffler commercial, think of Uncle Charlie in his hard hat; if it's a baby-powder commercial, think of your cousin Kim who just became a new mother.

Sometimes in a cosmetic commercial, you as the spokeswoman may be asked to use a teasing, sexy approach. The aim is to encourage the woman viewer to identify with you. "Oh, she's very provocative." In this case, I recommend you pretend that you're talking to a boyfriend.

If you're talking to another character, invent some background for your relationship in the commercial. "We went to college together ten years ago, and now because of our husbands' business moves, we again live near each other. We're very good friends."

Discover some quality in your partner that's like the character he or she is playing. While you're waiting in the waiting room and have a chance to work with your partner in the scene, there are a couple of little exercises that can help you build rapport.

Watch your partner and describe to yourself everything he's doing. Now he's lifting his hand to his eye. Now he's scratching his forehead. (This also helps your concentration.) Another exercise is to copy physically what the other person is doing as though in a mirror image.

If you're talking to the product or about it, you will be holding it, handling it, wearing it, eating it, driving it, using it, or simply admiring it. Be sure of your relationship with it. If the product is a Milky Way candy bar, think of how you used to love chocolate as a kid and squeezed all the candy in a Whitman's Sampler for one with a soft caramel inside. Remember, how you feel about the product is how the viewer will think of it.

The "Business"

The "business" is the physical activity you must perform in a commercial.

When you go into the audition room, it helps to create your own little set. Look around for a stool (most audition rooms have one) that serves as a makeshift worktable. Look around for props. They can help you refer to the product or object you're talking about more naturally. A scarf can substitute for a freshly laundered towel. A wallet can substitute for a shaver.

A few hints:

- Hold the product or prop toward the lens, just below it. You don't want to let it hide your face.
- If you're working with a partner, both of you can look at the product under the lens, and thereby cheat toward the camera instead of staring into one another's eyes.
- Perform each action deliberately. For example, if you're asked to hold up the towel and touch it to your face, complete the action of holding it up before you touch it to your face.

How to Handle One-Liners

You find out you have one line and you think, Ah, good, I don't have to do a script breakdown. This should be a cinch.

If you're lucky, you might get a complete script and have access to a storyboard. From them, you will gain some idea of what's going on and at least be cued in by the line ahead of you. This doesn't always happen; you may well be given a sheet of paper with one lonesome, disoriented, orphaned line on it.

All of the following suggestions are to give you—and the viewer—the sense that something has been going on before in the scene, that you're not just in limbo.

- Ask the casting director to cue you into the line—even if you have to give him the question to ask you.
- Ask him to pan the camera to you just before you say the line. *Or*—
- Just before you say the line, step into the picture.
- Give yourself some business—you're folding laundry or reading the product's back label. This way you can look up and say the line into the camera.
- If you're a model, stand or sit with your back to the lens and swirl your head around and say the line into the lens. This accomplishes two things: It shows off your hair and adds a little energy to the audition.

No Lines

You have no lines but have to pantomime some business. Not a cinch either.

Once you get into the audition room, either you will be shown a storyboard showing what you're to do or your business will be described to you by the casting director.

Ask to see yourself on the monitor going through the action. This is one time where you should insist.

As I just mentioned, take your time. Keep the action simple and deliberate. Do only one piece of business at a time. For example, the business is to drink a cup of coffee. You've never tasted the brand before and you must react favorably. Go through it slowly first. Take a tentative sip. And then another sip. Let us really know you're tasting it. Savor it. You may be asked to speed the action up. Do so, but be sure that the steps are still separated—in other words, don't show that you like the taste at the same time or before you taste it. (I've seen it happen.)

Work on the Opening and Closing Lines

Sometimes the only chance you have to show your personality is in the opening line, before you get into the sell part of the commercial. There will be a little opening handle the copywriter has put in to set up the commercial. It is known as the attention getter. Try it in different ways—with charm, with intensity, with comic flair. The last line usually is a call to action—that is, to buy the product. It is the last impression you will leave with the people who will judge your performance. Make it count.

Try to memorize both lines so you will not have to rely on cue cards and will be free to give them your all.

Changing Your Reading

As I mentioned earlier, the director usually makes his entrance at one of the call-backs. He may ask you to change your interpretation drastically, or script changes may require you to alter your reading. (Agency people may be busy working out bugs in the script up to the last minute.) Even when the script remains the same, you may be given a whole new slant. They may say, "Let's try this as a hard-sell commercial." You may have to strengthen your objectives. Or try it a little bit more laid back. Or, if it's a comedy, do it a little broader.

Now's the time to both remember and forget your script study. First follow the director's specific direction without question. If you really think it works better your way, say "Can I just try it this other way?" Show the director you have done the script study. Be firm in your convictions, but know when to give in.

Here are some scripts and suggested ways of handling them. Have fun!

SOLVE SHAMPOO

Open on young woman with Full head of beautiful hair.	YOUNG WOMAN: You're looking at problem hair!

Woman smiles at viewer's disbe-
lief.

You think it's beautiful.

Dissolve to woman looking unhappy with prewashed hair.

You should have seen it an hour
ago—limp, dull, lifeless . . .

Cut to Solve Shampoo bottle.

Here's my problem solver! Solve
Shampoo with pH 4.

Pull back to woman just finishing
lathering up hair. Slowly dissolve
through to opening shot of smiling young woman gently swing-
ing hair on shoulders.

It thoroughly cleans and leaves
my hair in perfect condition . . .
healthy, shining, full and soft to
the touch.

Move in on close-up of Solve
bottle.

Solve Shampoo with pH 4 has
solved my problem. Let it solve
yours.

Character:	Young woman getting ready to go to a party. You are warm and charming.
Whom you are talking to:	A roommate or younger sister, perhaps.
Objective:	To convince her to try Solve Shampoo by sharing your experience of having miserable-looking hair, us-ing the shampoo, and looking great afterward.
Study:	Try to recapture the time when you were going out on an important occasion and you felt you looked just awful. (It may not have been a hair problem, but the feeling was the same.) Recall how you felt at some time when you felt you looked just knockout: happy and glowing.
Check:	Practice repeating the phrase "Solve Shampoo with pH 4." All words should be clear but roll easily off your tongue—no stumbling with pH 4. Be careful of your S's.

CRYSTAL CLEAR DISHWASHER POWDER

Open on medium shot two women in kitchen standing at dishwasher. Go in on first woman holding up spotted glass.

1ST WOMAN: I'm so mad I've got spots before my eyes.

Cut back to two-shot.

2ND WOMAN: I don't blame you—and with your in-laws coming for lunch.

2nd woman takes glass from first.

Don't worry, I'll run home and get my Crystal Clear Dishwasher Powder.

Dissolve to cu Crystal Clear Dishwasher Powder.

ANNCR: Crystal Clear gets dishes and glasses perfectly clean—leaves no embarrassing film spots.

Dissolve to two women at beautifully set dinner table. 2nd woman picks up glass.

SFX: *Doorbell rings*

2ND WOMAN: Still seeing spots before your eyes?

1st woman looks admiringly at clear glass.

1ST WOMAN: No, everything's crystal clear.

Character:
: *1st Woman*—(about 25) Worried, nervous, recently married, unsure.
  2nd Woman—(about 30) Problem solver. Experienced housewife. Knowing, warm, motherly.

Relationship:
: You've been neighbors for two years and are good friends.

Objective:
: *1st Woman*—To get some sympathy for your predicament and, more, be given a solution.
  2nd Woman—To help your neighbor by solving her problem. In physical terms, to make her give a sigh of relief and smile.

Study: 1st Woman—Try to find a time when you were in a
             tight fix and saw no way out. For example, rushing to
             catch a train and finding your car battery dead.
             2nd Woman—Your child fell and hurt her knee. You
             try to comfort her with a Band-Aid.

BANK UTOPIA

Open on long shot male bank executive with pointer in hand standing before chart.

EXECUTIVE: Days of high interest gone? Not at Bank Utopia. We offer recessionproof interest and it's fully insured. Here's how it works.

Move in to medium shot. He points to information on chart.

EXECUTIVE: Our interest rates for a six-month Utopia account are what you would ordinarily receive for a two-year money-saving certificate. How do we do it?

Dissolve woman customer walks into bank. Shakes hands with him as she sits at his desk.

EXECUTIVE: For full details, step into any local branch and see your Utopia banker. The Federal Reserve stands behind us. Bank Utopia. It's all in the name.

Character: You're the pillar of the community. You know what
                 you're talking about.

Objective: To get viewer (person you're talking to) to come in,
                 sit down, and listen to your advice.

Whom you are   While you'll want to talk to someone whom you feel
talking to: warmly toward, you still have a businesslike author-
                 ity. Perhaps you could be talking to your nephew.

Study: Pick a situation when you gave advice to a nervous
                 person, perhaps about buying a house or a car.

CHOCO-MOUNDS

Open on young and older truck drivers in truck cab. Older one is driving.

OLDER TRUCK DRIVER: (*Teaching kid the ropes*) You'll find, kid, when you've been driving as long as I have, there's no substitute for a hot meal.

Move in on young truck driver who is tearing open a Choco-Mounds bar.

YOUNG TRUCK DRIVER: Maybe not, but I'm glad I brought along these Choco-Mounds.

Pull back to include two truck drivers.

OLDER TRUCK DRIVER: Still eating kid stuff?

Cut to cu Choco-Mounds.

YOUNG TRUCK DRIVER: (*Offers Choco-Mounds*) Try one, it'll give you some quick energy and staying energy.

Pull back to older truck driver reluctantly taking Choco-Mounds.

OLDER TRUCK DRIVER: Tell me another one.

YOUNG TRUCK DRIVER: No, Choco-Mounds has protein. I bet there's enough staying power in it to last us to the Kansas City Diner.

Dissolve cu older truck driver about to take another bite from Choco-Mounds bar.

OLDER TRUCK DRIVER: Hey, this Coco-Mounds tastes pretty good. Protein, huh? Y'know, kid, I bet we can make it to Albuquerque.

Character: *Older Truck Driver*—You might have a scowl throughout the commercial until the end when you eat and enjoy candy bar.
Young Truck Driver—You might take on a good-natured, innocent attitude. You're just happy to be driving along and enjoying yourself. You've always wanted this kind of job.

Objective:　　*Older Truck Driver*—To teach younger man about life on the road. Keep him in his place. The trick here is not to give in too soon.

Young Truck Driver—To make friends with older truck driver by sharing your food (the candy bar).

Study:　　*Older Truck Driver*—Imagine going to the movies with a girlfriend and having your little brother tag along.

Young Truck Driver—Imagine you're a kid trying to win over your older brother. Go back to your childhood and think of how great it was to eat your favorite candy.

RUSTY'S

Open on young reporter, at table in Rusty's (a fast-food restaurant). He's got camera equipment, etc., on table next to him.

FRED: (*Exhausted*) all day long I chase news stories . . . (*Cheers up*).

He picks up hot dog.

. . . my favorite one is Man Bites Dog.
That's why my favorite hangout is Rusty's.

Cu of hot dog and bun with "100% beef" supered over it.

Their 100-percent beef hot dogs on a bun are a treat I've enjoyed since I was a kid.

Hand putting mustard on it.

I like to cover them with Rusty's special spicy mustard. Then I head for Rusty's salad bar.

Dissolve to salad on table and pull back to see Fred, hot dog in one hand, salad fork in other.

Crisp lettuce with fresh juicy tomatoes, onions, and crunchy green peppers, and lots of salad fixings.

Pull back to reveal Rusty's logo over shoulder. Go in on logo.

Hot dog! That's Rusty's! They've got my buy-line.

Character:　　You're a reporter. You might try glasses for this. You might try talking fast in a slightly higher register to give energy and enthusiasm to spot.

Objective:	To get other person to try Rusty's by showing obvious enjoyment of food.
Whom you are talking to:	A buddy, or a new girlfriend.
Study:	Imagine you've been on a five-mile hike and you're starving.

MINTCOOLS

Couple in posh hotel suite. Woman is searching through chest drawers. Pull back to include man at doorway.

MAN: What are you looking for? Donna, there are people out there waiting to meet you.

Woman looks up, throws her arms out.

WOMAN: I can't find my breath mints.

Dissolve to medium shot. Man offers woman Mintcools

MAN: Here, try my Mintcools.

WOMAN: Oh, no, I hate that medicine taste.

Move in on man's hand holding package of Mintcools.

MAN: They really taste like mint and they really keep your breath fresh. Ready to meet your public now?

Gives him a kiss.

WOMAN: I'm in mint condition.

Cut to package of Mintcools. Super: "improved."

ANNCR: Mintcools. You owe it to your public.

Character:	*Woman*—Attractive best-selling novelist. Could be a little wafty. *Husband*—A take-carer type. Managing her career.
Objective:	*Woman*—Worried about garlic in dinner she's just had. Nervous about reception. Must find breath mints. *Husband*—Wants to convince her that breath mints will solve her problem. This will then calm her down and get her out to reception, which is his larger objective.

SAMPLE STORYBOARD

COUPLE IN POSH
HOTEL SUITE.
WOMAN IS SEARCHING
THROUGH CHEST
DRAWERS.
PULL BACK TO INCLUDE
MAN AT DOORWAY.

MAN: What are you
looking for? Donna,
there are people out
there waiting to meet
you.

WOMAN LOOKS UP,
THROWS HER ARMS
OUT.

WOMAN: I can't find my
breath mints.

DISSOLVE TO MEDIUM
SHOT. MAN OFFERS
WOMAN MINTCOOLS.

MAN: Here, try my
Mintcools.

WOMAN: Oh, no, I hate
that medicine taste.

MOVE IN ON MAN'S
HAND HIOLDING
PACKAGE OF
MINTCOOLS.

MAN: These are the
new improved
Mintcools.

PULL BACK AS WOMAN
TRIES MINTCOOL AND
SMILES.

MAN: They really taste
like mint and they
really keep your
breath fresh. Ready
to meet your public
now?

GIVES HIM A KISS.

WOMAN: I'm in mint
condition.

CUT TO PACKAGE OF
MINTCOLS.

ANNCR: Mintcols. You
owe it to your
public.

Study: *Woman*—Imagine looking for a diamond ring that you've lost, just before going to meet the person who gave it to you.
Husband—Imagine calming down a child who must go to the dentist and is making a scene in the reception room.

14

Day of the Shoot

A set on the day of a shoot is often hectic, relaxed, interesting, boring, tense, fun, tedious, glamorous, maddening, and, most of all, confusing. For instance, when things seem to go wrong, you may think it's your performance at fault. No one gives you a clue. Believe me, not to worry. More times than not, it isn't you, as this story illustrates.

As it happened (so Bernie Owett, the creative director who was there, told me), actor John Ritter, star of "Three's Company," was performing in a Listerine commercial. The scene, shot outdoors, was of a couple who had just used the product and, with the sunset behind them, were going in for a kiss. Simple enough action, and, in Ritter's eyes, performed just as directed. Around the twentieth take, he began to wonder what he was doing wrong. When the director at take eighty-four (yes, really, eighty-four), said, "Okay, we'll go with that," Ritter was baffled—eighty-four was no different from the others.

A year later Ritter was still worrying about it and when he came upon Bernie on a Hollywood set he jumped at the chance to ask about it. "How come eighty-four takes?" he asked. "Was I that bad?"

"Not at all," Bernie explained. He and the award-winning cameraman, Vilmos Zsigmond, were simply trying to catch the setting sun at the precise moment before it dropped into the horizon.

All that fretting for nothing.

The day of the shoot can be a fun and rewarding experience if you know what to expect, how to act and react, what to do, where to go, and how to make your performance special. And so, the reason for this chapter. In it I hope to give you an honest, informative, and reassuring preview of the day.

Signing In

When you walk into the film studio, if they have a reception area, please don't wait there, or in any empty office. Go directly to the stage set, ask for the A.D. (assistant director), and sign in. Be on time and make yourself known. Important people may have anxiety attacks if you can't be found.

No Stand-ins

In children's commercials, two or three children are booked for each part. On the day of the shoot, if one gets sick, another will step in.

This is not true in adult commercials. There is no actor or actress on the set to stand in for you. In dollars and time, the consequences can be catastrophic. Many commercials cost over $100,000 for a day's shoot. To add to it, the agency could miss their air date, bollixing up their whole marketing plan.

In only one case have I had talent not show up. The person, who shall remain unnamed and unappreciated, was a professional football player. Professional actors and actresses will show up on the set even if they're feeling quite ill.

Of course, an emergency can come up, in which case, notify your agent or casting director at once—even in the middle of the night. As they say, the show must go on—especially true of a shoot.

The Assistant Director—Your Guardian Angel

You can stop worrying about details the moment you're in the A.D.'s hands. An A.D. has many functions in relation to the shoot, but for you, the talent, he is the person who will serve as your personal guide and handholder.

As I mentioned above, he is the first person you seek out. Your A.D. will

sign you in;

direct you to makeup and to wardrobe;

see that you get on the set in time;

advise you where to sit and wait;

take you to the director;

review the contract with you (the signing of the contract takes place on set);

see that you are ready and present when it comes time to perform;

advise you, if you have an emergency, how long you can leave the set and where to make necessary phone calls.

Note: It's rare in the case of an audition that you would be given permission to leave the set.

Day's Calendar

Most shoots run from 8:30 to 5:30 with an hour lunch break. Any time over 5:30 is considered overtime. Usually 7:00 is the cutoff time. The reason for this is that it's time for another meal break and studio crew costs really begin to mount. A typical breakdown of a shooting day goes like this:

7:30 Report to makeup and hairstylist.
8:30 Check wardrobe on camera.
9:30 Shooting begins (hopefully).
1:00 Break for lunch.
2:00 Back on set.
5:30 Wrap.

Lunch Break

Many people go out and politick during lunch, talk to the director or client, try to make an impression. Pretty actresses are often asked to have lunch with the client.

If you can get out of invitations, do. A festive lunch may make the break more cheery, but you could come back exhausted from having to be pleasant and witty. Far better to sit quietly by yourself, study your script, or just absorb what you learned that morning. Do anything that helps you be prepared and rested for the afternoon.

Shooting Begins

When it comes time to shoot, you will hear the A.D. or sound man shout, "Bells!" A bell will ring, signaling that a sound recording is to be made and you must be quiet. You will see and hear two wooden sticks being clacked together. This is called a "slate." The A.D. will read the slate. Take one. Sound. Action. You're on.

MARKS

As you rehearse for the camera, the director will have chalk lines drawn on the floor. These are called "marks." They indicate where you are to stand so you will be in the exact camera range and angle. Say you are directed to walk into a scene carrying a tube of toothpaste. From point of entry, you are to take three steps. Your mark, then, would be your stop spot.

Some actors are exciting marksmen. I worked with Michael

Landon out on the Coast, and he was a joy to watch. Given a direction to walk into a scene from a distance, he went through it once, adjusted the steps, and thereafter walked exactly to the same place and turned exactly the same way. It seemed instinctive with him, but of course it was the result of years of experience.

Unseen Marks

Let's say you are directed to pick up—but not drink—a cup of coffee. You must be able to lift the coffee cup to the exact spot desired. Such limitations I call "unseen marks." They take more concentration than you can imagine, especially since the shot is usually close up and you may even have to talk at the same time.

I recommend you practice off-camera. Do it over and over again so that you can do it without thinking. It's perfectly all right to ask the director, "How much of me is on camera? . . . Does my hand show when I bring the coffee cup in?" It can save a lot of uncertainty, give your performance confidence, and give you the mark of a pro.

THE DIRECTOR

The director is the man in charge of the shoot. He's involved in lighting, camera angles, dealings with agency people and their client, and in telling you, the talent, where to stand and what to do.

Directors often come out of a camera background. Many have marvelous visual and staging ideas, yet know little or nothing about acting. If you're a professional actor or actress, they expect you to know what to do.

On most sets, all ideas and complaints about performance go to the director. The agency producer is the person who receives and relays the information from the agency people to him. In the case of conflicting information, the director becomes a sort of mediator. For instance, the writer may say an actress is not being conversational enough, while the account man might complain that she's got to punch up the product name. "Look, fellows," the director will say when he meets with them, "you can't punch up every word and have an easy conversational tone." Once the conflict is settled, he will then give the actress the direction.

For the success of the shoot, it's up to you to work with the director so that it will be all brought together.

ACTOR MEETS DIRECTOR

You bring your acting talent to the commercial—your ability to motivate the part. The director brings his visual talent—his ability to make a scene work. So to speak, you must sing and dance together. If you luck into a director like Bill Alton, a former actor, you will receive knowing direction as well as support. But most often you may find the director does not talk to you in acting terms. He or she may say, "Have fun with it," or "Just talk as though you're having coffee with a friend."

It's up to you to translate a direction into motivation and action. If the director says, "Give it more energy," concentrate more on the particular product. If it's a washing machine, think of something you really want, maybe a new sports car or a trip to Hawaii—anything that will heighten your intensity.

If you worked your script out before and know your objective for each scene, you will naturally be more secure in your relationship with the director. Knowing he is more interested in the overall picture, you can take responsibility for your own performance. Remember, you both have the same goal—a successful shoot.

SPEAKING UP

If you're a beginner, you understandably may have apprehensions about following directions. Easily fixed. Listen hard and concentrate and you can't go wrong. You will not be directed to do anything that you can't do. Many film directors (Fellini, for example) have achieved fine things with people off the street.

If you're having difficulty, speak up, express your nervousness or failure to understand. It's the director's job to help you perform.

If you have a directing suggestion or some idea that may help, tell the director—but not in front of everyone. Take him aside and discuss it. This way the director does not have to worry that your idea may be contrary to the client's idea; he doesn't have to defend himself. What's more, he might want to take credit for it. Why not?

Many directors give directions privately, up close, face-to-face. Here's a chance to express your ideas. Remember, the director usually has more to risk than you do.

RELATIONSHIPS WITH OTHER ACTORS

"Occasionally you get mixed in with actors and actresses and there's a problem." So Andy Duncan, a leading TV- and radio-commercial and feature-film actor, told me at a luncheon recently. This happens particularly if one actor is from an improvisational background (which Andy is) and the other is not. As Andy explains it, the other actor may be reading the commercial word for word while he might be putting in conversational uh-uhs, ahs, and mms. He always tries to explain his method to the other actor—what he's doing. Of course, he believes in give-and-take.

You may find yourself in the same situation, and you'll have to be diplomatic. It pays, as Andy will attest. You're one of a family and you sink or swim together.

A few suggestions:

- Be open if the other actors want to go over the script with you.
- Do everything to support your fellow actors and actresses.
- Don't make yourself look good at their expense.
- Go out of your way to help a neophyte—especially help them with any questions they have.

REMEMBER, EVERYBODY WILL BE SUPPORTING YOU

The makeup person will be there to make your face look good; the hairdresser to style your hair true-to-type; the stylist to see that your wardrobe is camera-perfect. They will have consulted with the director and agency beforehand and come up with a look.

Fine, but what if you don't like what the hairdresser is doing to your hair? Speak up. "Oh, I don't feel comfortable with my hair this way." But listen, too. He is an expert. Something will be worked out. Besides, no hairdresser is going to change your hair radically from the audition.

After you're finished with makeup, hair, wardrobe, you will be checked out on camera under lights. "She's got too much makeup on," the director may say. "The hairstyle is too extreme—make it more natural," the stylist may add. "I'd put her in the checked blouse instead of the sweater," the cameraman may suggest. Such scrutiny may make you feel like a Betty Crocker cake that hasn't been frosted properly. But take heart, it's part of the process. And really everybody is for you.

IT'S ALL IN A DAY'S SHOOT

Sometimes actors and actresses complain to me that they don't get enough feedback from directors. You think you've given a Clio performance, but what do you hear? The director complains about the lighting, and the sound man yells that the sound isn't coming through clearly. When that finally gets straightened out, the director comes up to you and says, "Bring the bowl of soup one inch higher," or "When you tilt the greasy pan, will you tilt it just an inch more so we can really see how the grease has been removed."

Please don't feel that this is a reflection on your performance. Remember, the product is the star.

Sometimes, at day's end, the shoot that started off in a nice loose manner may seem to tighten to near breaking point. The client and all the agency people seem to be huddled together whispering. You think they're commenting on your lack of talent or training—or both. You have one more shot to go and you feel the director's sharpness is directed at you. Usually it's not. It is probably just a buildup of his day's trials with agency people and client, plus all the technical difficulties. Or the producer may have told him that if he doesn't get the shot now, they're going to go into overtime. All of this is piled up in his head. You're tired, too. Now's the time to bear and forbear, and to concentrate on doing your part.

KEEPING YOUR ENERGY UP

The day drags on. You been on the set since 7:30. You were told they'd probably shoot your scene after lunch. There have been all sorts of technical difficulties with lighting, and one scene suddenly looked clumsy on camera and had to be redone.

It's now 4:00, and there you sit. You haven't seen the other side of the camera. They knew that there was to be a scene with the other people and product shots; why didn't they just call you for an afternoon session?

As a matter of practice, you are required to be on set for the full day's shoot. This is because there are bound to be complications. In the above case, they probably counted on being ready for you at 11:00, but it didn't pan out. In any event, you can see it makes more sense that you wait than that the entire crew wait for you.

But a whole day—how do you keep your energy up? As I mentioned in the chapter on auditions, it's wise to bring along a mystery or your knitting or another script you're working on. May you go for a walk? Absolutely. You may want to go off to another room and jog or meditate. Of course, you will let the A.D. know where you'll be.

LOCATION

When a commercial is shot "on location," it means the shoot takes place outside the film studio. Sometimes you'll just go to a nearby location for the day. Transportation will be provided from the studio to the location and back. If the location is near to your home, you may ask for directions and drive there on your own. Very often you will be required to stay overnight. If so, the film company will make all the arrangements for accommodations.

Weather Day

Although locations are chosen for their good weather, the shoot could be rained or snowed out. You could be stuck on location for several days while the clouds roll by. Naturally you will be paid for delays. Often, clever production managers will have arranged some alternative indoor shooting that can take place. Take enough clothes and crossword puzzles with you to pass the wait.

Clothes

You'll need clothes to wear in the evening when you're not wearing your official shooting wardrobe. You may wish to take along a bathing suit for an after-shoot swim. *Big caution:* Take along suntan lotions, hats, and anything else to prevent sunburn. You're often standing around waiting for a shot to be set up. They thought it would take five seconds, but it's taken a half-hour and you're fried.

Location Logistics

Sometimes, when you go on location, you are asked to make your own travel reservations. More likely, they'll be made for you. The union requires that travel and lodging be first-class. Both items plus expenses will be paid for by the client. Ask your agent ahead of time what is the per diem. (See chapter 22.)

Above all, get directions straight. Know which airport you're to go to. Know what hotel you'll be staying at. Often someone from the studio will meet you. If something happens and they don't, you can get a cab and go to the hotel. Know the full name of the person you are to contact. Know the name of a backup contact. Know the name, address, and phone number of the film company.

Location Temptations

It's a custom on location for people to have dinner together. Fine. Go and enjoy yourself. But if everyone wants to stay up drinking the night before the shoot, don't do it. No one will forgive you the next day if you constantly have to have Murine poured into your eyes and you can't remember your lines.

To put it another way, holiday atmosphere or not, don't leave your professional attitude back home. Get plenty of rest, eat lightly, do not drink too much alcohol. Remember, others may be able to sit in the back and nap, but you're out there facing the telltale camera.

Let me assure you, the fun part will come. There's usually a wrap-up party to look forward to. Also, there may be time after the shoot to shop and sight-see. I know it may seem silly to sit around on a set all morning when you could be shopping for souvenirs, but there can be many changes in shooting plans and you may be needed. However, if it looks like you could steal away for a period, be sure to ask the A.D.'s permission to leave the set.

Where and When Will the Commercial Run?

Recently on a Shield soap commercial, the fact that I had already told the performers that it was going to be a national network run didn't seem to matter. Once on the set they asked a "suit" where it was going to run. "Oklahoma," he replied. Now, that was true, but it was also going to run across the country. Result: The actors frantically called their agents to find out if it was so and got themselves and everyone into an uproar.

A set is really not the best place in the world to pick up such information. Frequently the people there know little or nothing about air dates, etc., and if they do, they don't want to discuss it. Of course, you want to know how the commercial will run. But do ask before the shoot and believe the right people, either your agent or the casting director.

Okay, It's a Wrap

Shoot's over. While you're waiting to turn on your TV and see yourself selling Shield soap, send thank-you notes to directors, producers, casting director. Tell them you enjoyed working with them and hope to work with them again.

How to Get Rehired

Another job may come up involving a director with whom you've worked. While this director is reviewing your final audition tapes, he'll remember that you are great to work with. Since a director's opinion counts heavily, chances are you'll get the job. Many times, he will forgo a performance with a brilliant but difficult person for a performance with a competent and pleasant person.

Of course, talent counts, but how you treat everyone you come in contact with counts as much. Don't be phony, but do acknowledge the work of the makeup person, the hairdresser, the stylist. Be as civilized as possible. Help make the machinery run smoothly. Along with your performance, it can make the difference between being in one commercial or being "in commercials."

15

Voice-Overs and Radio

YOU HAVE SUCH AN INTERESTING VOICE

The other day a producer stepped into my office waving a script and saying, "Vangie, we have to have another voice for the track on this commercial. The client wants someone who has more authority." She then quickly read me the script, described what she was looking for, and explained why the current voice wasn't working.

When she was done, I got up from my desk and headed for my special voice-over cabinet. I opened the door and viewed the hundreds of little boxes inside. I chose six boxes and gave them to her. The voice in one of those little boxes will earn $25,000 to $50,000 from this account alone.

What Is in Those Boxes, Anyway?

Magic? Not quite. Each of these 7″ × 7″ boxes contains an audiotape of someone's voice. If you were to play one of the tapes, you would hear that voice delivering several commercials. The tapes are of beginners and pros, males and females, young and old.

The story above illustrates only one instance when I refer to these tape boxes. Most of my audition calls require me to be familiar with the actors' voices. As your chances of doing radio commercials or voice-overs depend on your being represented in my voice-over cabinet, I intend, in this chapter, to show you how to get your tape there. You must know what kinds of voices are most in demand. How to discover if you have the right voice, and how you fit in. How you can develop your voice. How to put your sample tape together. How and where to distribute your tape. How to audition. But first, let's look at the opportunities for the right voice in this wide-open and lucrative field.

Opportunities

Although radio commercials and voice-overs comprise the majority of jobs, they are not the end of the opportunities for the right voice. Let's take a quick survey of the field.

RADIO

Voices are needed for:

Dialogue commercials—slice-of-life dramatizations, comedy skits.

Straight announcer commercials—often two announcers are used to punch up copy points.

TELEVISION

Voices are needed for:

Sell over the product.

Announcer interrupting minidramas.

Call-to-buy tags at ends of commercials.

Donuts (not the kind you eat)—These are commercials made with just openings and closings (voice needed). Like a donut, there's a hole in the middle. This is filled by local stations or distributors with a selling message—e.g., special sale announcement (another voice needed).

Dubbings—These are voices used in place of the voices of on-camera performers. This often happens when on-camera person can't act or has a poor voice or is not available for a revision.

Jingles—Singing voices needed.

Animated cartoons—The Flintstones need voices, so do Bugs Bunny, Superman, etc.

Demos—These are slide films made to test commercials. They are not aired but played to selected audiences (usually at a theater) called "focus groups." For economy reasons, drawings are used instead of live actors and actresses. Voices are recorded to play over drawings.

Scratch tracks—These tracks are used to edit film—e.g., to time the segments of commercials. They are rough and not used as final recordings. Frequently a voice is used other than that of the announcer who will deliver the on-air commercial. (Jobs for two voice-overs.)

Industrial films—These are information films used within a company. They are looked upon as a type of commercial, though they may run anywhere from thirty minutes to two hours. These are sometimes done through the advertising agency.

Without question, there's plenty of work out there. What's more, if you have a great voice, you might even become rich doing it. Joan Ellis, head of Jefferson & Ellis, a large talent agency in Chicago, told me that she knew of at least ten voice-over people there who made over $400,000 a year and the average was $60,000. In New York and Los Angeles, centers of TV commercials, you can imagine the figures. Something to talk about!

How Do You Know You Have the Voice for It?

Hearing your own voice without the help of a tape recorder is like seeing yourself without a mirror. At best, the impression is blurry. So before you decide that doing radio commercials and voice-overs is your thing, buy, beg, or borrow a tape recorder. Then practice and listen and practice and listen some more.

How to Practice

Above all, speak freely. Keep the tape recorder running during a prolonged conversation with family or friends. It will be the most honest likeness you can get. In the beginning you might catch yourself performing rather than conversing, but you'll soon forget the tape recorder is listening. When you play the tape back, chances are you'll say, "That's not me." Reserve judgment *and* the tape. You'll want to refer back to both.

Once you've become accustomed to the sound of your voice, you're ready to perform. I wouldn't do a commercial right off; select a monologue instead. Read something from a book, a play, something with which you're not too involved. When you play the tape back, listen with both ears.

- Listen for pitch. Do you sound high, squeaky? Is your voice so low it's muffled, reverberates?
- Listen for volume. Do you speak in a whisper? Do you speak as though you want to be heard above a crowd?
- Listen for resonance. Does your voice have a full quality? A warmth? Are there nuances of tone? Is it dull? Nasal? Flat? Throaty? Metallic?
- Listen for articulation. Do you mumble? Does your voice sound as though you talk without moving your lips and tongue?
- Listen to how you communicate. Velvety tones don't mean a thing if people, mesmerized by it, don't pay attention to what you are saying. You must talk to your listeners on a one-to-one basis; telling them about the product or service and having them pay attention is the whole point of commercials.
- Listen for speech defects. Do you stutter? Do you lisp? Do you sibilate (whistle your s's)? If you have a speech defect, there's no point in going into commercials, unless you're willing to spend time and money and put pebbles in your mouth to overcome it. Otherwise you'll be blocked out of most commercials.

Books to read: *Freeing the Natural Voice,* by Kristan Linklater, and *The Use and Training of the Human Voice,* by Arthur Lessac. Both are published by Drama Book Specialists, 150 W. 52nd St., New York, N.Y. 10019.

Involving Others

Your own two ears may help in diagnosing and correcting your voice problems, but you'll soon want the judgment of other ears. I suggest you put together choice portions of your tape studies and play them for some friends, hopefully critical, and anyone in the business, hopefully friendly.

Possible Evaluations and Positive Suggestions

Eventually, you probably will arrive at one of the following evaluations. Of course, you want to know where to go from there, and so, my suggestions:

EVALUATION: I'm perfect right now and I'm ready to make up a sample tape to send around.

SUGGESTION: Go to it. See your tape on my cabinet shelf!

EVALUATION I feel I need voice development. I don't seem to project or come through strongly.

SUGGESTION: Work with a singing teacher to help your breathing and voice quality.

EVALUATION: My diction is sloppy. I tend to slur, garble words, not articulate well.

SUGGESTION: Work with a speech coach. Practice reading aloud slowly, exaggerating good diction.

EVALUATION: My voice and diction are acceptable, but my delivery is tentative and my pacing erratic. I'd like to learn a little technique.

SUGGESTION: An acting or an accredited announcer school is your best help. Take classes from someone who works in the field. Get a professional slant.

Note: Many schools have professional equipment and will help you put together a professional tape. Many will also teach you how to make contacts, etc.

Caution: Be sure you use a school that's licensed if licensing is required in your state.

Learning Your Craft

Teachers may develop your voice. Schools may develop your techniques. But neither develops your confidence and credits like job experience. From the start, get all you can.

Get into college film. Get into college radio. Get on cable. Get on local radio. Get on local TV—if you have a special hobby, etc., you might try for a talk show. Volunteer to work with amateur filmmakers. Volunteer to do sales films, etc. Volunteer to be the voice for slide film presentations. Get a job demonstrating and selling in a department store. Get a job selling by phone. Volunteer to make calls for your favorite politician. One proviso in the last two suggestions: Don't put me on your lists.

Important: While you're doing your special thing, keep reading commercials by yourself with a stopwatch in hand. Most top announcers seem to have a built-in time sense. They know how much to get into twenty-eight seconds or fifty-eight seconds, and how to "pick up two seconds." Reading commercials aloud is the best way I know of developing this skill.

Putting Your Act Together

Assuming you have no professional help, I've compiled aids to help you develop a tape that will stick in the mind's ear of a casting director.

In all, there are two factors you must decide upon before pressing the "record" button.

1. What is your voice type?
2. What material suits your voice type?

Let's go into each in detail.

CHOOSING YOUR TYPE

You'll want to put together a tape that indicates some range, yet emphasizes your strong points. It should be true to your type. The best way to identify your type is to listen to radio and television. Close your eyes and concentrate on the voice. You'll notice that similar products usually use similar types. After careful and frequent listening, you'll begin to notice how voice and product or service complement each other—how the voice delivering a food commercial drips with appetite appeal; how the voice delivering a cosmetic commercial has a seductive quality.

Voices fall into the following general types:

Straight announcer:	Informative, clear, strong voice
Hard-sell announcer: (often used for retail)	Like a straight announcer, but a stronger, more intense selling style is called for.
Cosmetic: (also used for travel)	Soft, seductive, poetic, gentle, sexy, evoking images.
Food:	Warm, appetite appeal, often folksy, usually lighter-type voices.
Corporate:	Dignified, low-key, informative, strong in quality, but delivery is laid-back.
"Character," female:	This is often called "something different," "a little kookie," a little rasp in the voice.
"Character," male:	This can range anywhere from blue-collar macho to the regional dialect to just a slight edge to the voice.

Announcer or Actor?

Usually, a request for talent goes something like this: "We need a voice for Jumbo Flakes. We'll need an announcer—a lot of copy," or "We need a kookie voice—we'll probably need an actress." The fact that most announcers are actors doesn't seem to matter; it's a way of defining types.

When an announcer is called for, the quality wanted is authoritative, informative—not to be confused with the old-fashioned insincere, deep-voiced type heard on old radio commercials. Of paramount importance is the ability to deliver a great deal of copy in a short time, make it understandable, and still give it color. To get the speed and clarity necessary for this kind of delivery, one top voice-over announcer visualizes himself as a captured CIA agent giving information to his rescuers before his captors return.

When an actor is called for, the requirements usually are for a low-key, slow, conversational delivery. The tone often leans toward character, often borders on the folksy. Mason Adams, who recently starred as the managing editor on "Lou Grant," is famous for his warm, folksy voice-overs. In case you are neither the staccato, bite-'em-off, spit-'em-out type of announcer nor the other extreme, the gentle whimsical actor type, try for a range in between. Choose material accordingly.

Note: Now is the time for all good spokeswomen to start developing tapes that include an authority approach. Up until now, women's voice-over tapes have featured kookie, warm, pleasant-housewife, or sexy, sultry types. Let's add the voice of authority to it. The potential in this area is exciting.

A Suggestion on Selecting Your Type

If you've decided you can do two types of voices that are far apart in range, give one up. Resist the temptation to put a hard-sell spokeswoman and a Donald Duck voice on one tape. Choose one style and stick to it.

WHAT MATERIAL TO CHOOSE

Of course, your voice type will determine your material. Choose commercials that best show off your individuality within a type. As an announcer, you may range from soft sell to hard sell or a variety of character-type commercials.

How to Get Commercial Material

Ask your friends in the business for commercial scripts that have already been broadcast. There should be a few among them that you can adapt to your style.

If you're starting out and have no professional samples, use or paraphrase an appropriate on-air commercial. You can select and tape one from off the air. If you have a gift for it, write your own material. Remember, especially at the beginning, keep your material range narrow.

Putting Your Tape Box Together

Please, don't act as your own studio technical director. Once you have your act together, go to a professional studio to have your tape made. The professional sound will give you the needed advantage to enter the fast track.

Before you make your tape and send it on its way, you should know these few technical and practical points:

- Tapes should be recorded on reel-to-reel tapes at 7½ rpm.
- Put four to six commercials on the tape.
- Sound effects and stock music should be included where appropriate (your recording studio will put these in).
- Sizes of reels in their individual boxes are usually 4" to 5" in diameter.
- Your name and phone number should be on both the box and reel.
- On the inside of the box, list the commercials by product.

Distributing Your Tapes

Your voice tapes are in a box. Your name and information is clearly noted on them. Now where will you find names to send them to? How do you get them on the desks of casting directors and producers? A direct approach can work. Personally, I set aside a time every week to listen to the voice-over boxes that pile up on my desk. Most casting directors and producers do listen to unsolicited tapes. Still, sooner or later, and the sooner the better, you'll need an agent.

What an Agent Will Do for You

Some agents will help you distribute your tape. Some agents, particularly in New York and L.A., will add another very important tape box to casting directors' and producers' files. It's called a "master reel" and on it are the voices of a number of their clients. I find these reels very useful in searching for a particular type of voice or in experimenting with different voice possibilities. I suggest you ask prospective agents if they make up master reels.

Your agent will also guide you as to the kinds of commercials you should do, the accounts you should work on. Tricky career decisions frequently come up. At one point, just doing a demo will lead to a job as spokesperson on a major account. At another point, you may do two or three commercials and they may not even run. Your agent can help you determine the best choice for your career.

Which Agent Is Best for You?

You're already doing on-camera work; you want to do voice-overs, too. You already have an agent: If your agent hasn't recognized your voice-over potential, let him hear about it. Get him to help you develop a tape. Some agencies have a specific person who deals only with radio and voice-overs. It's good to get yourself into both departments; it can mean more work.

You're planing to concentrate on voice-over only: Find an agent who specializes in voice-overs. These people frequently handle the most wanted voices. If you're starting out, don't be put off; it can be to your advantage. A call comes in, the talent is not available, they'll suggest some lesser-known talent in the same category. Your chance to shine.

You're just starting out: If you're going the on-camera-actor and voice-over route, go to one of the larger agencies that have both departments. If you're going to make voice-over your niche, go to an agency that is very strong in radio and voice-overs. You can be fairly confident your tape will be listened to. Agents like Charles Tranum listen to every tape that's sent to them. Ask around. Also see chapters 9 and 11 on how to get an agent and how to get an interview.

The Audition from Reel to Real

Your tape has either won you an agent who has sent you out on the audition or it has inspired a direct call from a casting director or producer. There you are on your way from the ad agency's reception room to the audition room. Unlike an on-camera performer, you have not been kept waiting too long in the reception room. That's because you must be paid for any recording and waiting time after one-half hour. Good and bad for you. No cooling your heels; no time to study your script, which is usually given to you when you sign in.

Once at your destination, you'll find yourself in an audition room. Our one professional room at J. Walter Thompson is "floating" (soundproof). This room has all of it—wonderful equipment, wonderful sound, broadcast quality. You might land there, but if it's busy, we'll probably record in my office, using a portable tape recorder. Don't feel cheated. The machine is fine for audition purposes.

ON-YOUR-FEET SCRIPT POINTERS

Once inside the audition room, you'll have to think and work fast. Before the tape starts spinning, you will be given the script and enough time to read it. As the time is limited, let's look at how you can make the most of it:

- Ask if there's a storyboard.
- Ask what kind of music will be used.
- Note the product. It will be the clue to your delivery.
- Mark up your script. Underline major copy points. *Note:* you may not always be given the entire script.
- If you're doing a voice-over, keep in mind that the listener should not be aware of or distracted by the quality of the voice; your delivery should interpret or highlight the picture—never be intrusive. You probably have given it the right delivery if, on playback, your delivery sounds relatively laid-back.
- If you're doing a radio commercial, the delivery should have color, interest.
- If more than one voice is called for, you will need to make yours distinctive. For instance, the voice of the announcer telling about the vitamins in a One-A-Day capsule should not sound like the young husband (on camera) who has just taken one.
- If your part in the commercial is to interrupt action or to do a tag and you are not given a script, ask what the other voices sound like or what the rest of the commercial is about.
- If you're auditioning for a voice-over, ask to see a storyboard; if not available, inquire about the video (picture) portion. (Whenever possible, producers record the voice track as the announcer watches the pictures.)

TAPES SPINNING—TIME TO SPIN YOUR TALE

You will usually be asked to try the copy first—that is, to do it your way. This is the time to concentrate. Forget your own sound and make sense of the commercial.

Think of the commercial as a minidrama with a beginning, middle, and end. Keep the storytelling aspect of it in your delivery. Tell the story to one person. The opening line of a commercial is the grabber. Make the most of it to get your listener's attention. The middle of the commercial leads from problem to solution. Keep the interest sustained. The leitmotif, the key selling phrase, is repeated several times throughout the commercial. Make it stand out. At the ending, there's the call to buy—the appeal to try the product and live happily ever after. Make it strong. Remember, the story is about the product; make sure you pronounce its name clearly.

TAKING DIRECTION

You feel you really gave it a great reading, and you probably did. But after your first read-through, it's time to listen to directions and listen carefully. What's said may not make as much sense to you as the way you see it, but following the directions is the way that will win you the commercial. That doesn't mean you have no say, but it's probably better to suggest, and, if your suggestions are not accepted, to give in. If you feel you'd like to hear a playback, ask, "Could I just listen to part of that last take please?" Why not?

DON'T FORGET TO LEAVE YOUR CALLING CARD

Remind them you were there. In case the advertising agency doesn't have your tape box on file, leave one behind. If you are also an on-camera talent, leave your picture and résumé as well.

Other Voices: Singers

Although the old Pepsi-Cola-Hits-the-Spot types of commercials have changed their tunes to more sophisticated compositions, the people who sing in commercials are still called "jingle singers."

To become a jingle singer, you must be able to read music fast and give the exact vocal rendition required. If your diction is super-clear (hard to find in these yah-yah-yah days), you have an advantage. Once music producers find the talent with the unique combination, they usually stick with them. If you're it, the rewards can be music to your ears. A simple music tag at the end of several different commercials can really multiply the figures on your residual checks.

Jingle singers are usually chosen by music producers, who often form little singing repertory groups. New York, Los Angeles, Chicago, Atlanta, and Nashville have many such groups. You will, of course, have to submit a tape of your singing voice.

And More Voices: Animated Voices for Animated Commercials

People who can invent a voice for a cartoon have a very special talent indeed. The Mel Blanc, Herschel Bernardi, and Joe Silver voices—of Porky Pig, Charley the Tuna, and Ajax, respectively— have become legends in their time. And rightly so, for they have raised their talents to an art, imbuing their cartoon voices with the exact degree of realness and mimicry.

If, like Lucille Bliss (the Smurf voice), you've been talking in different voices since you were so high, you're probably a natural for this field. When Lucille was a child, her mother, a concert pianist, used to take her along on concert tours. As it was hard to find new playmates during her short stays in different towns, she invented little friends for herself with special little voices. Later she used one of these voices as a Smurfette.

You'll probably have to head for the scene of the action, L.A., to get work. Most probably you'll have to establish yourself as a feature-film cartoon character. The people who do commercial animation often use performers with whom they've worked on a feature film. It's a hard field to break into, but, once in, a profitable and fun one.

There's Gold in Those Golden Tones

There's a pile to be made in radio commercials and voice-overs— probably more nuggets than for on-camera work. For one thing, you're not visible. Your voice is not that identifiable to the average listener. Except for a direct conflict, you can do as many commercials as you want without worrying about overexposure and thus being excluded from jobs. And then, there is usually more than one commercial involved in radio and voice-overs. A client may want fresh visuals using different performers, but as a rule he'll want continuity in the voice-over. Sometimes you may end up doing six or eight commercials plus tags for one account. You are paid for each one. That's a lot of loot. Let's look at some facts and figures:

A voice-over session is for two hours. You may do several commercials within that time. The session fee is $225.60 and is applied against one commercial. You will receive $225.60 for each commercial you record thereafter. A reuse payment guarantee for each commercial (thirteen uses within a thirteen-week period for a Class A program) works out to $943.50.

A radio session is for ninety minutes. You may do a number of commercials within that time. The session fee is $110 and is applied against one commercial. You will receive $110 for each commercial you record thereafter. A reuse payment guarantee for each commercial (twenty-six uses in thirteen weeks) works out to $635.

EXCLUSIVITY

The same exclusivity rights that apply to on-camera talent apply to voice-overs. You could ask why this is so when the general public isn't that aware of your voice. The fact is, people in the business are very aware of voices. If your voice is on commercials extolling the heavenly virtues of two competitive airlines, it could justifiably upset both sponsors. Lest you be sued for speaking out of both sides of your mouth, be sure to have your agent check out conflicts.

I hope in this chapter I've helped you a little to discover if you have the voice for commercials and how to sell it. Now let's get on to print models—another door.

16

The Beautiful Way into Commercials

I love working with the beautiful people—the fashion and cosmetic models.

Considering how I've been carrying on about the craft of acting, and especially if you're in the business, my ardor may come as a bit of surprise to you. Where is the casting director's usual gripe—"She's great-looking, but she can't do a line"?

I happen to believe that the stock complaints about models are just that—stock. I know models can develop the person-to-person kind of acting that TV commercials require. Modeling, after all, is a form of show biz. People who go into it usually have it in them. And thank the Big Casting Director in the Sky they do, for they are often the only ones who have the look we need.

If you need more reasons for my enthusiasm for models, let me tick them off.

Models are often less inhibited than actors. Models, in projecting their own personalities, are more willing to make changes and try new ways. Models know how to create an effect without words: a feeling, a mood, an energy, a sexiness.

That said, I hope in this chapter to achieve two things: to encourage guys and gals to go into modeling as a stepping-stone to commercials; and to open up to the print model the career-broadening and lucrative world of TV commercials.

Ideal Training Ground

Print-photographer studios and fashion runways are natural training grounds for commercials. In a way, they are the model's stage, the model's film studio. I encourage actors and actresses to do some modeling just as I encourage models to learn acting. Together these crafts make a winning combination.

But since you're starting from the modeling side, let's investigate just how it trains you to do commercials.

Modeling helps you gain poise. You learn how to move. You learn about clothes; how to wear them.

Modeling makes you aware of how you hold your body; how you appear to others. It teaches you how to correct faults in your posture—e.g., how to stand so your legs will not appear bowed.

Modeling teaches you how to relate to the camera—how you and the camera and the photographer create a picture. This is invaluable as the basic rules that apply to print apply to TV.

There's no question, if you've gone through the rigors modeling demands—contacting, posing, keeping yourself up—you're "in shape" for doing TV commercials.

Are the Physical Requirements for Print and TV the Same?

With one exception, the requirements are exactly the same. We want the same fabulous faces and figures as print photographers do.

FOR WOMEN
Large, wide-set eyes
Beautiful thick hair

Good facial structure
Clear skin
Perfect teeth

FOR MEN
Broad shoulders
Well-proportioned body
Rugged, interesting-looking face

The one big exception: In print modeling, aside from being photogenic, you must meet strict height and size requirements. Most model agents won't take on models unless the women are at least 5'7" and a perfect size 8; the men 6' and size 40 R. In TV commercials, except for fashion commercials (a designer-jean commercial, for example), there are no strict height or size requirements.

If you don't meet print standards, however, you will have to take a different route into commercials. Even though top New York and L.A. model agencies have TV departments, they will not take you on, even on a free-lance basis; they have groomed their roster of fashion models for commercials and are strictly committed to them.

How do you get an agent if you don't meet print requirements? Look around. There just may be agents in your city who handle all kinds of models. For more information on types of agents, see chapter 11.

"In" Looks

The classic model look is always in style. But there are annual vogues. At this writing, the vogue is an exotic look: dark hair and heavy eyebrows.

As a "look" becomes more popular in print, it becomes more popular in television. Some years ago, brunettes were not used in moisturizer commercials because they were associated with oily skin. Not anymore, at least not currently. Sally Kandle, casting director of N. W. Ayer, recently booked Esmé, a dark-haired beauty, for a moisturizer. Models like Janice Dickinson, Eva Voorhis, and Julie Wolfe, other beautiful brunettes, are also appearing in commercials for makeup and skin-care products.

A Magic Door into Commercials

Very often you don't even have to knock. If you're a model, doors fly open. The reasons are apparent:

• You're visible. There you are on the cover of or inside the covers of top fashion magazines. Casting directors, producers, clients see you, want you, call and ask for you.

• You're in a position to make contacts. Some of the people who do print shoots also do commercial work. They will certainly help you break into commercials, zip you past secretaries.

• Your portfolio speaks for you. You've had extraordinary opportunities to develop a great one. Models who work with fabulous photographers naturally acquire fabulous pictures.

Measuring Up—It's Only the Beginning

Having doors open for you is not necessarily enough. A TV commercial is not the same as a magazine cover. To succeed in TV, you have to *forget you're a model and think actress or actor.*

As I said earlier, so many models come in on interviews and pose as though there's a photographer in their heads calling out, "Look sexy," "Widen your eyes," "Don't purse your lips," "Keep your face turned to the right," etc. Some are so afraid to disturb their faces that they hardly blink.

If I had one thing to advise a model, it would be to forget about your looks. Your look is fine or you wouldn't be up for the commercial. Remember, I've seen your picture. As a casting director, I'm interested in the person behind that face; I want to see your warmth, your enthusiasm, your naturalness, some indication of how you'll perform in the commercial.

Let me stress one thing. Since you're a wanted commercial

type to begin with, you really owe it to yourself to study acting. If you've jumped straight to this chapter, go back and read through chapters on learning your craft, auditions, and script breakdown.

What Model Has the Time?

You're running around town on bookings all day—sometimes as many as six in one day. Often your bookings run until nine or ten o'clock at night. You're too exhausted to talk, let alone take acting lessons. I know it's tough; still, others have done it. Mary Denham, for instance, was a top model when she broke into commercials. All the time that she was modeling, she studied acting. Eventually, thanks to her natural and cultivated gifts, she became a much sought-after spokesperson. If you can't give it all that effort, even a few improvisational classes to get you started in the right direction would be a help.

Audition Versus Booking

I can almost understand it when a model decides to take a definite print booking rather than go on a TV audition. I can almost understand it when her booking runs late and she shows up at 1:00 or 2:00 that afternoon for her 10:00 A.M. appointment. After all, a model's time is money.

Almost understand, I said. If you seriously want to get into commercials, you really have to take responsibility in your bookings. That means you don't go to print go-sees that will prevent you from getting to auditions. If you're going to be late for an audition, you call and say so. If you're held over on a shoot, you call your agent and have him or her call the agency casting director.

Dressing the Part

On a go-see, people look through your book. On an audition, they look at you.

Now, I know that when you're coming straight from a *Cosmopolitan* cover shoot with sexy hair and makeup, it's not always easy to do a quick change to a young lawyer type. But it would help put you on an even footing with an actress who doesn't have the same problem.

How should you dress? Models are expected to dress well. So, for example, if you're up on a cosmetic commercial, be trendy— clothes in fashion, makeup in fashion. Still, before you go on a shoot, pack a blouse into your satchel. If you get the impression you're overdressed, you can always go to the ladies' room and change, and at the same time take your makeup down.

If you're a male model, jeans, slacks, sport shirt, sweater are acceptable attire—open-to-the-waist shirts are not. If you're up for a spokesman job, dress like a spokesman—wear a suit and tie or a blazer and slacks.

Somehow top models like Anette Stai and Scott Webster always seem to come to auditions dressed the part. Maybe that's why they're top models. Of course, if you're on a shoot, you may be tied up until the last minute and simply unable to make a switch. Explain the problem to your interviewer and bring along an appropriate picture. The reality is that a TV audition is different from a print go-see, and you have to approach it in a different way.

Portfolios

Unlike actors and actresses, you're fortunate to have a lot of pictures that help you win a commercial. As mentioned earlier, you're doubly lucky, because photographers shoot in action, and these shots make terrific samples.

Since you'll probably be working in both print and commercials, I suggest you do what many models do: (1) Keep your portfolio in two sections—one section for fashion, the other section for commercials; (2) put your glamour shots in the fashion section—e.g., a cover of European *Vogue* or an editorial in the *New York Times* fashion magazine. These shots most likely look more exotic, posed. Put your more natural, animated shots in the commercial section. If you're a female model, your makeup will be daytime. You'll be wearing skirt, blouse, sweater, and your hair in a natural style. If you're a male model, you'll be shown wearing jeans or a sport shirt.

Before you go on an audition, find out as much about the commercial as possible. Will you be wearing a bathing suit? Will you be wearing jeans? Will your hair be in a certain style? Pick out shots you have that are closest to the part and bring them along on the audition.

Models and Agents

As I mentioned earlier, most of the big model agencies have television departments that handle their print models exclusively. If you're one of their top models, it's all you need. As you get plenty of calls, their functions are to check out your availability and conflicts and to work out your scheduling.

For many print models, however, a model agency's TV department may not work. Some models may need to expand their range to young husband and wife types. If you fit into this slot, I suggest that, in addition to your print agent, you seek out talent agents who will promote you as an actor or actress. In looking for a talent agent, you will have to follow a slightly different procedure than you would with a model agency. Along with your portfolio or composite, you'll need an 8 x 10 glossy head shot. Naturally, you will have to demonstrate that you have acting ability. Vangie words of wisdom: Be sure you select agents who respect your talent. When I've asked for a model, I've had agents say snickeringly, "Well, you can try her." Often agents simply don't know their models' potentials. It's up to you to convince yours that you've got what it takes.

Note: If you live in a less commercial-oriented area, you'll probably find there are two or three agents who handle both print models and TV-commercial talent. It's a convenient way to work in both fields.

Opportunities for Male Models

You can blame it on the times, but although a female model can succeed in commercials without knowing how to deliver a line, if you're a guy and you can't act, your chances are near zilch. Because of the high cost of commercials and the changes in women's life-styles, male models are simply not used as handsome escorts as they once were. Unless the commercial calls for only an elegant look—such as a wine commercial—an actor will usually land the part.

Now for the good news. Male models who can act are often preferred over actors, especially as spokesmen. How often I hear "We want a good-looking guy who can act." Max Brown and Dave Bailey are two examples of models who fill the bill. Both have emerged from print modeling and are now tops in their category.

More good news. A male model who can act is often whisked off to be in soap TV series or films—as happened to Jack Scalia and Nick Nolte.

Their stories are not all that unusual. If you've got the looks, and if you develop your acting ability, it should pay off, especially if you get that one big break. . . .

Two Different Worlds
and the Differences Between Them

Modeling and doing TV commercials are two different games.

As a print model, you can go around to photographers in blue jeans and shirts and expect they'll envision you in flowing gowns or vested suits.

As a TV-commercial performer, you must present yourself in a stylish contemporary manner—look very "with it." You just can't expect clients, businessmen who often make the ultimate decision, to have the knowledge and imagination to mentally dress you up.

As a print model, you can get away with coming in with no makeup and your hair in a rubber band. Most photographers just need to see your facial structure and hair color and quality to visualize you on the cover of a magazine.

As a TV-commercial performer, you must look the way you'll appear on the TV screen. Believe me, it's very difficult to tell a client that with eye makeup and hair done, this girl will really look ravishing.

As a print model, you're the star.

As a TV-commercial performer, the product's the star. You're the attention getter and sales clincher.

As a print model, you often strike and hold artful poses.

As a TV-commercial performer, you must develop a natural way of moving.

As a print model, you don't have to say a word beyond "cheese" or "whiskey."

As a TV-commercial performer, you will often be required to deliver lines. You must study acting.

As a print model, your goal to be a top model is limited by age and weight. And for the most part, one successful shoot leads only to another shoot.

As a TV-commercial performer, you are not as limited. You can go from model to housewife to spokesperson. Commercials can open doors to feature films, TV series, etc. One successful commercial just could make you a star.

As a print model, you're booked for a special time. A definite job and the money are enough incentive to be on time.

As a TV-commercial performer, getting an audition is no assurance of getting the job. Still, the importance of being on time is theoretically the same. Miss the audition, miss your chance at the commercial.

As a print model, you do your work and make your modeling fees, which can be as high as $2,000 to $5,000 a day. (In certain very competitive areas, like liquor or cosmetics, print models get bonuses if the ad continues to run after six months; such windfalls, though increasing, are still few and far between.)

As a TV-commercial performer, thanks to residuals, a day's shoot can keep earning money for you. Some models make as much as $50,000 in residuals from one commercial. Of course, you don't get as many jobs as a print model.

As a print model, you're often booked or given a job from your portfolio. You sometimes don't even have to show up for an interview. Your portfolio is sent over to the photographer who books you.

As a TV-commercial performer, you have to audition the particular business and lines you're going to do. Your résumé and portfolio are important, but ultimately what gets you the job is how well you audition.

As a print model, you're usually one of just a few sent up on a job. They've usually seen your book before. Two or three people pass on you. There's a good chance you'll get the job.

As a TV-commercial performer, you'll usually be one of many people competing for a commercial, and there are many people okaying you. Thus the odds against getting the job are greater.

Schooling

At a luncheon recently, Nina Blanchard told a group of us a story that to me points up why models should study acting.

As she tells it, she and one of her models appeared on a TV talk show. The model, all luscious 5'10" of her, staggered (she was a bit tipsy) out on the set decked in a simple T-shirt, shorts, and high heels. Once at her destination, she draped herself around the TV host, nearly knocking him to the ground. She then proceeded to sit down and wave and giggle at the audience and tell interminable stories. Nina tried to shush her to no avail.

The day after the show was aired, Nina felt it was such a disaster (as did some of the people in the audience) that she called and apologized to the host. Several other people called, too—but not to apologize. Among them was the casting head of a network who was interested in the girl for a series, and a famous director. Here Nina had been bugging her on how you had to work hard, study, be dedicated, and eventually after ten years you'd make it—and all rules thrown to the winds, the model does it in one evening. Nina, who teaches at UCLA, wondered how she could face her class.

Thinking, Well, this is it, Nina sent the girl out on the various interviews. This time the girl was cold sober and dead shy. She just sat there. When they asked her to read lines, she couldn't do it. In a state of nervous collapse, she came back to Nina pleading, "Please, never send me out on anything with lines again."

Now, one conclusion could be: Never appear on a TV show tipsy unless you want to become a star. But seriously, think of the marvelous opportunity she missed. Maybe just one good improvisational class could have helped her cash in on her smashing appearance.

Faraway Fields

As a TV-commercial model type today, the world is your stage. American model types are wanted in many foreign and exotic places. Currently there's a lot of work for female models in Japan and South America.

I would think knowing the basics of a language would be essential. Good thing to think about if you're a high-school student and searching for subjects that will help your future career as a model.

And Fields Not So Afar

I've indicated in this chapter that doing TV commercials can lead to careers in film, TV series, etc. I would like to underline that since you already have looks going for you, with a dedicated attitude toward learning the craft of acting, the future for you is unlimited. If you've ever watched TV talk shows and heard the question "How did you get started?" asked of a successful actor or actress, you know the chances are very good they'll answer, "Commercials."

17

Why Not Your Child?

Once upon a time there was an Ivory Snow baby. The baby was a three-month-old boy, and wearing Ivory-soft diapers was his first job in commercials.

As the little boy grew, it was discovered that he had a lot more going for him than coos and gurgles: He was a natural for commercials.

When the little boy was 8 years old, he auditioned for his first movie and won the starring role over 5,000 children.

A fairy tale? Not at all. I can attest to its truth. I worked with this little boy on a Kodak commercial. He was so terrific we wanted to sign him to a long-term contract, but the movies beat us to it. Both working with and observing the boy, I saw a natural and unspoiled child, extremely friendly, outgoing and comfortable with adults. He never seemed to tire. People on the set told me he was willing to do the same scene over and over again and at the end of a long day's shooting come out laughing and telling jokes.

All the time, in the background was his supportive mother—a very important part of this story.

The little boy's name, in case you didn't guess it, is Ricky Schroder, veteran of Madison Avenue and, since his starring role in *The Champ,* a television and movie star.

Now, before you pin all your hopes for your child on this one story—wait. It's not why I put it at the head of this chapter. I simply wanted to underline what the chapter is essentially about—namely, the kinds of qualities your child will need, even if he or she does one commercial, and how you can tell whether your child possesses them.

I mentioned that Ricky's mother was a very important factor in his success. Your role in your child's success is equally important. Together, you're the winning combination. But before we go on, let's look at the market. Just what are the statistical chances of getting your child into commercials.

100,000 Commercial Jobs for Children Every Year

In the last five years, the use of children in TV commercials has had by far the most dramatic growth over any category. This includes the much-in-demand housewife type.

But then, you might have guessed it. Every time you turn on your TV, you see children selling children's products, children selling adult products such as detergents, cars, cat food, and packaged goods of all kinds. Advertisers have recognized a basic fact: Children are great salespeople.

"Wow," you say, "there's a chance for my child!"

You're right. There is. But first, let's cut those 100,000 jobs down to size. Your child has competition, and plenty of it. There are about 30,000 talented youngsters out there already vying for these jobs.

"Okay," you say, "but the odds are still pretty good. If you divide thirty thousand into a hundred thousand, that still comes out to three and a third jobs per child a year."

Unfortunately, it doesn't quite work out that way. Some children get far more than their mathematical share.

On the other hand, 100,000 jobs is still a pretty big target to shoot for, and I honestly think the odds of getting at least one of them are good—in fact, provided you know the market and prepare properly to meet its requirements, quite good.

About Piggy Banks and Autograph Books

Children are paid on the same scale as adults. A child can earn as much as $30,000 for one commercial (one day's work). And it can be a route to stardom. It was for Ricky Schroder. It was for Brian Uttman, who went on from commercials to TV and movies. It was for Quinn Cummings, Kristy McNichol, Brooke Shields, et al.

Both fame and fortune are attractive and human goals. But to me (here I go being idealistic again), the chance that doing commercials gives a child—the chance to develop himself or herself— is the best part. Many parents tell me their children are more confident, more at ease with adults, and more conscientious as the result of the experience.

But let's get down to your child and you and try to get a clear picture as to whether getting into commercials is right for your child and if you have the qualities to promote him or her.

What Kid Wouldn't Want to Be in Commercials? And Who Shouldn't

Before you take one step, there's one basic question you should ask yourself: Does your child really want to be in commercials?

The answer is crucial. In the beginning, you will, of course, ask your child how he or she feels about doing commercials. But be wary of the answer, listen for undertones. Remember, children often say yes and go along with things because they want to please.

HOW DO YOU KNOW IF YOUR CHILD REALLY WANTS TO BE IN A COMMERCIAL?

Brian Uttman's mother was quick to see the early signs. Like Ricky Schroder, Brian started his professional career in commercials. His interest in acting and his aptitude for it were apparent even before that. When he was in the fourth grade, so his mother told me, he was doing plays in his neighborhood with other children. After that he went into a semiprofessional children's "little theater" that toured New England. Obviously he loved to perform, and the same is probably true of most of the children who make it in commercials.

FIFTEEN WAYS TO TELL IF YOUR CHILD IS RIGHT FOR COMMERCIALS

It's not easy to be objective about your own child, but try honestly to answer the following questions:

Does your child like most foods? This is a must, as many commercials require children to eat with enthusiasm.

Does he or she have good teeth? With very few exceptions, braces are unacceptable.

Is your child athletic and well coordinated? This is important because many children's commercials require strenuous play.

Is your child nice-looking in an average sort of way?

Does he or she have a warm, outgoing personality?

Can your child communicate easily with adults?

Does he or she take directions easily? Enjoy participating?

Do friends, or perhaps even strangers, remark to you about what an attractive or outgoing or funny child you have?

Does your child enjoy the company of adults? Is he or she spontaneous around older people?

Does your child make up games or "playact" with friends?

Does he or she enjoy being the center of attention?

Is your child a leader?

Does your child take part in school plays or pageants? (This could be very important since producers and casting directors consider this to be acting experience.)

Is your child funny? The ability to make people laugh is one of the rarest and most sought-after gifts in all of the entertainment industries. If your little boy has freckles and wears glasses and looks like a pint-size Woody Allen, be sure he wears those glasses at an audition. There is tremendous demand these days for "character" children.

Is your child patient? Does he or she mind doing the same thing over and over again? Does your child have stamina? Commercial-making can be a long and arduous business and your child may be asked to perform the same routine over and over again.

If you answered yes to most of these questions, your child may well have that certain magic something of which child stars are made.

WHAT THE PROS LOOK FOR IN CHILDREN

Now that you've given your child your own evaluation, let's look at some professional requirements.

Age. Most commercial jobs call for children between the ages of 6 and 12. If the child looks younger than his or her actual age, all the better. An 8-year-old who looks 6 has an inside track. For apparent reasons, he or she is more emotionally mature, yet looks the right age for a younger part.

The age for infants in commercials is 6 months to 18 months. Again, if they're small and look younger, all the better. There is rarely a call for a child in the terrible twos, but children can begin to work again when they're about 4.

Looks. For many years the big "look" in children has been all-American—blond hair, fair skin, conventionally attractive. This has changed. Still, whatever the child's ethnic background, most advertisers look for children who say "average." The character child is a possible exception, but anyone too different might distract from the real star, the product.

Personality. From your own personality evaluation of your child, you might guess some of the qualities agents, producers, and casting directors look for in children. In general, they want natural, unspoiled, spontaneous, intelligent, energetic, well-behaved children. Also, as a child for the most part will be in the hands of strangers, we look for those who are able to function independently of their parents.

Let me repeat that one of the prime attributes we look for in children is an unusual amount of patience. A child may be asked to say the same line, munch the same cereal, or open the same door twenty-five or thirty times. The child who rebels after the second take is not likely to get many jobs in the future.

Rosemary Bryant, one of the best-known "children's agents," says the main thing commercial-makers look for is a child who is not afraid of strangers, who says hello to the doorman, postman, and of course the agent.

Are You a Peanut-Butter Mother?

A director friend of mine tells the story of the time he was doing a peanut-butter commercial. The commercial called for a little boy to eat a peanut-butter sandwich. Not much of a chore for most kids.

The first take was ruined when another actor blew a line. The second take was interrupted by a passing fire engine. Similar misfortunes plagued the eleventh and twelfth takes.

By this time, the poor child had consumed the equivalent of four peanut-butter sandwiches in about a half-hour. When my director friend suggested that perhaps they'd better use a different child, the peanut-butter child's mother shouted, "Absolutely not! My boy can do it. He's a trouper."

The boy *was* a trouper. Nevertheless the thirteenth take was ruined by the sight of a child being sick.

If the child had been an adult, they would have waited for him to recover and go on. Not so with children. There are always several standbys eager to jump in when such mishaps occur.

If, in the above story, you recognize similar tendencies in yourself to hover over and push your child, you had better deal with
them before you think of getting him or her into commercials.
The worst thing you can do to a child's career is to get a reputation for being a "stage mother," the generic term for any peanut-
butter mother. In this business, the word spreads as fast as a scoop
of Skippy on a slice of bread.

Selma Rubin, a well-known children's manager, says she pays
more attention to parents than to children when conducting interviews. She feels parents have to be flexible, and she's not interested in working with those who seem to be in it only for the
money. All of the agents I've spoken to agree.

It's Up to You

More important than your reputation is how your behavior affects your child.

It's up to you not to let your ambition get in his way.

It's up to you to convey to him that the fun part is the doing,
the experience. For instance, that auditioning is like playing; that
getting the job's just a bonus.

It's up to you not to blame him for not getting a particular
commercial and not to let your own disappointment show.

Okay, you're sure that you and your child have what it takes to
make it. What next?

Getting Started

If you're like most parents, you probably picked up this book and
headed straight for this chapter. It's understandable. But just as
there are some major differences between approaching the commercial field as an adult and as a child, many of the things I've
said in earlier chapters also apply to children. For instance, the
same techniques employed in finding which agencies handle what
accounts should be used in finding work for your child. So please,
after you've read both chapters on children, go back to page one

and get an understanding of the scope of the commercial world your child will be entering.

SAY, "BORDEN'S CHEESE"

Your first step is to get out your camera and start taking dozens of pictures of your child. Adult actors need only one or two pictures, but casting directors, managers, and agents like to see several photographs of children. Brian Uttman's mother sent out snapshots to thirteen agents on her first foray into the commercial field and received eleven responses.

Once your child is established, you may want some professional pictures. There are many routes you can take in obtaining professional photographs (see chapter 6), but at the beginning, snapshots will do just fine. Below are some guidelines for your picture-taking.

Taking Pictures That Get Attention

Take color pictures. Color photographs serve two functions. They give an agent or manager an idea of your child's hair and skin coloring. In casting, they are used to match a child with the adult actors who will play the mommy and daddy in the commercial.

Take caught-in-the-act pictures of your child—eating, laughing, playing, etc. Natural, unposed, spontaneous, candid shots that show your child's personality and enthusiasm are ideal.

Take tight close-ups. A picture of your child looking through the lens at the person taking the picture communicates a sense of intimacy. Again, a natural expression is what you're after.

Take a full-length shot. This gives the viewer an idea of your child's height and proportions (fat or thin) and is also helpful in casting commercials where there are other children or adults involved.

GETTING THE PICTURES READY FOR MAILING

Put name, address, home phone, or contact phone on the back of every picture. If the picture is big enough, you should also include height, and weight, and date of birth.

Include a letter. The letter should serve the same function as a résumé. Include any relevant information, such as experience in local theater, drama groups, or previous television appearances. Also include all the information that is on the back of the photograph.

Your letter should also note your child's school hours, and—very important—how quickly you can get him or her to a last-minute interview or audition. With children, many jobs are won or lost simply on the basis of availability.

Be sure also to indicate whether your child is missing any teeth. This may sound silly, but sometimes it is very important.

TO WHOM DO YOU SEND PICTURES?

You will send your pictures to casting directors, agents, and managers, but to each for different reasons.

Casting directors do not usually give general interviews to children. If your child's pictures are appropriate, he will be called directly for an audition. This is because we often are looking for children without experience, and a spontaneous reaction to a particular scene is the desired quality.

On the other hand, managers and agents do give general interviews, and in sending them your child's picture and data, your goal will be quite different, as I will now explain.

What Is a Manager and What Does He Do?

A manager is a professional person whose business it is to take an overall, long-term interest in the child he represents. His main function is to guide the child's career and recommend appropriate courses of action.

If your child is just starting out, a good manager can be price-less. Although they are not allowed to solicit business, they can help sell your child's ability to good agents. And as they work with many different agents, they are likely to get wind of almost all the good opportunities.

Managers are also valuable for a child who is in constant de-mand or whose family knows little or nothing about show busi-ness. They can be very supportive and take the burden of sched-uling from harried parents.

In the beginning, at least, a manager will get involved in such everyday details as the need for a child to get a haircut, see a dentist, take dancing lessons, and so on. He will help you get résumés and pictures together. He also has more time than an agent to devote to your child, since the average manager handles only about twenty children.

Many managers started out as mothers of professional children or as child actors themselves. They know all the pitfalls of the profession and most are very sympathetic to the child.

Selma Rubin, the manager I mentioned earlier, believes a man-ager should have a farseeing view of a child. "You can't just look out for today," she told me. Sometimes, she explained, this means discouraging a child from taking a certain commercial if it means possibly losing a role in a major film. Selma has turned down both commercials and TV series for one of her prodigies, Irene Cara, who appeared in *Fame,* because she believes Irene is destined to be a "superstar" and at that point Selma felt discretion was neces-sary.

Basic Questions to Ask a Prospective Manager

How long have you been in the business? Obviously someone who has been around the block a few times is more likely to be productive than someone just getting his feet wet.

Whom else have you handled? Managers are a lot like athletic trainers: The more winners they have produced in the past, the more they are likely to produce in the future.

How many agents do you work with and how soon will my child get an interview with some of them?

How much do you charge? This is a must question because managers, unlike agents, are not bound by any union (SAG or AFTRA) regulations; they can charge whatever percentage a client is willing to pay. The usual rate for a manager's services is 15 percent for jobs that come directly through them and 10 percent for jobs that come through an agent. In the latter case, the agent also gets 10 percent.

How long will our contractual agreement be, and are there any special stipulations? A manager can sign your child up for several years. Although managers' contracts are fairly standard (you can buy one in stores that sell standard contracts), I advise you to read the fine print and all the addenda. It's not a bad idea to have your family attorney take a look at the contract. Some managers ask for residual fees from jobs your child got before signing with them. In such instances, you have to decide whether it's worth it or not.

To Have a Manager or Not to Have a Manager

My feelings really come down to this: You need a manager if your child is having trouble breaking into the business, or, conversely, if your child is very successful.

Many of the managers I talked to suggested that it's best to let a child explore the opportunities of commercials for a while before committing themselves to a manager.

I'd say that if your child is a big hit right from the start and is only interested in commercials, one of the good agents who specializes in children will more than fill the bill. Later on, if you develop further career goals, a manager can offer a great deal of help and guidance.

What Is an Agent and What Is His Function?

An agent's main function is to solicit business. He is the one who calls a casting director and sells a particular child for a commercial.

Agents are vital to the whole process of breaking into the business. Your child may get along without a manager (50 percent of child actors have managers; 50 percent don't) but there is no way to succeed without an agent.

How Does the Process Work?

A typical situation might work like this: A casting director is assigned to cast a commercial that involves children. He calls all the agents he works with and gives them a breakdown of his needs. The agents then recommend some of the children they represent. If a child is represented by several agents, the first agent to call would get the commission.

How Many Agents Can You Have and How Do You Find Them?

You've noticed that I indicated your child could have several agents. That means as many as will take the child on. There are, however, exceptions. Many agents will take children only on an exclusive basis. That means your child must use only that agent. In return, the agent actively seeks work for the child and gives advice on how his or her performance can be improved. In other words, the agent acts as a manager.

Not all agents take on children as clients. On the other hand, there are some who handle children only, and some who handle both adults and children. The lists of agents and managers who handle children in appendixes D and E should point you in the right direction.

There are obviously more agents in the big television cities like New York and Los Angeles, but nowadays commercials are made almost everywhere and you should be able to find someone good—and union-approved—without traveling too far.

What Percentage Does an Agent Get?

The maximum permitted by SAG is 10 percent of the child's earnings. Run, do not walk, to the nearest exit if any agent suggests he is entitled to a bigger share of the pie. And on the way home, stop at the nearest phone booth and let your local SAG know about the incident.

What Are the Other Expenses?

Actually, the cost of starting out is less for a child than for an adult. For one thing, the fact that you can send snapshots eliminates the photographer's fee. You should be able to keep your basic package (picture and mailing) down to a minimum.

Also, in the beginning, formal training, singing, dancing, or acting lessons are not a must. It's your child's charisma that counts. If in time your child becomes relatively successful, you may of course want to invest in various kinds of lessons.

There are, however, enough other costs involved. There's hairstyling, clothes, and transportation to and from auditions, and baby-sitting fees for children staying at home. And of course there are union fees. All in all, it can be expensive, so be sure you know what you're doing. Shop around for the services you need.

Note: Save all your receipts. Working expenses of this type are tax-deductible.

Okay you know the odds. You've analyzed your child's abilities. You know what the experts are looking for. You're sure you have the qualities to make your child's venture into commercials fun and rewarding. You've taken pictures. You know about managers and agents. In other words, you're set to go. Now, what will the experience be like?

What It's Like for Your Child to Be in Commercials

If you watch old movies on TV, you're probably familiar with the scene of Shirley Temple or Judy Garland, all dressed in ruffles, about to do a routine for a hard-bitten agent.

"Okay, kid," he says as he bites on his cigar, "let's see what you can do."

The child performs. The agent shifts his indifferent pose. He sits up and takes notice, images of fame and dollar signs lighting up his eyes.

Even if you haven't seen one of these movies, you probably have some apprehension about what auditioning will be like for both you and your child. You envision either heartless rejection or instant success.

Let's see what your child's audition is really like.

The General Interview

There you are, sitting in the agent's or manager's reception room. Jenny, your daughter, who had a good night's sleep last night, is sitting next to you. *Note: Unlike Ms. Temple and Garland, Jenny is dressed in regular clothes—jeans and T-shirt, or whatever she normally wears.*

A buzzer rings; the secretary or receptionist picks up the phone, nods. You're next, she tells you, putting the phone down. Or, more likely, she says that the agent or manager would first like to see Jenny alone.

In the latter case, your heart sinks, you get that first-day-of-school feeling—or worse, you feel you're sending your child out into the cold, cruel world.

Let me assure you that the person on the other side of the door is usually very sympathetic toward children. As I said earlier, many agents and managers were child actors themselves, or are parents like you who started out by guiding their children's careers. If they are reputable, they got that way by understanding children, not by pushing them or reducing them to tears.

WHAT HAPPENS INSIDE THE AGENT'S OR MANAGER'S OFFICE

Your child will not usually be asked to perform. Most agents and managers are primarily interested in a child's personality: whether he is shy or freezes up around strangers. They are looking for more than a child who is photogenic; independence and ability to concentrate are also key factors.

Says Joy Stevenson, a West Coast agent, "When children come to see me, I try to put them at ease and ask them questions like 'What do you like to do best?' 'What's your favorite food?' I just talk to them to see if they're going to wiggle, look at the floor, look at the ceiling, or if they're going to look right at me and have a conversation with me. That's the child I'm looking for."

Kathy Dowd, a well-known children's manager in New York, echoed that thought. "There are some children who are adorable but who don't want to be bothered with the adult world. I'm looking for the child who talks to the garbage man and the cabdriver. He loves to get attention and his face lights up when he talks."

Tylar Kjar, an agent in Denver, says he always interviews the child first, then the parent. He also says he tries to make absolutely certain that the interest is genuine, not just a passing fancy. Before he takes on a child, he wants a commitment from the parent to take the process seriously.

Marcia of Marcia's Kids warns parents to beware of the "grandma syndrome." This occurs when a child comes in, is asked to sing, and clams up. The mother says something like "But you sang so well in the car for grandma." Very few interviews and auditions, Marcia points out, are held in a car singing for grandma, so you'd better be sure your child really wants to be there. The main things that she looks for are honesty and spontaneity.

HOW TO FIND OUT THE RESULTS

If an agent or manager says he can't use your child, try to find out—politely—why (out of earshot of your child, of course). It may be something as simple as the fact that he already has several children of that type. Agents and managers generally try to avoid taking on too many children of similar types, because they wind up competing against themselves. Ask the agent if he can recommend someone else you might approach.

Let me repeat, I would be wary of any agent or manager who makes extravagant promises the first time he sees your child or who wants you to make a big investment in photographs or training.

The Audition Room

Let's assume that all has gone well. You have an agent and you've just gotten your first call to go to an audition. What can you expect? Well, let me give you a little picture of what the scene will be like.

In the first place, on this trip you will be going to an advertising agency or a casting service. When you arrive at the audition room, you'll find seven or eight adults sitting around and perhaps ten to twelve children, usually of the same sex and age. In winter, coats and sweaters will be piled all over the seats. It will be very noisy.

Your first challenge will be to get to the receptionist, stepping over sprawled children on the way. (Children's auditions always seem more of a cattle call than adult auditions because they must be held after school hours. The whole audition, therefore, is fitted in between 3:00 and 6:00 P.M.)

When you get to the receptionist, be sure to ask if this is the Fritos audition for 7-year-old girls or whatever. On more than one occasion, I've heard of families waiting for hours in the wrong waiting room.

Check your appointment time, sign in, and ask for the script and storyboard (see chapter on auditions). Ask also if there are any other special instructions. If there is no script or storyboard, you can find a seat and relax.

You can, of course, save yourself another trip if you also ask where the bathrooms and water fountain are.

SITTING IT OUT

As you sit and wait, you'll be tempted to concentrate on the juicy gossip that's being exchanged among the adults, many of whom will have played and replayed this scene many times and gotten to know each other. You'll hear things like "We've just been over to the Colgate audition. They've been looking for two months." Or, "We've been up on *Annie* auditions seven times. We're pretty sure we're going to get into one of the national companies." Tales of auditions, call-backs, some boasting, some complaining, will fill the room. One mother I know brings a good mystery and ignores all the conversation; others love the camaraderie.

It's important that your child not take the competitive undertones too seriously. And, in my experience, they rarely do. Many of the children become friends and often resume games from one audition to another.

HOW TO HANDLE A SCRIPT

If there is a script, then it is more helpful for you to prepare your child a little for the audition than to pay attention to the gossip. First, read the script and make sure you understand it. If there is something you don't understand, go back and ask the receptionist to explain. If she doesn't know the answer, she will ask someone else connected with the audition.

If there is dialogue, go over the script with your child. Explain the meaning of anything she doesn't understand. Feed her cues and let her respond. Do not, however, coach her on inflection or an exact reading. This is especially important if the child is very young. She will receive instruction when she goes into the audition and it will be more difficult for her to unlearn a particular reading of the line. Remember, the casting director is looking for spontaneity. All children, especially younger ones, will either act naturally or they won't act at all. An older child, if his parents have "groomed" his performance, will almost invariably overact and not get a part.

Don't pressure your child to memorize. We had an audition recently and the mothers were told that their children would be asked to sing "You Are My Sunshine" or some other song they knew. A couple of mothers panicked and tried to teach their children the song very quickly. Naturally, their children did not do well in the audition because they were so busy concentrating on remembering the words. Fortunately, the director saved them by asking them to sing a song that they knew and their natural abilities came through.

Infants and Preschoolers

Since it is not necessary to wait until after school hours, infant and preschool auditions are usually in the morning. Let your agent know nap hours so that your appointment can be scheduled at a time when the baby has a good chance of being awake and alert.

You may be asked to take off the child's outer clothing, so make it easy for yourself by not having complicated buttons and snaps.

Bring with you any bottles or extra diapers you'll need. Casting offices have changing rooms.

It's important to make your child as comfortable as possible. And be prepared for noise. An infant audition can make a construction site sound like a library by comparison.

The Audition and After

Once your child goes into the audition, the whole matter is pretty much out of your hands. However, you might suggest to her that she have a good time, that it's all right to talk or ask questions, and not to worry if she doesn't know the answer to every question she's asked. You might also tell your child, "You may be put in front of a camera. Someone will tell you what to do just like when we take pictures at home."

There often will be several adults in the room where the children audition—the casting director, the art director, the scriptwriter, a representative of the client, and others. I've seen as many as twelve people involved in this process together.

Your child will usually be asked if she likes the particular product involved, as well as questions about age, school, and so on. Don't try to give her the "right" answers in advance. There are none. The questions are being asked primarily to get an idea of the child's personality. The freer she feels to respond and talk, the more likely she is to get the job. Just let your child answer the questions as fully and honestly as she can.

GOING HOME

After the audition, your child may want to tell you what happened inside, or may want to leave immediately. I've noticed that older children sometimes refuse to reveal anything in front of the others—they become embarrassed.

I think it's important at this time for you to concentrate on whether the child found it interesting or had fun rather than asking questions like "Did you get it?" or "Did the people inside like you?" Something like "Gee, you weren't in there very long" is apt to be devastating.

Talking about where you're going next on the trip home can ensure pleasant memories for your child and avoid needless pressure.

GETTING FEEDBACK

You can call your agent or manager the next day for any feedback he might have gotten. I would do this when the child is not around so that you have time to interpret the comments in a way that is constructive. I would share this information only with the child involved. If she wants to tell the rest of the family, let it be on her initiative.

If your child is considered a likely candidate, chances are you will get a call-back in three or four days. With tight schedules in the advertising business, you'll rarely be called to let you know that your child didn't get a part.

Call-Backs

You and your child are back at the advertising agency's reception room. This time the child population has diminished considerably. You are on your first call-back. A call-back means essentially that they've narrowed the field. There are usually two call-backs, and obviously your chances improve as you go on.

For more information on call-backs, see chapter 12.

The Director and What He Will Look For

The first or second call-back is the point where the director of the commercial comes to the forefront of the screening process. To help you understand what he expects of your child, I asked some well-established directors what they look for.

"I look for real kids, kids that people can relate to as if they were their own," said Richard Perkins.

"I look for curiosity, enthusiasm, sensitivity," said Maurice To-
bias. "I look to see how long they can be attentive, how patient
they are with other children. I look to see if they're team players."

Added David Impastato: "I try to stay away from pretty, clean-
cut, perfect kids. I look for uniqueness of response, something
that isn't just a typical smile with shining teeth. I try to avoid kids
that are wise guys and have all the jokes and patter. I also check
out their mothers. If the mother is a nervous wreck, I know I'm in
trouble if I cast that kid. If the mother is calm and not on some
kind of ego trip, I feel reassured."

Before the Shoot

Be sure to check with your agent/advertising agency/film company to see if your child should get a social security card and a work
permit (e.g., in New York it's necessary for children under 16 to
get work permits). They'll also tell you how to obtain these if
necessary.

The Shooting Day

At last the day has come. You and your child are entering a film
studio. It is the day of the shoot, and your child is first choice to
play in it. Very heady stuff; but along with a certain amount of
glamour, you'll probably find it a long, workaday day, full of details.

Of course you're on time. As mentioned before, unlike adult
shoots where there is one actor for each part, there are several
eager mothers and children there ready to stand in if you're not.

FIRST THING, FIND THE A.D.

Your manager or agent has given you the name of the A.D.
(that's film talk for "assistant director") to whom you're to report.
He will sign you in and send you to the wardrobe department.

It's extremely important that you find and report to him. I've
seen situations where an all-points alert has been sent out, only to

find a parent and child sitting quietly in an empty office in which "someone" had told them to wait.

Remember, shooting time is valuable. Even if you're only a few minutes late on the set, calls will go out and your child might well lose the job.

THE SET

Cameras everywhere; people setting up props, fixing lighting; people in knots discussing various shots. You and your child are at last on the set and it's exciting. Don't worry about where you should sit or when your child will be called—you will be taken care of. But it might be some time before your child will perform before the camera.

Be prepared. You'll do a lot of sitting around even after your child gets into the hands of the director. Dozens of small technical details can make the hours go by slowly. This is where patience comes in (remember, we talked about it as one of your child's chief attributes). Bring along things to amuse both you and your child during the long waiting periods. One mother I know started a successful business knitting children's clothes on the set. The more commercials her daughter got, the more wool she bought, until finally she had a business going.

LEAVE IT TO THE DIRECTOR

The same advice I gave on handling a script applies to the shoot. It is important to stress to your child the importance of following the director's instructions. For example, you've always told your child to chew her food carefully before swallowing. During a shoot, she will probably be asked to take only one bite, then spit it out. Impolite maybe, but it avoids the kind of peanut-butter episode I mentioned in the previous chapter.

Most Good Directors Are Children at Heart

Most good directors have developed their own little ways of getting the best performances out of children.

George Gomes built a special wall through which only the

camera lens could be seen. His reasoning is that this helps the child concentrate and not be distracted by all the people on the set.

Steve Horn once solved a familiar problem in an ingenious way. The child was supposed to open a kitchen cabinet and take out a bag of potato chips. After a few takes, the little boy complained, "I already did that." Steve had gone to the trouble of finding out that the boy loved baseball cards, and Steve had brought some along for just such an emergency. For every good take the boy would do, Steve would hand him a new card. The footage turned out terrific.

Most people on the set have tricks in working with children. Shooting a commercial with Ricky Schroder and his dog, Howard, it was the dog trainer's brilliant idea to rub liverwurst on Ricky's neck. This saved Ricky the trouble of coaxing Howard into an affectionate frame of mind. Needless to say, the dog followed him around all day.

Bill Hudson, a well-known children's director, believes so much in spontaneity that he won't give very young children their lines until they're in front of the camera and ready to roll.

TOOTH FAIRIES, RED SPOTS, AND "MANY A SLIP 'TWIXT CUP AND LIP"

Many things can happen along the way that can make the business of getting your child into commercials discouraging. Naturally, you want your child to succeed and will do your best to bring it about, but the fates don't always cooperate.

If you wake up on the morning of an important audition or shoot and discover that the tooth fairy, or measles, or chicken pox has made a surprise visit to your house during the night, bite the bullet and cancel the appointment. The commercial-makers will respect you for it. On the other hand, they'll never forgive you if you bring in a sick, unhappy child or one with no front teeth— especially if he was supposed to sell the merits of sugarless gum.

At a shoot, if your child, because of too much peanut butter or whatever, is replaced by another, yield with good grace. Other opportunities will come up, and if they don't, maybe your child is trying to tell you something.

Mishaps do occur, but don't look for them. Chances are, good fortune will win the day, and one day you will turn on your TV set and, lo, there will be the rewarding result.

19

OTHER DOORS

THERE'S A COMMERCIAL FOR PRACTICALLY EVERYONE

You're not an actor or actress and you're not a top fashion model—but, oh, how you'd love to get into commercials, or even do just *one:* see yourself on the other side of the tube and collect some of that luscious money.

Pie in the sky? Not at all. Getting into commercials and selling a real Mrs. Smith kind of pie or any other product is an obtainable goal. I see it happen every day.

The other day, for instance, an advertising manager from Kodak, one of our biggest clients, called and asked if I would see someone who wanted to get into commercials. Of course, I said I would. Now, before you say, "Okay, here's a story about 'pull,'" hear me out. When Bess Goodman, a woman in her sixties with a wonderful character face, walked into my office, I immediately went into the instant typecasting that goes on in my head when I interview an actor or actress. In her case, it was librarian, manicurist, switchboard operator, schoolteacher, bridge player, dowager. Bess Goodman could stand on her own.

I asked Bess if she was a friend of the advertising manager or any of his clients. "Absolutely not," she said. "I've never met any of them." How did she get such an impressive sponsor? Here's the story she told me.

Bess had been thinking for some time about being in a commercial. She had done some local community theater, been a Sunday School teacher, worked some for the Fresh Air Fund and part-time in real estate. Obviously there was a performer in her.

As she lived in Rochester, New York, Bess first contacted Eastman Kodak Company, home base for her, and was referred to the photography illustration department. Before she knew it, she was off for test shots armed with her props: glasses, a book, a couple of changes of blouses, jewelry, some makeup, and hair appliances. The test shots turned out to be winners and a photograph session was set up. Out of it came photographs that appeared in local ads and promotion material. Her kids began to call her "Mom the Model."

Later Bess grew more ambitious and had a voice tape made up at a local audio studio. She sent pictures and tapes to the advertising manager who had recommended her to me, and followed up with several calls. Upshot? He offered to introduce her to his advertising agency (us), and, lo, there she was in my office.

Although I had nothing for Bess then, I, too, was impressed with her. Since then, she has called me several times. Last heard from, she was making notes of any commercials she saw using older people and sending her pictures and résumés to the manufacturers or advertising agencies of the products advertised. She feels, as I do, that it won't be long before she lands a commercial.

Bess Goodman is finding one door into commercials. There are many other doors. In this chapter, I hope to open some of them to you. First, let's start with the most common category—Real People.

Real People

Allen Funt of "Candid Camera" fame always used to end his show by saying. "Someday, somewhere, someone may come up to you and say, 'Smile, you're on "Candid Camera." '"

I say, Someday you will be in a supermarket and someone may walk up to you and say, "Hey, you're in a commercial."

More likely, however, the interviewer will say, "We're doing some market research and we'd like to ask you some questions about our product." In other words, you'll not be the only one contending for the commercial. Before I tell you what you can do to be the pick of the crop, let me suggest that when you go shopping, plant yourself in a strategic spot. Pause a little longer at the frozen-food department or the check-out counter—there's more light for the camera there. And don't get dressed up to do your marketing. Advertisers are on the lookout for what are called "real people," everyday man-on-the-street people.

HOW IT WORKS

Market-research companies and people like Laura Slatsky of People Finders, a New York–based casting service, are ever scouting for possible people to endorse products. They usually send sales representatives and interviewers to malls and super-markets and such likely spots. Bob King is one of the most famous interviewers. The back of his head has been shown so many times on TV that some of his friends like to rush up behind him and ask if they can have their pictures taken with the back of his celebrat-ed head.

Picking names out of the phone book is another method scouts employ. So don't slam down the phone if someone calls and says, "We're conducting a survey."

I know what you're thinking: It's all chance. That's not entirely true. Some is design. You can tempt the fates. And you don't have to live in a big city to do it. Market-research companies often choose smaller areas because they're easier to cover. Since they often pick someone who knows a lot of people in town to act as liaison, some people have taken the initiative by forming film divisions in their communities; instead of waiting to be ap-proached, they let market researchers and film companies know about them. Why not knock on this door? Once you have your foot in, opportunity might just let you in.

Testimonial letters are also a proven way to get on an advertiser's research list. Write an honest letter to the manufacturer about your experience with its product. (See sample letter on p. 109.)

TIPS ON WINNING THE COMMERCIAL

Here are some pointers on how to win testimonial commercials.

1. Relax. Be yourself. Be spontaneous. Do not go out of your way to impress.

2. Use ordinary language. Speak the way you usually do.

3. Be specific. Mention the brand name. Tell what you like about the product. If you can, make it personal and colorful. I remember one mother talking about how a bleach made her daughter's nurse uniforms look so white that when she went to work in the morning she looked like a bottle of milk.

4. Pause before you answer. It's natural to take time to think.

5. Complete your sentences. Complete your thoughts. Keep your replies short.

6. Don't do a commercial. They want your spontaneous answers.

7. If you stumble, that's okay. Remember, they picked you for your naturalness.

8. Be sincere. Don't try too hard to please. Mean and believe what you say.

9. Be warm, open. They're looking for caring people.

10. If the job requires further interviews and auditions, dress for them as you usually dress. They must have liked the way you dressed, otherwise they wouldn't have picked you.

11. Trust the interviewer to help you. They're experts in drawing out people. You can trust them to be warm, friendly, and to put you at ease.

Note: You don't have to join the union to do a testimonial commercial. But who knows? You might find you're good at it, go on to study, and one day take off for New York or Hollywood.

A COLD IN THE NOSE AND OTHER
MINOR ACHES AND PAINS

Sometimes when I'm doing a general interview, I feel like a nurse. I'll ask an actor or actress, "Do you have arthritis? Do you have sinus trouble regularly? Do you have dry skin?" True, I'm interested in people who do commercials, but not quite so interested as to inquire about their minor infirmities. I ask these questions because my agency handles products that relieve these particular minor complaints and I'm looking for people to perform in commercials advertising them.

If you qualify as a "real person," you actually have a much better chance than an actress or actor to appear in commercials like these. Drug and pharmaceutical companies aim for believability and if you've seen a commercial where the very real person can't peel an orange or hold a frying pan because she has arthritis, you can understand why these endorsements ring true.

Kinds of Aches and Pains That Can Win You a Commercial

Here is a list of physical problems that could win you a commercial and possibly make you hurt less.

Frequent headaches
Sinus trouble
Muscle aches
Back trouble due to muscle aches
Arthritis of the hands or shoulders
Athlete's foot
Hemorrhoids
Skin disorders such as acne, psoriasis, flaking skin

Liver spots on your hands or face can also turn out to be an unexpected asset.

As many of the above problems may not be apparent to the

*eye, the networks will not run the commercial unless they have
an affidavit from the endorser showing that he or she really has or
had the problem and that the medicine does/did help.*

How to Air Your Complaints

In an earlier chapter, I told about the actress who calls every
time she has a cold in hopes that we may be casting for a cold-
remedy commercial. Fine. But how do you, an unknown, go about
turning your runny nose into a job in a commercial?

Get the *Standard Directory of Advertising Agencies* (available
in libraries) and look up the agencies that handle the drugs and
medications that you use to relieve your aches and pains. Write a
letter to them and enclose a picture of yourself. This picture
should not be a professional shot. On the back of it, put the health
problem you have. Don't forget to include your name, address,
and telephone number.

A sincerely written letter to the manufacturer, praising the
product and what it did for you, is also an ideal way to get attention.

Extras

As an extra in a commercial, you won't be one of the cast of
thousands escaping a towering inferno or storming a castle. You'll
be the person at the table next to the man who has ordered cream
cheese without a bagel; the man sitting on a barstool in a beer
commercial. And unlike the stereotyped Hollywood extra, you
will be valued as a talent.

I had not been in casting long when I discovered what being an
extra could mean to a performer. I remember a producer coming
back from a shoot waving a picture and raving about the extra
with a terrific look. "We definitely must use him," he said. When
I looked at the picture, I was surprised to see a top on-camera
performer. It turns out that many on-camera principals supplement their income by working as extras. It leads to contacts, and
often more jobs as principals. It upgrades careers.

A GREAT WAY TO GET STARTED IN COMMERCIALS

If you've done one commercial and lucked into getting into the union, do "extra" work and do a lot of it. You'll get exposure. You'll make on-the-set contacts. You'll get on-the-set training. You'll have a chance to learn from other mistakes and pick up all kinds of technique pointers. And you'll make money for your acting lessons.

HOW TO GET "EXTRA" WORK: ADVICE FOR PROS AND BEGINNERS

It's not uncommon, come the end of a day, that I'll receive a call that goes something like this: "We've been given the money to put a few extras in the drugstore scene. No audition is necessary—just have them come in." This is where a notation on your picture stating that you do "extra" work pays off. For after I have the specs, I go through my files with an eye for those performers who also work as extras. So do put "I do 'extra' work" on your résumé. Put it in big letters after your phone number and answering-service number.

Since film companies often hire extras, you should also contact them. Call and ask to speak to the casting director or someone in the production office. Ask how you can get on their extra list. If you can't make a phone contact, write a note to the film company stating that you are a member of the union and are interested in doing "extra" work. Attach it to your picture and résumé.

Of course, you're interested in the money. How does $210.75 for the day sound?

Print Models

When I want a "look" and I can't find it among the actors and actresses (and I often can't), I head straight for the print-model file. In it are pictures and composites of people who pose for ads in newspapers, trade magazines, brochures, promotion material, catalogs, etc. I'm sure, with their experience in modeling, they know how to relate to and come alive before the camera. But as I riffle through my files, I look for something more: Can he do a line? Has she learned to act?

If you're a print model and you've never taken acting lessons, I can't push you hard enough to do so. If you're a neophyte—have done just a few catalog pictures for your father's business—most of my previous chapters on pictures and résumés, interviews, auditioning, etc., should also serve as a helpful minicourse. I do, however, have some special advice for those of you who fall into a few specific print categories. I suggest you scan the titles below, and if you fit under one, read through.

BEAUTIFUL OR PRETTY GIRLS WHO ARE NOT THE REQUIRED HEIGHT

If you come to New York, make the rounds, and find that you're too short to be accepted by one of the top fashion agents, please don't go home. Find a print agency that handles more-average types and start studying acting. Nancy Fields of Ted Bates agrees with me that there are plenty of commercials waiting for you.

THE FULL-FIGURED WOMAN

There may not be a big demand on television right now for the full-figured woman (Jane Russell in the eighteen-hour-bra commercial is a charming exception); however, as people start to realize that fat can be fashionable, there is more and more acknowledgment of the more ample figure in print advertising. Clothing manufacturers have finally started to make flattering clothes directed to this market. Local clothes manufacturers are beginning to use the larger woman in local television commercials. Model agents are starting departments especially for the full-figured woman. Genny Green of Plus Models says that the demand has never been greater. Large cities such as New York, L.A., and Chicago now have agents who exclusively handle the large-sized woman.

If all these possibilities are not available in your area, promote them. Suggest that your talent agent create a division that handles your type. Approach local department stores and see if you can get them to include you in their fashion shows. Encourage your local television station to do a fashion show directed to the full-figured market. Do your share in giving television commercials a new breadth.

TWINS: DOUBLE YOUR PLEASURE, DOUBLE YOUR RESIDUALS

We're currently running a Double Cheeseburger, Double Whopper commercial for Burger King, and guess whom we're using. Twins in commercials do seem to go in cycles. One of the most famous is the Doublemint commercials.

Most of the twins seen in these commercials usually started in print. While most agents keep a file of twins, when there's a call for them, there's always a search. Any publicity or print ads involving twins are usually noted.

But why wait to have your picture clipped and filed away? Send your picture and résumé to advertising agencies and manufacturers of products. It may stimulate their thinking. A note about auditions: Be sure you dress identically and wear your hair in identical style.

BEGINNERS—OR THE BESS GOODMAN WAY

How often I've had an account person send me an ad with a note attached: "The client sent this to me as an example of type. Do you think you could check out if the model can act well enough to be in our new campaign?"

There's no question, if you're a type you see in ads—an attractive housewife, pleasing-looking executive, have a weather-beaten character face—print work is your door in. I recommend you do as Bess Goodman did: Start in your hometown; contact local advertisers and advertising agencies. Chances are as you gain experience and an interesting portfolio, you will be able to move on to commercials.

Body Parts

HANDS

A hand comes into camera range with a teaspoon and measures out instant coffee into several cups. A hand comes in and rushes through cascades of freshly shampooed hair. These hands are performers in commercials. And if people say you have beautiful, expressive hands, this area may be your door in.

Do You Have the Hands for It?

Compliments are only your first clue that you may have hand-model hands. Your hand type, how the TV camera sees them, how they perform on camera—in short, professional standards—will determine your success.

To be a hand model, your hands should fit into one of these commercial types:

Female housewife hands: Average-size, fingers not too long, nails not too long. Unless you want to specialize in "before" shots (not much work there), hands should not be rough and red.

Female cosmetic hands: Long fingers; long, rounded, smooth nails; no knobby knuckles, no cuts or blemishes.

Male hands: A good regular-size masculine hand.

Male cosmetic hands: Smooth, aristocratic hands; long fingers; little hair.

Male blue-cuff hands: Strong, broad, but not *too* large.

To be a hand model, your hands should be handy, dexterous. You'll sometimes have to pick up a cup or spoon from a specific angle and hold it in a particular way so that the product can be seen. Demonstrations are particularly difficult. Hands must be steady. I'll never forget the bartender I employed who got a case of the shakes when he poured beer. If you're the nervous type, but determined to be a hand model, better learn to shake in your boots.

Important: If your hands seem to meet the requirements but are large, skip this section and go on to other body parts. Heaven forbid your hands dwarf or overwhelm the product.

Handling the Job

Hand modeling is often done last, after the on-camera talent has left. You're tired, you've been hanging around the studio all day, and now your work begins. You may have to hold your arm in an awkward position for a long time. You may have to make tiny, careful movements. Jean Rayner, a successful hand model, told me about the time she had to hang upside down so that her hands could enter the picture from the top of the frame. This caused her veins to swell, so she had to hold her arms up between takes.

Clearly, this is not a job for someone who doesn't have stamina. Better ask yourself if you do before you pursue this area. If you do, there's work, the competition is not too heavy, and the rewards are good.

Hand Maintenance

Top hand models like Jean Rayner and Linda Rose are very careful to keep their hands in good shape. They avoid difficult chores that might cause minor cuts, bruises, or broken nails. For the household chores they do, they wear rubber gloves with hand moisturizers.

It's probably harder for male hand models to take care of their hands, but apparently that doesn't mean they have to stop doing manual work. Greg Fortune, one of the top male models, built a house and hand-modeled at the same time. I recommend Linda Rose's book *Hands,* published by Simon & Schuster, New York, for special hand-care tips and exercises.

LEGS

Since the camera magnifies, legs that cause hardhat crews to ogle are too heavy for the camera's eye. To be a leg model, you must have long, slender legs and not too large feet.

As in all body-part work, this pursuit requires stamina. I've heard some real war stories from leg models. One told me about lying on a studio floor wiggling her feet in the air for hours while the photographer tried to get the exact shot. Another told about climbing stairs for hours while the cameraman tried to follow the movement of her pantyhose fabric minutely. Obviously, it's not for the weak-kneed.

FEET

Beautiful feet are as scarce as hen's teeth. I know firsthand. I once had to find a pair of feet that were to belong to a 30-year-old woman. The leg models that came in had bony feet. Others came in with one good foot, the other marred by a bunion or corn or some such imperfection. (With the kind of shoes we wear today, no wonder.) When I finally found a 16-year-old with two perfect feet, long toes, and no blemishes, I felt as if I had discovered Cinderella.

If you have such perfect feet, take an instant picture of them and send it to the advertisers of foot treatments. If your legs are also great, send pictures to hosiery manufacturers as well.

OTHER BODY PARTS

Occasionally, a facial feature is used unconnected with a face. All you see is an extreme close-up of eyes or teeth or hair; the camera never pulls back to reveal the face.

These commercials always amaze me in that so often the one feature shown suggests the whole. I remember on a Long and Silky commercial, we used a girl who had the longest hair we could find. It extended all the way down to her knees. Even though she did not face the camera, many people wrote in to find out the name of the "beautiful Chinese girl" who appeared in the commercial. They imagined her face based on her beautiful long black hair.

And then there was the model who did a toothpaste commercial that showed only her perfect teeth. The commercial ran so often that even the check-out girl at the model's supermarket recognized her perfect smile. Since her face in the commercial was considered unrecognizable, she did not get residuals (see chapter 21). She felt cheated, and I think rightly so.

Actually, such disembodied work as the above isn't called for that frequently. For the most part, when special features like beautiful teeth or gorgeous lashes are needed, the face also appears on camera. However, if you have a perfect feature and just average looks, you're not out. Be sure to write to those agencies that handle products suitable to your special feature. Often a pretty face or a nice-looking face is acceptable if, say, the teeth are perfect enough or the search has been going on long enough.

Special Skills

I don't know if performers are just shy about making their special skills known or they don't think they matter. But it can be frustrating for a casting director, not to mention unrewarding for you, if you don't bring whatever special skills you may have to our attention. I'll show you just why in this scenario:

"We'd like to get an expert ice skater for this commercial," says a voice at the other end of my phone. "I'm sure we can't afford Dorothy Hamill," the voice continues, "but even if we could, we need someone with long red hair."

"I'll see what I can do," I say.

I go to our ice-skating file. No one there who skates and has long red hair. Okay, now I go through our pretty-young-women file, looking at résumés for long red hair and, under "Special Skills," expert ice skater. Still no one. I then look under "Dancers." Often dancers can also figure-skate. Still no one.

Scene changes to you with long red hair sitting there in your ice-skating costume reading this book.

Now why weren't you in my "Special Skills" file? It's true you may have sent me your picture and it wasn't filed, but more likely you never mentioned the fact that you are a champion figure skater.

This is all my way of saying that if you are an expert—really special at something—don't just include it under "Special Skills" along with typing and changing diapers. Send me special notice of it. If not a picture, at least send a note. If you have a publicity clipping, better yet. Send it. If you're an already established actor or actress, this is a good excuse to recontact people, a chance to jog people's memory with a fresh look at you. If you're a beginner, it's a good way in.

Over 65

In the last few years, I have found a big increase in the number of older people attending my classes. Some of my students started out in the theater (there was no television then), stopped to raise a family, and now would like to bring their fantasies to life. Some hope to make commercials a second career. Whatever their backgrounds, as the population age mounts, there will be more need for them in commercials and more older people going into them.

GRANDMOTHER AND GRANDFATHER TYPES

There seems to be a split in the way we envision our older citizens. On the one hand, we see them as athletic and taking an active part in community and political affairs. On the other hand, we still cling to images of the sweet white-haired old lady with a black ribbon and cameo around her neck or the old man with his trousers hitched up by suspenders.

Commercials today reflect this dichotomy. You may fit into one or both ends of the spectrum—but whatever, I suggest you carry your type(s) to the extreme.

If you're the modern grandparent type, have your pictures radiate life, health, and attractiveness; show yourself shopping, playing golf, dancing, etc. If you're the traditional-type grandparent, have your pictures suggest warmth, gentleness, kindness; show yourself knitting, smiling at a child, or holding a photo album. In either case, be sure you look like the clichés used in commercials.

Shakespearean and Classical Actors

If you've been working in the theater for years and never tried commercials, I recommend you take a television course. If you've never done any acting, a good basic improvisation class will loosen your inhibitions and, besides, be fun. True, once you're ready, you won't be as much in demand as a 30-year-old housewife type, but there's at least one commercial with your name on it.

The sections on print, infirmities, testimonials, and schools are important sections for you to peruse.

Experts

Just recently I had a call for a home economist to do a Reynolds Wrap commercial for cable. It was accompanied by an enthusiastic recommendation from the client: "We have someone on staff I think would be really good for it." I said I'd be glad to see her, and did so, along with seeing several other food experts.

The client was right! His entrant won the audition, did the commercial, and was good. In fact, so good that the producer, who also works on other accounts, recommended her to them. A commercial star was born.

She was at the right place at the right time, you say. Sure, but if you're a home economist, chef, or caterer, you don't need luck. Agencies who create food-related commercials are looking for you. Let them know you're there. Go to the library, get the *Standard Directory of Advertising Agencies,* and look up the agencies that handle accounts compatible with your expertise. Send your picture and résumé to them, along with a letter stating that you're not only knowledgeable in the food area but, through various teaching sessions and seminars (search your mind for this), you know you could perform well on camera.

There are many other areas of expertise that advertisers are interested in—wine connoisseurs, race drivers, dog breeders, etc.—and many reasons why they'll want you in a commercial. For instance, a manufacturer of a luxury product may want to show that people of taste and knowledge buy this product. We recently did a campaign for Samsonite where we needed design experts such as interior decorators, furniture designers, clothes designers, etc. We found them through agents and friends of friends, but here's the important part for you: Those who had pictures and résumés were considered first. Incidentally, it turned out to be good publicity for those selected as well as for Samsonite. So have those pictures and résumés made and send them out. The same advice given above for home economists goes for all areas of expertise.

Celebrities

Just as money makes money, celebrity makes celebrity. And commercials are the way to make both. If you've written a book, you're a prime candidate. A best-seller on money or economics, for instance, is very helpful in getting you a commercial. Can't you just hear the lead-in? "In these times when everyone is trying to save money, Mr. Celebrity, author of *How to Save Pennies,* will tell you how you can by buying our product, Penny Candy."

Whatever your claim to fame, I recommend that you and your agent put your heads together and figure out which advertisers could use you. Once pinpointed, send pictures and biography materials to them.

If you're a local celebrity without an agent, there are ways you can parlay your success on your own. If you've won a local beauty contest, for example, contact the advertising departments of local department stores. Use your imagination. Watch TV commercials and match your celebrity with products. Look up the products and their advertising agencies in the *Standard Directory of Advertising Agencies.* Once you've found them, send clippings, pictures, and relevant information. Be sure to include your name, address, and phone number.

Other Suggestions

In this chapter I've tried to open other doors into commercials. Now it's up to you to enter one. But in case you don't get in, don't give up. There's still one sure way into commercials: Buy a company and do your own. If that's not feasible, you still could get your pets and house into a commercial. Read the next chapter for ways to do it.

Pets, Pads, and Patios

People aren't the only ones who get into commercials. Cats, dogs, horses, parrots, and apartments and houses, too, are often part of the cast. And contrary to belief, they're not necessarily owned by animal trainers or producers. People like you often own the setters and settings used in commercials—and get good money for them.

This chapter is for those of you who have ever thought your pet would be great in a commercial, or that your home would make a perfect setting for a commercial. In it, I hope to answer all your questions as to how to get them into commercials and to allay your concerns about whether it's worth it.

Animals, Animals, Animals

Although "ferocious" beasts are sometimes used in car commercials (cougar, lynx, etc.), you probably do not currently own one. But you may own one of the domestic animals most often used in commercials—dogs and cats, or perhaps horses or parrots. Does your pet have the qualifications to be in a commercial? Let's briefly look at the points required for each.

DOGS

While mixed-breed dogs are often quite marvelous-looking, purebreds are usually used in commercials. This is because dogs in commercials usually have to perform tricks, and since it's hard to find a dog with a bagful of them, two or more dogs are often used to play the part of one dog. For instance, a dog may be used who can fetch and carry a ball; another who can chase a toy Gravy Train. Since it must appear that the same dog is doing both tricks, naturally the dogs must be identical-looking. Not easy to find in a mixed-breed.

Also, standby dogs are needed for dog-food commercials. If after several takes Spot gets tired of wolfing his food, Rover takes over. With thousands of dollars riding on the commercial, the sponsor, of course, can't have a stuffed, bored-with-his-food dog ruin a take.

Training

Dogs who would cause Barbara Woodhouse, famous British dog trainer and TV star, to say "Naugh-tee dog" need not apply. Dogs who aspire to a career in commercials must be well trained. That means willing to work on the set, able to perform without you, and able to get along with the other dogs on the set. Don't worry, your pet will be in good hands. If you're not a professional trainer, there will usually be one on the set.

It's also extremely important that your dog be a good eater— that is, short of taking bites out of people. Sponsors like a dog that will dive in and really lap up the food. Dainty eaters are not used as much because they don't give the impression of really enjoying the food.

Exception to the above! If you're famous like James Whitmore, you may get your untrained dog or dainty eater into a commercial with you. But as in Whitmore's case, your dog probably will have to be patiently trained. It's up to you to decide if it's worth it.

CATS

I've had friends with big-bellied old cats hint that their Sphinx or Elliott would be perfect for commercials. Sorry, cats are chosen for their beauty and attractiveness. A famous exception is Morris, the 9-Lives cat, who was "discovered" at the ASPCA.

If your cat can push the phone receiver off and say "Meow" when the grocer asks his order, you're that far ahead. But whatever wins your cat a commercial, you need not worry about his welfare on the set. Since cats generally are not easily trainable (do I hear a *yeow* from cat lovers?), an expert trainer will be there.

How to Get Your Pet into Commercials

As you can't very well make the rounds with your dog, cat, horse, or parrot, I recommend you do the next-best thing—take color snapshots of your pet and send them around.

A few photographic hints: Show the animal in profile. If your dog's a pointer, show him pointing. If your dog catches Frisbees, show her jumping into the air catching one. By all means show a picture of your animal eating. If you animal does remarkable tricks, you might send a videotape of him or her doing them. (While writing this chapter, I received a letter and two pictures from someone who had a dog who could climb trees. "She can walk and balance and turn on limbs as small as 4 inches in diameter." I'm still figuring that one out. Should this dog be used in a commercial for cat food or dog food?)

Once you have great sample shots, send them to animal trainers who you know work in commercials. If you live in a large city, check the *Yellow Pages* for names of trainers; call them and ask if they do commercials. Send photos or tapes to animal agents (see Appendix G). Send photos to pet-food advertisers, both the agency and the manufacturer. If you know a particular film company in your locale that does pet-food commercials, contact it. The film company production manager is usually the one who tracks down dogs and cats and other animals to be used in commercials.

THE JUNGLE OUT THERE

Okay, so you own a cougar.

The "ferocious" animals used in commercials are almost exclusively cast through the film companies via trainers. And thank heavens for that. I prefer to keep a safe distance from the whole subject. Once I was on a set for a honey cereal where a bear proceeded to eat not only the cereal but also the bowl and finished off with a big bite out of the table.

My other encounter with the beasties was with a black panther that performed in a perfume commercial with a beautiful black-haired, green-eyed model. In the commercial, the model was supposed to run through the grass with the black panther. Unfortunately, she was menstruating and the cat, as is the way of cats under such circumstances, kept leaping at her. Although declawed and defanged, the panther managed to make both the model and me very nervous. So, please, I beg you, if you have a beast who'd love to get into commercials, call a trainer with good contacts—and don't call me.

How to Get Your Wonderful House or Apartment into Commercials

When a commercial is shot on location (outside a studio), the question "Where?" is naturally discussed at the first preproduction meeting. When it comes up, an art director or agency producer sometimes mentions a location they've used previously. Sometimes someone suggests his or her own home. But after the initial go-around, the film or production company usually takes over. If the setting is an apartment or house, they bring out photos of several possible sites. These photos are obtained from location-hunting services they employ and are of places owned by people like you. How can you put a picture of your house or apartment among them? Let's look at some of the ways.

REAL ESTATE WANTED

Your house may have one, two, or three fabulous, desirable features. It may have a sweeping driveway that would make a marvelous setting for an elegant car commercial, or an antique country kitchen that conjures up nostalgic smells and images of steaming home cooking. But generally the houses picked for location shots combine *both* interesting interiors and exteriors, for very often one part of the commercial is shot outside a house, the other part inside.

What they look for in interiors: Big rooms are in demand; lots of windows, some picturesque bay windows; old-fashioned kitchens; living rooms with exposed beams and generous fireplaces. Access space is important, for even though just a small section of a room is needed, there must be space to accommodate crew and equipment. However, if a small room is just perfect, a compromise may be reached and the number of people hanging on the camera cut down.

What they look for in exteriors: Contemporary, average-income houses are the most requested. However, a wonderful Victorian or extremely lavish mansion is also frequently called for. Interesting driveway entrances; backyards with patios; and streams and ponds are all in demand.

APARTMENTS

If you watch TV commercials carefully, you'll see that the apartments usually have a sophisticated, "with-it, " bachelor-pad atmosphere—sleek decor, dramatic skyline view, terrace. If you live in New York, getting your apartment into commercials may be a practical way to help pay high rent and maintenance. Of course, you'll have to get building or landlord permission.

LET THERE BE LIGHT

Because filming requires lots of light, film companies look for houses open to natural light—sunlight pouring through windows;

porches or terraces without shadowy overhangs. Still, where there is light, there are shadows; and so, even under the best circumstances, film companies usually use artificial light in conjunction with natural light. If your house or apartment is selected for a commercial, they will be interested in how much electricity it can carry. But don't worry about blown fuses—film companies usually bring their own generators in trucks parked outside your house or building; cables carry the extra electricity needed into your house or apartment.

In addition to light sources, most film companies seek out houses or apartments with light rooms—white walls, light floor, light tones of furniture, anything that will reflect light.

HOW MUCH MONEY CAN YOU MAKE?

I doubt if you could make a substantial living renting out your house or apartment for commercials alone. You can make anywhere from $750 to $3,000 per day, but a commercial usually involves only a few days at most. A feature film, however, might involve weeks.

WILL MY HOME OR APARTMENT BE WRECKED?

No. And this is the part that always surprises me.

Often, for a shoot, minor architectural changes are made—a door removed, a gate put up, walls painted. Furniture or paintings are sometimes moved about or removed (frequently the film company brings its own). But in the end, everything is returned to its original state. Honest, you can be assured of it. Of course, if you like the pale peach walls the commercial called for, you can keep them.

WHAT ABOUT BREAKAGE?

The film company's insurance will reimburse you. Usually, you will have to find the replacement. Obviously, you'd put away your Aunt Ida's Ming vase.

HOW DOES IT WORK?

There are local finding organizations that search out houses and apartments in their area suitable for location sites. When a commercial calls for on-location filming, the film company usually contacts one or more of these sources. They, in turn, are shown pictures of and given information about possible sites. From these, they make their selections, which, as we discussed above, they will show at the preproduction meeting.

Let's say your house or apartment is chosen. At your convenience, the film company will visit your place and discuss the terms with you. Here are some questions you should be sure to ask:

- How much money will I get paid for overtime? (Usually the money you will receive will cover a ten-hour minimum. Overtime is beyond ten hours.)
- Will I be reimbursed for other lodging I may have to take during shooting? What about food?
- Will you repaint or will I receive the money to have it done?
- Will you repair or replace damaged articles directly or will you reimburse me?
- Will you pay for materials that require cleaning?
- Who will do the reimbursing, the film company or the finding company?

All of these questions are usually handled up front and in a very businesslike way.

WHAT ARE THE DRAWBACKS?

Providing you don't find yourself in the rare situation where some property is damaged, I think the drawbacks are mainly emotional. Although in the beginning many people feel a little powerless—especially when they can't use their own phone—after the first shock, they find an attitude that works for them. In fact, most find it to be fun.

I'M READY TO RENT

All right, you've weighed the pros and cons. What do you do

next? If you can, you go to the experts. Locations Unlimited-type organizations are located in most large cities. Reading the trades is a good way to track them down, as they advertise to film companies in them. Also, chambers of commerce and industry organizations are interested in encouraging filming in their areas. Many have film councils that, as part of their services, help find locations for production companies. Names are available in trade directories listed on page 103.

Or do it yourself. Get your neighbors and friends interested and form your own Locations Unlimited. Then list your group with the chamber of commerce or contact film companies in the nearest large city.

GETTING YOUR HOUSE OR APARTMENT READY TO AUDITION

If you're dealing with a Locations Unlimited-type organization, they will do most of the preliminary work for you. But in case you're doing it yourself or forming a group, there are three aspects of a site you must present in detail: pictures, measurements, and electrical capacity. After reading what this involves, you may, in the end, decide it's far better to go with the experts.

Pictures. You'll need instant shots of your house (exterior and interior). This means front, side, and back shots of exterior plus shots of grounds. For the interior, you'll need long shots of rooms plus individual shots of special areas such as fireplaces, alcoves, etc.

Measurements. Rooms and accesses to rooms must be measured. A floor plan must be made noting doorway measurements and heights of ceilings.

Electrical capacity. The location of every socket and fuse box must be listed.

Note: Bartering can help you lessen expenses. For example, if you know a photographer who needs a location, offer him your apartment or house in exchange for a good set of pictures.

WHAT ARE YOUR CHANCES OF SUCCESS?

Firms like Locations Unlimited are always looking for new customers because it is so much cheaper for a film company to rent an apartment or house for a shoot than to build a set. Your chances of success depend mostly on how "right" your house is.

One caution: Don't become too successful, like the person I know who "rented out" her New York town house. Although it took her a little time to get started, when word got around about what a great location site she had, she had no problem in renting her rooms for photography or commercials on a regular basis. Soon, however, the neighbors started complaining about the film company trucks tying up the street. She finally had to limit her bookings to print shoots.

If you'd like to supplement your income from renting out house, hearth, and pets by doing commercials yourself, go back to chapter 1 before you read the next chapter, "The Business of the Business."

21

The Business of the Business

You're a performer and, even if you can afford one, you're also your own business manager. To succeed in commercials, you can't be one without the other.

I love the creative part of my work—seeing people, developing them, picking the right person for the right part. That's what attracted me to casting. But there are other things involved—negotiations, contracts, phone calls, and a lot of paper work. At the beginning I resisted this, I have to admit—after all, I was a creative person. But then I came to realize that the business aspects and the creative aspects go hand in hand, and you have to be adept at both in order to succeed. I now enjoy them both.

The Fundamentals

Every business has its own procedures, its own vocabulary. As a commercial performer, you are a member of a profession governed by contracts. You are daily involved with time, money, working conditions, legal agreements. You use technical terms and should know what they mean. It goes without saying, the more knowledge you have of what you're about, the better able you will be to protect your rights, get what's coming to you, and possibly save yourself from being sued. So please learn your business.

Your Spot

An office. Every business needs one.

The first thing I recommend is that you look around your house or apartment and find your spot. If the phone is already sitting on it, all the better.

One can accumulate a lot of paper in this business of doing commercials. But today, with all the organizers and ingenious ways to use space, you can literally operate in a closet. You can use wall space for books and bottom space for files. Whatever your space, with a little planning, you should be able to have at your fingertips your appointment books, journals, notebooks, pictures, résumés, the whole works necessary to carry on your business.

Above all, do it your way. If you can keep everything in order and in its place, good for you—you'll save time and aggravation. If you're messy, be consistently so, and learn how to operate in chaos.

ITEMS TO KEEP TRACK OF

With the list below as a guide, you should find it easier to decide how much space you'll need and to select your spot.

Pictures
Résumés
Appointment records
Personal-growth notebook
Contact files, both mail and phone
Receipts for all expenses
Journal of daily expenditures

Record of commercials currently running
Record of income
Letters releasing you from commercials no longer running
Publicity material
Clip files, notes, reviews
Union information

First Things First

You wouldn't go up on a commercial without having your act together, would you? By the same token, you shouldn't put up your "Open for Business" sign without clearly knowing these terms and what they mean to you.

- Principal performer
- Extra
- Exclusivity
- Conflicts
- Holding fees
- Residuals
- Union

Your SAG or AFTRA contract book (get one—it's the best $3.50 you'll ever spend) will inform you of the others.

PRINCIPAL PERFORMER AND EXTRAS

When your agent or a casting director calls you for a job, you will assume that it is for a principal part. Extras are usually hired without an audition. Let's look at what separates a principal from an extra.

You are a principal (performer) if

A. You appear in a close-up shot on camera ("close-up" means neck up).
B. You speak a line or lines of dialogue.
C. Although you may have no lines, you are identifiable and in

the foreground and you are identified with the product—for example, in any of the following ways:

1. You are in a stationary shot, drinking a bottle of Pepsi-Cola.

2. You are in a silent (no dialogue) shot and are demonstrating or illustrating a product—e.g. you are opening the door of a new Ford.

3. You are reacting to a voice-over message—e.g., while the announcer tells how you can have it your way, you point to the pickle you want on your hamburger.

You are an extra if *you are not identified and involved with the product in any way.* For example, you are walking in front of a bank as a man counts money, but you do not react to him or the money.

EXCLUSIVITY AND CONFLICTS

Although these two terms are used interchangeably, there is a difference. Exclusivity has to do with the advertiser. Conflicts have to do with you, the performer.

Exclusivity. The advertiser has a right under union contract to demand that you do not perform in any commercial advertising a competitive product while he is paying you to advertise his. Exclusivity applies only to principals and identifiable voice-overs. Extras and unidentifiable voice-overs, such as cartoon voices, are not bound by it.

Conflicts. You have a conflict when you are already contracted to be in a commercial advertising a product or service competitive with the one in which you are about to be asked to perform.

As there are often varying interpretations of what products or services comprise a conflict, let's go into specifics.

1. A product or service is not considered competitive if it is manufactured or offered by the same advertiser. Example: You

could do a Kraft cheese and a Kraft mayonnaise commercial.

2. A product or service is not considered competitive with another product or service simply because the manufacturer has in his line a competitive product or service. Example: You could do a L'Oréal shampoo commercial and a Clairol hair coloring commercial even though both companies manufacture both products.

3. Products or services, although in seemingly different categories, may be considered competitive if they make one or more similar product claims. Example: You could not perform in both a soap commercial and a deodorant commercial if both claim to stop body odor.

Note: It sometimes happens that an advertiser may want to tie you up on one or several products, even though the product(s) may not be in direct conflict with the product advertised. Example: A candy-bar manufacturer may want to tie you up on gum. In case of such a tie-up, you are entitled to scale and a half.

HASSLE-SAVING GUIDELINES

When you are asked to perform in a commercial, be very clear about what the product or service is and what it claims to do. The consequences of overlooking a conflict—being fuzzy or trying to fudge on gray areas—can be costly. You can be sued not only for the money paid to you but for the cost of the entire commercial production as well.

To avoid legal complications and losing money:

1. Make sure your agent has talked to the casting director and checked out all the product claims and all the gray areas.

2. If a manufacturer wants to tie you up with several product claims, talk it over with your agent and decide whether it's worth it or whether you should ask for more than the going scale-and-a-half rate.

3. When you get the commercial, double-check: Read it carefully and check claims.

4. Be sure you have written release if you've appeared in a competitive product commercial. Don't take a verbal okay.

5. Don't rationalize. If you know you are indeed a principal in a competitive product commercial, don't talk yourself into thinking that actually you are only on camera for a few seconds and no one will recognize you.

Nonexclusive Commercials

Commercials produced for cable only, seasonal commercials, test-market commercials, and nonair commercials either require no exclusivity or are negotiable. This is because of their limited run and limited audience. A seasonal commercial, for example, is related to a particular season such as Christmas or Mother's Day.

Test-market commercials are used to test the product in a specific market, often in one or two small cities. Usually this means a limited run. If the product is a success, the run is expanded and the commercials are used on a national basis. The advertiser may request exclusivity on a national or local basis. This is negotiable.

Nonair commercials are commercials not intended for broadcast use. They may be used to elicit audience reactions, or for copy testing, or as demos to present to clients. There is no exclusivity demanded of you, unless extra payments are arranged.

HOLDING FEES

Starting from the first day of employment (e.g., rehearsal, shooting day), an advertiser must pay the talent (you) a holding fee, equivalent to a session fee, each thirteen weeks. (The original session fee is applied against the first thirteen-week cycle.) This payment allows the advertiser to use the commercial during the cycle. If the advertiser neglects to make the holding-fee payment within twelve business days, they lose the right to run the commercial.

The holding fee may be applied against residuals if the commercial is in use. If the commercial is not run on the air, but the manufacturer wishes to retain (hold on to) the right to run it, you will still receive the holding fee. For you, this becomes a minimum guarantee during the twenty-one-month contract.

RESIDUALS

Residuals, also called "reuse payments," are the moneys paid to a principal for the times the film or tape of his or her performance goes on the air. Residuals may seem like easy bucks, but it's money rightly due you. If something for nothing makes you feel guilty, consider this: As your commercial runs repeatedly, you become identified with the product, and so a competitive advertiser cannot ask you to sell their products. This reduces your opportunity for employment. So enjoy your residuals—you're entitled.

How a Commercial Runs, Holding Fees, and Residual Payments

When you are called on an audition, you must be told the anticipated usage of the commercial. The kind of residuals you will receive will depend on

- What category it runs under—e.g., network program or wild spot?
- How much it is used in the particular category—e.g., if it is a wild spot, does it run nationally or locally?
- How many months the commercial runs.

I consulted with Joanne Masciotti of our talent-payment and labor-relations department to give you as understandable definitions as possible of the following categories. (Consult your SAG and AFTRA books for exact payments due you in each category.)

A broadcast commercial. If the commercial is a regular commercial to be used on network and regular TV stations, it is called a "broadcast commercial." Provided there's a minimum fee of $750 for on-camera work and that the network usage occurs before cable usage, the fees paid you will cover cable usage.

If the commercial is produced for cable use only, cable-commercial terms of conflict and payments are special.

If it is subsequently used as a broadcast commercial, additional moneys must be paid.

A commercial is considered a "wild spot" if it is broadcast by noninterconnected single stations, or if it is independent of any program except a local participating program—that is, one that is available to more than one sponsor.

In either case, you are paid on a thirteen-week-cycle basis. The size of the area where your commercial runs makes a difference in the fee. This figure is arrived at by what is called "unit weighting." For example, a city the size of Philadelphia is a six-unit weight. A smaller city the size of Baltimore is a two-unit weight. You'll find charts in your SAG contract telling you precisely how much you should be getting per unit.

All other uses of a commercial are considered program uses. These commercials are shown on a network basis—usually across the country and paid on a per-use basis. Compensation for use of program commercials is divided as follows:

Class A Use	Telecast in over 20 cities
Class B Use	Telecast in 6–20 cities
Class C Use	Telecast in 1–5 cities

Obviously, compensation for Class A usage is greater than for Class C.

Dealer commercials. These are commercials produced by the manufacturer to be distributed to dealers. In turn, the dealers buy time on their local stations. Often the dealer's name and location are tagged on. There are two six-month rates for dealer spots; one includes New York City and one doesn't.

Points of negotiation. When you're starting out, you'll probably be working in your own local area and receiving local minimum payments. As you gain experience, you will want to be more selective and consider some of the other points that may mean more money. For instance, commercials running network or in large cities pay better than those in smaller cities. Following are some of the questions you or your agent might ask as points of negotiation:

- If it runs network, what does it run, Class A, B, or C?
- If it runs on a wild-spot basis, how many cities will it run in? If it runs in only a few cities, will you be given a guaranteed minimum? Will it run in one region or on a national basis?
- If it runs in a test market, how long will it run there? Will you be given a cutoff date beyond which it will be taken off the air? Will you be paid as though it were running on a national basis?
- Is it a product where you're sure of getting a Class A program commercial? You don't want to get stuck on a test commercial that pays the minimum scale and jeopardize your chance for the network commercial.
- How much exposure? Are you the spokesperson? Are you in a vignette? As a spokesperson with a strong identification, you get more exposure than if you're one of a couple in a vignette. The former can give you needed exposure. It can also result in people saying, "Oh, he's all over the place," even though you are doing just one commercial.
- Does it run in L.A. or New York only? If the commercial runs heavily in New York or L.A., many people in the industry see it and assume that it's running all over the country. You may be getting L.A. rates, but people in the business think you're on a national commercial.

How long must you pay your agent a fee? On the morning of the shoot, when you sign your SAG standard contract, you will be allowing the advertiser to use the commercial for twenty-one months provided he pays the required holding fees. Your agent is entitled to a 10-percent commission on the residuals from the commercial during these twenty-one months. After that time, if you agree to allow the agency to renew the commercial at scale, your agent is not automatically entitled to a commission. You must receive at least 10 percent above scale for your agent to deduct commission. If you become a star during the interim, you may consider renewing the contract only if there is a great deal more money involved. Usually, however, the contract is renewed with a moderate increase that also allows your agent to continue to collect his commission.

Keeping track. It's important to keep track of when your twenty-one-month contract is up. Before that time (at least sixty days), you or your agent must notify the advertising agency (or employer) in writing that you want a release or that you wish to renegotiate the terms. If you fail to do this, your contract is automatically renewed for a second twenty-one-month cycle at scale. If you notify the agency in writing and they fail to contact you or your agent to discuss new terms but continue to run the commercial, you should notify your union.

Who will pay your residuals? Payment is made by the advertising agency that hires you. Usually, the agency uses the services of T and R, Talent and Residuals, or a similar payroll service (I know we do). Via computers, and supervised by our talent payment department, they keep track of all the complicated procedures involved in keeping records of when, where, and for how long a commercial runs and how much the performer is due. You will receive information on your check stub or an attached form telling you exactly what usage the payment covers.

Keeping your own records. I recommend you do as many performers do: Keep good records. Keep cards of each of the commercials you are doing, how they are running, when the twenty-one month period of each expires, and when you've received your last holding fee. Be alert to cost-of-living adjustments. In other words, keep tabs on the computer; it has been known to be human.

JOINING THE UNION

In most states, and in most circumstances, in order to be hired for a commercial, you must be a member of the union. To do film commercials, you must be a member of the Screen Actors Guild (SAG). To do videotape or radio commercials, you must be a member of the American Federation of Television and Radio Actors (AFTRA). To be an extra in L.A., you must be a member of the Screen Extras Guild (SEG).

As a member of the union, you must be a professional performer who makes his livelihood from it. The main purposes of the
union are to see that its members receive employment preference
and that any person who wants to join meets professional requirements. For this protection and for many other services—such as
regulation of working conditions; negotiation of contracts; pen-
sions; monitoring usage of commercials; etc.—you must pay a fee
to join, and then pay annual union dues.

What Must You Do to Join the Union?
You must have a promise of a union-regulated job. The producer (or advertising agency) must present to the guild, in writing,
facts showing

1. that you have had sufficient training and/or experience to
qualify for a career as a professional film actor, and
2. that you intend to pursue this career and to be available for
employment.
3. If you have an agent, mention it—it helps to confirm that
you're a professional.

You don't have to join the union for your first shoot. You are
given thirty days to join the union, during which time you may do
any number of commercials (lucky you!). After that time you
must join the union for your next job, and in fact you are called a
"must join." The initiation fee to join SAG is $600.
Since there is less competition outside of New York and L.A.,
it's often easier to get into the union outside of these cities. Once
you belong to SAG, no matter where, you're considered a member.

Exceptions or Waivers
In order for me to employ a nonunion performer for a commercial, I must get a waiver from the union—that is, a statement
allowing me to do so. I usually have to tell them the extent of my
search—the number of members I've interviewed who might fit

the requirements. This usually happens when the commercial calls for a specific unusual physical requirement or ability. Recently I had to find a champion weight lifter who didn't look like one. That wasn't so easy. There are also other situations where you don't have to be a union member to be cast:

- If you endorse a product.
- If a commercial is being filmed in a factory and you're an employee of the factory and appear on camera doing what you would *normally* be doing at work.
- If you work outside union jurisdictions (e.g., in "right to work" states).
- If you're a child under 7.
- If it's your first employment within the studio zone, and the producer can show that you have sufficient training and experience to qualify for a career as a professional motion-picture actor and that you intend to pursue that career and be available for employment in the motion-picture industry.

We've covered the terms that you should at least be familiar with before you go on an audition.

While residuals are where you'll make most of your money, let's look at fees you're entitled to along the way, starting with the audition.

Workaday Business

BASIC COMPENSATION, CONTRACTS, AND THE IRS

Come your first call to go on an audition, a whole new happy business responsibility begins. The chips come in and you have to keep track of earnings. Knowing such things as audition money due you and extra preproduction and day-of-shoot compensations, as well as how to read your contract and get the maximum tax deductions, can make the difference between your moonlighting as a waiter or being waited on. As I want all of you to work, hopefully your meal will not be served by another aspiring commercial performer.

The Audition Sign-in Sheet

Trite but true—time is money. As one of the main functions of a sign-in sheet is to compute overtime money due you, it is important that you know these basic rules that govern time spent on an audition.

- You must sign in when you arrive and sign out when you leave. The receptionist is required to have a clock on her desk.
- Moneys due you will only accrue from the time of your appointment.
- Early doesn't count—late does. It doesn't matter if you sign in early. However, if you're late for your appointment, the hour will only begin from the time of your arrival.

Moneys Paid for the Audition

As a principal, you don't get paid for your first or second auditions for the same commercial. That's why it's important that you sign the sign-in sheet and that you keep track of how many callbacks you go on.

You only get paid if you're kept waiting more than an hour from the time of your appointment. You will be compensated for any time after the hour in half-hour units—$18.75 for each half-hour.

On a third audition, you will be paid $75 and you will be required to be available for two hours. If after two hours you're kept any longer, you'll be paid $18.75 for each half-hour unit thereafter.

On a fourth audition, you may be kept for four hours. You will receive $150. For any additional time, you will receive $18.75 per half-hour.

Special Audition Fees

If you're required to memorize (not familiarize yourself with) a script, you are entitled to half a session fee. If you're a quick study, you may memorize the script, but that doesn't count. If you're given the script before the audition, it's usually just to study it and become familiar with it.

If you're required to improvise—that is, come up with some dialogue in a particular scene or invent a bit of business—you must be told this before the audition. Such an audition would be considered an ad-lib or creative session. You will receive $112.80 for one hour of improvisation. For any time after that, you will receive $56.40 per half-hour.

If you are asked to audition for the part of an extra, you will be paid for the audition. You will receive $26.35 per hour for each interview. There will be a minimum of two hours.

Preproduction Compensations

You've gotten the job. Hurray! The meter really starts running when you get a call for rehearsal, wardrobe shopping or fitting. All payments to you are based on an eight-hour session (shooting day). To eliminate confusion, I've based the following examples on the $300 minimum session fee. If you receive a higher fee, compute the time accordingly.

If you are called in for a rehearsal, you will be paid $37.50 per hour, or one-eighth of $300.

If the agency or film company asks you to come in with your wardrobe selections, you will be compensated for your time. If extra wardrobe is needed, the fitting usually takes place on the same day of the shoot (usually early in the morning). This counts as part of your regular workday. For example, if your fitting or wardrobe call is at 7:30 A.M and your shooting call is for 9:00, 7:30 is considered the time your session begins. If four or more hours intervene between the end of the fitting time and the beginning of the work call, and you're dismissed in the interim, the fitting will be paid as though it were on a prior day.

If your fitting or wardrobe call is on a day prior to the shooting day (at most, it's one or two days before), you will receive a one-hour minimum payment for each call (one-eighth of $300, or $37.50). After that, you'll be paid in fifteen-minute units ($9.88 per unit).

If the stylists take you on a shopping trip, you will receive the same payments as for fittings.

WARDROBE ALLOWANCE

If you wear your own clothes in the commercials, you will receive $10 for each nonevening-wear garment and $20 for each evening-wear garment.

Day-of-Shoot Compensations

Your call for hair and makeup will be on the day of the shoot, and will be considered part of your workday. If the call is for 6:00 A.M, that's when your workday begins.

If your session goes into overtime, you will receive time and one-half for the ninth and tenth hours. Under the current rates, that would be $56.25 per hour. Beyond ten hours you will receive double time for each hour in hourly units. Under the current rates, that would be $75 per hour.

SPECIAL SITUATIONS

The above compensations cover payment for the usual on-camera commercial. Depending on your role in the commercial, you may be entitled to more or less.

If you are asked to improvise and develop dialogue, you will receive an additional 50 percent per day for creative work.

For a voice-over session, you will receive $225.60. The producer may keep you for two hours. The $225.60 will cover the first commercial; for each additional commercial recorded, you will receive an additional $225.60.

For a radio session, you will receive $110 for ninety minutes. During the ninety minutes, you may do any number of commercials. You will receive $110 for each additional commercial after the first one.

As an on-camera extra, your session fee is $210.75. This is an unlimited buy-out. Unless specially negotiated, you will receive no residuals.

Stunt-man fees are based on the particular stunt. Also, there are very specific guidelines as to when a stunt player is required. If you're not a stunt player, you must be notified ahead of time of any hazardous business.

Dancers

This includes swimmers and ice skaters if their performances are choreographed. There are many special provisions for working conditions. Be sure you read the SAG contract section that delineates them.

Travel-Time Compensation

Any time spent traveling between the place of reporting (usually designated by the film company) and a location is considered travel time. It's up to you to keep track of the time. You are paid for travel time as follows:

If you leave for the location before noon prior to the shooting day, you receive a full day's pay.

If you leave between noon and 6:00, you receive a half day's pay.

If you leave after 6:00 P.M, you are compensated for the actual hours that you travel.

If you travel on the same day of the shoot, you are paid as though it were shooting time but not overtime.

Weather Compensation

Usually you are given a weather day when the location is outdoors. It simply means that if the weather does not allow the filming to take place, the shoot will be postponed until weather permits. In case of a cancellation, you will receive a half day's pay for the canceled day(s). You can see why it's important that you give advance notice to all involved of any schedule problems you may foresee.

SCREEN ACTORS GUILD
EMPLOYMENT CONTRACT FOR TELEVISION COMMERCIALS

Date_____ 19____

:tween Talent & Residuals, Inc., (T & R), Employer, and_____ (Player).

& R engages Player and Player agrees to perform services for T & R in television commercial(s) as follows:

ommercial Title(s) and Code No(s)._____ No. of Commercials

Excluding Lifts_____

CHECK IF APPLICABLE:
☐ DEALER COMMERCIAL(S)
☐ TYPE A   ☐ TYPE B
☐ SEASONAL COMMERCIAL(S)
☐ TEST MARKET COMMERCIAL(S)
☐ "NON-AIR" COMMERCIAL(S)

ich commercial(s) are to be produced by_____

r J. Walter Thompson Company, Producer, 420 Lexington Avenue, New York, New York 10017, acting as agent for

_____   _____
Advertiser   Product(s)

ty and State in which services rendered:_____ Place of Engagement:_____

☐ Actor/Actress   ☐ Singer—Solo or Duo   ☐ Singer—9 or more   ☐ Stunt Player
☐ Announcer (Commercial)   ☐ Singer—3–5   ☐ Contractor   ☐ Puppeteer
☐ Announcer (Billboards)   ☐ Singer—6–8   ☐ Specialty Act   ☐ Pilot

assification: On Camera_____ Off Camera_____ Part to be Played_____

ompensation: _____ Date & Hr. of Engagement:_____

ieck if: Flight Insurance ($10) Payable ☐ $_____
          Wardrobe to be furnished by Producer ☐ by Player ☐
          If furnished by Player, No. of Garments @ $7.50_____; @ $15.00_____Total Wardrobe. Fee $_____
                                    (Non-Evening Wear) (Evening Wear)

☐ Player does not consent to the use of his services in commercials made hereunder as dealer commercials payable at dealer commercial rates.
☐ Player does not consent to the use of his services in commercials made hereunder on a simulcast.

ie standard provisions printed on the reverse side hereof are a part of this contract. If this contract provides for compensation at minimum union scale, additions, changes or alterations may be made in this form other than those which are more favorable to the Player than herein provided. If this contract provides for compensation above minimum union scale, additions may be agreed to between Producer and Player which do not conflict with the provisions of the applicable Commercials Contract; provided that such additional provisions are separately set forth under "Special Provisions" hereof and gned by the Player.

ntil Player shall otherwise direct in writing, Player authorizes Producer to make all payments to which Player may be entitled hereunder as follows:

☐ To Player at _____
                                    (Address)

☐ To Player c/o _____ At _____
                                              (Address)

ll notices to Player shall be sent to the address designated above for payments and, if Player desires, to one other address as follows:

To: _____ At _____
        (Name)   (Address)

his contract is subject to all of the terms and conditions of the applicable Commercials Contract. Employer of Record for income x and unemployment insurance purposes is Talent & Residuals, Inc.

ALENT & RESIDUALS, INC., Employer

y_____

WALTER THOMPSON COMPANY, Producer

y_____
                                                        Player*

Player hereby certifies that Player is twenty-one years of age or over. (If not twenty-one years of age or over, this document must be signed by a parent guardian.)

the undersigned, represent that I am the_____ of the above-mentioned
                                    (Mother, Father, Guardian)
ayer and, as such, fully authorized and entitled to enter into this agreement in his/her behalf.

_____   _____
            Witness   Signature of Minor's Parent or Guardian

PECIAL PROVISIONS:

ayer acknowledges that he has read all the terms and conditions in the Special Provisions section above and hereby agrees thereto.

_____
                        Player*

IMPORTANT PROVISIONS ON BACK. PLEASE READ CAREFULLY.
A 2 6/79   WE ARE AN EQUAL OPPORTUNITY EMPLOYER

STANDARD PROVISIONS

1. RIGHT TO CONTRACT
Player states that to the best of his knowledge, he has not authorized the use of his name, likeness or identifiable voice in any commercial advertising any competitive product or service during the term of permissible use of commercial(s) hereunder and that he is free to enter into this contract and to grant the rights and uses herein set forth.

2. EXCLUSIVITY
Player states that since accepting employment in the commercial(s) covered by this contract, he has not accepted employment in no authorized the use of his name or likeness or identifiable voice in any commercial(s) advertising any competitive product or service and that he will not hereafter, during the term of permissible use of the commercial(s) for which he is employed hereunder, accept employment in or authorize the use of his name or likeness or identifiable voice in any commercial(s) advertising any competitive product or service. This paragraph shall not apply to off-camera group players (other than name groups) or to players employed in seasonal commercials.

3. OTHER USES (Strike "a" or "b" if such rights not granted by Player)

(a) Foreign Use

Producer shall have the right to the foreign use of the commercial(s) produced hereunder, for which Producer agrees to pay Player not less than the additional compensation provided for in the applicable Commercials Contract. Producer agrees to notify the applicable union in writing promptly of any such foreign use.

(b) Theatrical & Industrial Use

Producer shall have the right to commercial(s) produced hereunder for theatrical and industrial use as defined and for the period permitted in the applicable Commercials Contract, for which Producer shall pay Player not less than the additional compensation therein provided.

4. ARBITRATION
All disputes and controversies of every kind and nature arising out of or in connection with this contract shall be subject to arbitration as provided in Section 55 of the applicable Commercials Contract.

5. PRODUCER'S RIGHTS
Player acknowledges that player has no right, title or interest of any kind or nature whatsoever in or to the commercial(s). A role owned or created by the Producer belongs to the Producer and not to the player.

6. NATURE OF EMPLOYMENT
If by reason of this contract, Player is deemed to be an employee of Advertiser for any purpose, it is agreed that Player shall be deemed temporary employee only and that Player shall not be entitled to any rights or benefits granted to other employees of Advertiser by reason of such employment, and that the only compensation, rights and/or benefits to which Player is entitled are those specified in this contract.

Contracts—Or Why You Should Read the Fine Print

You will be asked to sign a contract on the day of the shoot. The assistant director (A.D.) will bring you the contract on the set. To make sure that everything is in order, ask for time to go off and read it before signing. Anything special about the contract will be checked off. Following are six items to look over. I recommend you look at the sample contract reproduced here and find where they are and what specifically is stated. In each case, is it what you agreed to?

- Type of commercial—dealer, seasonal, etc.
- Player consent to dealer commercials
- Player consent to simulcast (concurrent broadcast on radio and TV—e.g., a symphony concert)

- Classification (*Note:* There is a special contract for extras.)
- On Camera/Off Camera
- Compensation, Session Fee
- Special provisions

If you have any questions, ask the A.D. Call your agent if there is anything in the contract with which you do not agree. Remember, your rights and entitlement to compensation are explicitly stated in the contract. Once you've signed, you have agreed to them and have no recourse for redress.

Be sure to flip over the contract and check the standard provisions.

Right to Contract. This means you don't have a competitive commercial and therefore are free to sign the contract.

Foreign Use. Don't overlook this item. Do you want to grant the use of this commercial in other countries? If you don't cross this paragraph out, you've given the advertiser this right. But bring it up before the day of the shoot.

Your Income and Outgo and the IRS

I certainly don't recommend you cheat the IRS, but please don't cheat yourself. Take all the deductions you can. You don't need receipts unless you spend $25 or more at one time. My tax consultant recommends you keep a diary and make daily or at least weekly entries of your business and professional expenses. It's equally important to keep a record in the back of your diary of all your income as an actor. This should include your per-diem along with your session and residual earnings.

ALLOWABLE DEDUCTIONS

In making out your list of deductions, bear in mind that every deduction you make should be proportionate to your income. Also be sure you don't take off for expenses that have been reimbursed. Following is a list of a TV-commercial performer's usual allowable business and professional expenses. Your tax adviser may have a few more to add to the list.

- Complete costs of photos including mailing
- Résumés and publicity
- Agents' and manager's fees
- Telephone and answering service
- Clothes you wear exclusively for your work—including maintenance
- Dance clothes such as leotards, tights, dance shoes, etc.—including maintenance
- Drama and coaching lessons—diction and dance lessons, etc., included
- Local transportation to agents, managers, etc.
- Transportation to interviews and auditions (If you use a car, you can take a proportionate amount for auto expenses.)
- Thefts (Actors moving about are more susceptible.)
- Stationery and postage
- Hair care—including wigs and hair dye
- Union dues
- Trade papers and any other professional publications connected with the acting profession
- Gifts to people who have helped or can help you with your career
- Outside entertainment costs
- Professional research—including attending the theater for professional research
- Rehearsal-studio rental (You can't deduct rehearsals or practices conducted in your apartment.)
- Promotional theater tickets for agents, managers, and casting people to come and watch you perform—for future engagements
- Lodging and meals away from home
- Video- and audio-tape recorders and business equipment needed—typewriters, file cabinets, etc.
- Makeup
- Beautification expenses—including electrolysis

- Depreciation of all professional equipment—audiovisual gear, tape recorders, etc.
- All cable-TV costs, including installation fees and expansion of pay-TV channel charges
- Foul-weather gear for commercials shot on location
- Job-hunting expenses

The Bottom Line

It's very simple. No conflict here. You just take your audition fees, session fees, and residuals, smile all the way to the bank, and follow up, follow up, follow up. . . .

23

Follow Up

You've read through this book—or, more likely, picked out and pored over those chapters that are of special interest to you. Now for the reprise.

If you started this book with just a notion you'd like to get into commercials, and it has grown into a conviction but you haven't taken action . . .

Follow up with your appraisal of yourself and by finding your type.

If you've gone so far as to have defined your type . . .

Follow up by putting your act together—clothes, makeup, hair. Start inquiring about acting schools and register with one.

If you've reached the point where you've had pictures and résumés made and are ready to go on interviews . . .

Follow up by contacting everyone you know and every friend or relative of anyone you know who is in the business, and looking through the *Standard Directory of Advertising Agencies* for every account that handles commercials using your type. Start sending your picture and résumé to prospects.

If you're already making the rounds ...
Follow up with calls and charming notes reminding interviewers of you.
If you have one or several auditions coming up ...
Follow up each time by leaving your picture and résumé behind, sending a thank-you note, and phoning again.
If you have won a commercial ...
Follow up by leaving your picture and résumé on the set and sending a thank-you note.
If you're waiting for your residual checks to come in ...
Follow up and *follow up* and *follow up* some more.

And that goes for getting your children, pets, apartments, and houses into commercials. Do it and you'll find it will make the difference between a dream and success. *One proviso:* All the time you're following up, *keep making fresh contacts.*
And now good luck and see you or yours on the next commercial break.

Vangie

APPENDIX

Free-Lance Casting Services

NEW YORK   (*212 Area Codes*)

Adams & Sorel	39 Jane St.	242-5571
BCI Casting	1500 Broadway	221-1583
Jane Brinker	51 W. 16th St.	924-3322
Elaine Brodey	P.O. Box C, Lenox Hill Station	737-2721
Deborah Brown Casting	250 W. 57th St.	581-0404
Kit Carter & Assocs.	160 W. 95th St.	864-3147
Central Casting Corp. of New York	200 W. 54th St.	582-4933
Cereghetti Casting	119 W. 57th St.	765-5260
Colquhoun/Talbert Casting	303 W. 42nd St.	Unlisted
Complete Casting	240 W. 44th St.	382-3835
Contemporary Casting	16 W. 46th St.	575-9450
Johnny Deron	30-63 32nd St., Astoria	728-5326

Donna Deseta Casting	424 W. 33rd St.	239-0988
Lou DiGiaimo & Assoc.	150 E. 52nd St.	753-3590
Sylvia Fay	71 Park Ave.	889-2626
Feuer & Ritzer Casting Assoc.	1650 Broadway	765-5580
Leonard Finger	1501 Broadway	944-8611
Ginger Friedman	303 E. 83rd St.	424-1714
Maria Greco & Assoc.	888 8th Ave.	757-0681
Group 3 Casting	1414 Ave. of the Americas	758-1776
Herman & Lipson Casting	114 E. 25th St.	777-7070
Hughes/Moss Casting	1515 Broadway	840-2474
In Casting	226 E. 54th St.	752-5833
Iredale Assoc., Inc.	271 Madison Ave.	889-7722
Johnson-Liff	850 7th Ave.	757-9420
Michael Kara Casting	1650 Broadway	582-0132
Kramer/Nigro Co.	524 W. 57th St.	691-7130
Lynn Kressel Casting	157 W. 57th St.	581-6990
MCL Casting	300 W. 55th St.	246-9108
McCorkle-Sturtevant Casting	240 W. 44th St.	888-9160
Navarro-Bertoni Casting Ltd.	25 Central Park West	765-4251
Omnidance	1776 Broadway	957-8403
Lou Perry Major Casting	315 W. 57th St.	582-0953
Irma Puckett Casting	31 W. 16th St.	989-4498
Pulvino & Howard Ltd.	215 Park Ave. South	477-2323
Reed/Sweeney/Reed, Inc.	1780 Broadway	265-8541
Screenworks Ltd.	36 W. 62nd St.	246-1800
Barbara Shapiro Casting	111 W. 57th St.	582-8228
Shulman/Pasciuto, Inc.	1457 Broadway	944-6420
Simon & Kumin Casting	850 7th Ave.	245-7670

Skyline Casting	723 7th Ave.	869-9206
Joy Todd	250 W. 57th St.	765-1212
Dan Tyra-Danico	P.O. Box 1801, Grand Central Station, 10263	
Jack Weber Casting	484 E. 74th St.	861-0474
J.F. Wilhelm & Assocs.	234 W. 44th St., Suite 905	944-5978
Joy Weber	250 W. 57th St.	245-5220
Bill Williams	1501 Broadway	221-7111
Elizabeth Roberts Woodman	1650 Broadway	541-9431

FLORIDA

Marion Polan Agency	P.O. Box 7154, Ft. Lauderdale	(305) 379-7526
The Casting Directors, Inc.	1524 N.E. 147th St., N. Miami	(305) 944-8559
Barbara Diprima	1200 Biscayne Blvd., Suite 200, Miami	(305) 445-7630

CHICAGO

Alderman & Guerra Casting	679 N. Michigan Ave.	(312) 280-1900
BCI Casting	232 E. Ohio St.	(312) 266-8785

LOS ANGELES *(213 Area Codes)*

Anderson/McCook	3855 Lankershim Blvd., N. Hollywood	760-3934
BCI	1956 Cahuenga Blvd., L.A.	466-3400
Beck Bros./Video Den	336 Foothill Rd., B.H.	550-0659
Pamela Campus	846 N. Cahuenga Blvd., L.A.	464-3310
Casting Services/Bobbi Morris	439 S. La Cienega Blvd., L.A.	278-1030
Divisek Casting/Karen & Barbara Divisek	12166 W. Olympic Blvd., L.A.	462-1758

Kiyo Glenn	4567 Nagle, Sherman Oaks	762-5577
Marilyn Granas Casting	220 S. Palm Dr., B.H.	278-3773
Melanie Sherwood Casting	6305 Yucca St., #600, Hollywood	462-6817
Dorothy Kelly Casting	6534 Sunset Blvd., Hollywood	467-4282
Terry Kerrigan & Assocs.	4120 W. Alameda, Burbank	760-7636
Susie Kittleson Casting	1302 N. Sweetzer Ave., L.A.	652-7011
Kathy Knowles Casting	9044 Hollywood Hills Rd., L.A.	657-5687
Barbara Lauren	7135 Hollywood Blvd., #605, L.A.	876-6111
Judy Landau	568 N. Larchmont Blvd., L.A.	464-0437
Michael Lien Casting	336 N. Foothill Rd., #8, B.H.	550-7381
Sheila Manning Casting	470 S. San Vicente Blvd., #101, L.A.	852-1046
Margarette & Kennedy Casting	6815 W. Willoughby, Hollywood	462-4561
Phyllis Ricci	4150 Fair Ave., N. Hollywood	761-8257
Carl Shain Casting	921 S. Curson Ave., L.A.	935-6631
Carol Soskin	P.O. Box 480106, L.A.	553-6781
Tepper/Gallegos Casting, Inc.	7033 Sunset Blvd., #208, L.A.	469-3577
T.L.C./Booth	6671 Sunset Blvd., B.H.	464-2788
The Casting Room IPS—Barbara Richman	3518 Cahuenga Blvd. West, Hollywood	851-3595
The Voicecaster: Bob Lloyd	3413 Cahuenga Blvd. West, Hollywood	874-1933
Tammy Windsor Casting	14001 Peach Grove St., Sherman Oaks	501-3510

Agents

NORTHEAST*

CONNECTICUT

Joanna Lawrence Agency	82 Patrick Rd., Westport	(203) 226-7239
Connecticut Talent Agency	10 Bay St., Westport	(203) 846-3064

WASHINGTON, D.C.

Central Casting	1000 Connecticut Ave., N.W.	(202) 659-8272
Ann Schwab's Model Store	1529 Wisconsin Ave., N.W.	(202) 333-3560

BALTIMORE, MARYLAND

Faces Modeling and Talent Agency	1 Investment Pl.	(301) 321-9512
Taylor Royal Casting	2308 South Rd.	(301) 466-5959

BOSTON, MASSACHUSETTS

Cameo Models & Talent	392 Boylston St.	(617) 536-6004
Copley 7 Models & Talent	29 Newbury St.	(617) 267-4444
The Ford Model Shoppe	176 Newbury St.	(617) 266-6939
The Hart Agency	137 Newbury St.	(617) 262-1740
Bea Sprague	108 A Appleton St.	(617) 267-4211

NEW JERSEY

Joyce Conover Agency	33 Gallowae, Westfield	(201) 232-0908
Danline, Inc.	260 N. Michigan Ave., Kenilworth	(201) 245-5900

*Connecticut; Delaware; Washington, D.C.; Maine; Maryland; Massachusetts; New Hampshire; New Jersey; New York; Pennsylvania; Rhode Island; Vermont; West Virginia

The Meredith Agency	91 Overlook Ave., Wayne	(201) 694-7802

(*212 Area Codes*)

Bret Adams Ltd.	448 W. 44th St., 10036	765-5630
Agency for the Performing Arts (APA)	888 7th Ave., 10106	582-1500
Ambrose Company	1466 Broadway, 10036	921-0230
Abrams Artists & Assocs.	420 Madison Ave., 10022	935-8980
Richard Astor Agency	1697 Broadway, 10019	581-1970
Baldwin-Scully, Inc.	501 5th Ave., 10017	922-1330
Bauman & Hiller Assoc.	250 W. 57th St., 10107	757-0098
Peter Beilin	230 Park Ave., 10017	949-9119
J. Michael Bloom	400 Madison Ave., 10017	832-6900
Don Buchwald & Assocs.	10 E. 44th St., 10017	867-1070
Bill Cooper Assocs.	224 W. 49th St., 10017	307-1100
Cunningham-Escott-Dipene	919 3rd Ave., 10022	832-2700
D.H.K.P.R.	165 W. 46th St., 10036	869-2880
Francis Dilworth	496 Kinderkamack Rd., Oradell N.J.	661-0070
Marje Fields, Inc.	250 W. 57th St., 10107	581-7240
Gage Group, Inc.	1650 Broadway, 10019	541-5250
Hartig-Michael Agency Ltd.	527 Madison Ave., 10022	759-9163
Henderson-Hogan Agency	200 W. 57th St., 10019	765-5190
Hesseltine-Baker Assoc.	165 W. 46th St., 10036	921-4460
Int'l Creative Mgmt. (ICM)	40 W. 57th St., 10019	556-5600
Jan J. Agency	222 E. 46th St., 10017	490-1875
Joe Jordan Talent Agency	200 W. 57th St., 10019	582-9003

The Lantz Office, Inc.	888 7th Ave., 10019	832-1010
Lionel Larner Ltd.	850 7th Ave., 10019	246-3105
Sanford Leigh Ent.	527 Madison Ave., 10022	752-4450
Lester Lewis Assoc.	110 W. 40th St., 10019	921-8370
MMG Enterprises	250 W. 57th St., 10019	246-4360
Marge McDermott Enterprises	216 E. 39th St., 10016	889-1583
M.E.W. Company	370 Lexington Ave., 10017	889-7272
William Morris Agency	1350 Ave. of the Americas, 10019	586-5100
Oppenheim-Christie	565 5th Ave., 10017	661-4330
Fifi Oscard Agency Ltd.	19 W. 44th St., 10036	764-1100
Harry Packwood Talent Ltd.	342 Madison Ave., 10017	682-5858
Dorothy Palmer	250 W. 57th St., 10019	765-4280
Perkins Talent	156 E. 52nd St., 10022	582-4511
Raglyn-Shamsky Ltd.	60 E. 42nd St., 10017	661-6690
Eric Ross Assoc.	60 E. 42nd St., 10017	687-9797
Bernard Rubenstein Agency	215 Park Ave. South, 10003	460-9800
Dick Rubin Ltd.	60 W. 57th St., 10019	541-6576
STE Representation Ltd.	888 7th Ave., 10019	246-1030
The Honey Sanders Agency Ltd.	229 W. 42nd St., 10036	947-5555
William Schuller Agency	667 Madison Ave., 10021	758-1919
Monty Silver Agency	200 W. 57th St., 10019	765-4040
Susan Smith	850 7th Ave., 10019	581-4490
Starkman Agency, Inc.	1501 Broadway, 10036	921-9191
Sutton Artists Corp.	119 W. 57th St., 10019	977-4870
Talent Reps, Inc.	20 E. 53rd St., 10022	752-1835
Michael Thomas Agency	22 E. 60th St., 10022	755-2616

Tranum, Robertson & Hughes	2 Hammarskjold Plaza, 10017	371-7500
Bob Waters Agency	510 Madison Ave., 10022	593-0543
Ann Wright Representatives	136 E. 57th St., 10022	832-0110
Writers & Artists Agency	162 W. 56th St., 10019	246-9029
Babs Zimmerman	305 E. 86th St., 10028	348-7203

PENNSYLVANIA

Philadelphia Models Guild	1500 Locust St., Suite 3414	735-9558

THE MIDWEST*

CHICAGO, ILLINOIS

A Plus Talent Agency	666 N. Lakeshore Dr.	(312) 642-8151
David-Lee Models	64 E. Walton St.	(312) 649-0500
Geddes Agency	1522 John Hancock Ctr.	(312) 664-9890
Shirley Hamilton, Inc.	620 N. Michigan Ave.	(312) 644-0300
Emilia Lorence Ltd.	619 N. Wabash	(312) 787-2033
Playboy Model Agency	919 N. Michigan Ave.	(312) 751-8000
Stewart Talent Mgmt.	212 W. Superior, Suite 406	(312) 943-3131

SOUTHFIELD, MICHIGAN

Affiliated Talent & Casting Svc.	28860 Southfield Rd., Southfield	(313) 559-3110

MINNEAPOLIS, MINNESOTA

Creative Company, Inc.	430 Oak Grove	(612) 871-7866
Gem Models & Talent	5100 Eden Ave.	(612) 927-8000

*Illinois, Indiana, Iowa, Kansas, Michigan, Missouri, Minnesota, Nebraska, North Dakota, Ohio, South Dakota, Wisconsin

Eleanor Moore Agency, Inc.	1610 W. Lake St.	(612) 827-3823
New Faces Models & Talent	310 Groveland Ave.	(612) 871-6000

MISSOURI

Monza Talent Agency	911-1 Main St., Kansas City	(816) 421-0222
White House Studios	4532 Holly, Kansas City	(816) 931-3608
Talent Plus	326 N. Euclid St., St. Louis	(314) 367-7890

OMAHA, NEBRASKA

SR Talent Pool, Inc.	206 S. 44th St.	(402) 553-1164

OHIO

Familiar Faces	254 Oak St., Cincinnati	(513) 559-9336
Glamour Model & Talent Agency	140 N. Main St., Dayton	(513) 222-8321
Dorian Leigh Model Agency	1375 Euclid Ave., Cleveland	(216) 579-1188
Limelight Assoc., Inc.	3460 Davis Lane, Cincinnati	(513) 631-8276
John Robert Powers	5900 Roche Dr., Columbus	(614) 846-1047

MILWAUKEE, WISCONSIN

Rosemary Bischoff Agency	924 E. Juneau Ave.	(414) 273-7393

THE WEST*
PHOENIX, ARIZONA

Bobby Ball Agency	808 E. Osborn	(602) 264-5007

*Alaska, Arizona, California, Colorado, Hawaii, Idaho, Montana, Nevada, New Mexico, Oregon, Washington, Wyoming

Plaza Three Talent Agency	4343 N. 16th St.	(602) 265-3000

CALIFORNIA (OTHER THAN LOS ANGELES AREA)

William Adrian Teen Models Agency	520 S. Lake Ave., Pasadena	(213) 681-5750
Artist Management	2232 5th Ave., San Diego	(619) 233-6655
Mary Crosby Talent Agency	2130 4th Ave., San Diego	(619) 234-7911
Demeter & Reed Ltd.	70 Zowe St., San Francisco	(415) 777-1337
Frazer-Nicklin Agency	3600 Pruneridge Ave., Suite 115, Santa Clara	(408) 544-1055
Grimme Agency	207 Powell St., San Francisco	(415) 392-9175
Manikin Manor Talent	2410 Fair Oaks Blvd., Sacramento	(916) 486-1811
Model Management, Inc.	1400 Castro St., San Francisco	(415) 282-8855
Tina Real Agency	3108 5th Ave., San Diego	(619) 298-0544
Rib Mirrors	54 Park Terrace, San Francisco	(415) 383-5540
Cindy Romano Agency	P.O. Box 1951, Palm Desert	(619) 346-1694
Dorothy Shreve Talent Agency	729 W. 16th St., Costa Mesa	(714) 642-3050

LOS ANGELES   (*213 Area Codes*)

Abrams-Rubaloff & Assocs., Inc.	8075 W. 3rd St., L.A.	935-1700
Bret Adams Ltd.	8282 Sunset Blvd., L.A.	656-6420
Agency for the Performing Arts, Inc.	9000 Sunset Blvd., Suite 315, L.A.	273-0744
Carlos Alvarado Agency	8820 Sunset Blvd., L.A.	652-0272

Fred Amsel & Assocs., Inc.	291 S. La Cienega, Suite 309, B.H.	855-1201
The Artists Agency	10000 Santa Monica Blvd., Suite 621, L.A.	277-7779
The Blake Agency Ltd.	409 N. Camden Dr., No. 202, B.H.	278-6885
Nina Blanchard Agency	1717 N. Highland Ave., Hollywood	462-6241
J. Michael Bloom Ltd.	9220 Sunset Blvd., Suite 1210, L.A.	275-6800
The Boyd Talent Agency	4605 Lankershim Blvd., N. Hollywood	506-7835
Iris Burton Agency	1450 Belfast Dr., L.A.	652-0954
Carey-Phelps-Colrin Agency	1407 N. LaBrea Ave., Hollywood	874-7780
Century Artists Ltd.	9744 Wilshire Blvd., Suite 206, B.H.	273-4366
Rita Chandler & Assoc., Inc.	8833 Sunset Blvd., Suite 405, L.A.	855-0641
Charter Management	9000 Sunset Blvd., Suite 1112, L.A.	278-1690
Commercial Actors Agency	8500 Wilshire Blvd., Suite 604, B.H.	855-0422
Commercials Unlimited, Inc., Sonjia W. Brandon's	7641 Beverly Blvd., Suite 400, L.A.	937-2220
Contemporary-Korman Artists Ltd.	132 Lasky Dr., B.H.	278-8250
The Craig Agency	8732 Sunset Blvd., Suite 265, L.A.	855-1448
Creative Artists Agency	1888 Century Pk. E., Suite 1400, L.A.	277-4545
Bernyce Cronin & Assocs.	539 S. La Cienega Blvd., L.A.	273-8144
Cunningham-Escott-Dipene	261 S. Robertson Blvd., B.H.	855-1700

Diamond Artists Ltd.	9200 Sunset Blvd., Suite 909, L.A.	278-8146
The William Jeffries Agency	8455 Beverly Blvd., B.H.	651-3193
Judith Fontaine Agency	6525 Sunset Blvd., Suite 512, Hollywood	467-6288
The Gage Group	8732 Sunset Blvd., Suite 750, L.A.	652-8833
Dale Garrick Int'l Agency	8831 Sunset Blvd., Suite 402, L.A.	657-2661
The Gersh Agency, Inc.	222 N. Canon Dr., Suite 204, B.H.	274-6611
Dennis-Karg-Dennis & Co.	470 S. San Vicente Blvd., L.A.	651-1700
The Granite Agency	1920 S. La Cienega Blvd., Suite 205, L.A.	934-8383
Greene's Creative Expressions	439 S. La Cienega Blvd., Suite 110-112, L.A.	278-9902
Beverly Hecht Agency	8949 Sunset Blvd., Suite 203, L.A.	278-3544
Henderson-Hogan Agency	247 Beverly Dr., Suite 102, B.H.	274-7815
Ray Hunter & Assocs.	132 Lasky Dr., B.H.	276-1137
Int'l Creative Mgmt. (ICM)	8899 Beverly Blvd., L.A.	550-4000
Toni Kelman & Assocs.	7813 Sunset Blvd., L.A.	851-8822
William Kerwin Agency	1605 N. Cahuenga Blvd., L.A.	469-5155
D.H.K.P.R.	7319 Beverly Blvd., L.A.	857-1234
Tyler Kjar Agency	8961 Sunset Blvd., Suite B, L.A.	278-0912
Caroline Leonetti Ltd.	6526 Sunset Blvd., Hollywood	463-5610
The Light Company	113 N. Robertson Blvd., L.A.	273-9602

Robert Longenecker Agency	11704 Wilshire Blvd., Suite 200, L.A.	477-0039
Grace Lyons Agency	8730 Sunset Blvd., Suite 380, L.A.	652-5290
M.E.W., Inc.	151 N. San Vicente Blvd., B.H.	653-4731
MGA (Mary Grady Agency)	10850 Riverside Dr., Suite 504, N. Hollywood	985-9800
Mishkin Agency	9255 Sunset Blvd., Suite 610, L.A.	274-5261
Wm. Morris Agency	151 El Camino Dr., B.H.	274-7451
Burton Moss Agency	113 N. San Vicente Blvd., Suite 202, B.H.	655-1156
M.T.A. Agency	4615 Melrose Ave., L.A.	661-9888
Dorothy Day Otis/Jack Rose Agency	6430 Sunset Blvd., Suite 1203, Hollywood	463-7300
Pacific Artists Ltd.	515 N. La Cienega Blvd., L.A.	657-5990
Ray Rappa Agency	7471 Melrose Ave., Suite 11, L.A.	653-7000
Sackheim Agency	9301 Wilshire Blvd., Suite 606, B.H.	858-0606
Honey Sanders Agency Ltd.	721 N. La Brea Ave., Suite 200, L.A.	938-9113
Norah Sanders Agency	1100 Glendon Ave., Penthouse Suite, N. Hollywood	827-8932 824-2264
Peggy Schaefer Agency	10850 Riverside Dr., N. Hollywood	985-5547
Don Schwartz & Assocs.	8721 Sunset Blvd., Suite 200, L.A.	657-8910
David Shapira & Assocs.	15301 Ventura Blvd., Suite 345, Sherman Oaks	906-0322

Lew Sherrell Agency	7060 Hollywood Blvd., Suite 610, Hollywood	461-9955
Smith-Freedman Assocs.	9869 Santa Monica Blvd., Suite 207, B.H.	277-8464
STE Representation Ltd.	211 S. Beverly Dr., Suite 201, B.H.	550-3982
Charles Stern Agency	9220 Sunset Blvd., Suite 218, L.A.	273-6890
Sutton, Barth & Vennari, Inc.	8322 Beverly Blvd., Suite 25, L.A.	653-8322
Talent Group, Inc.	8831 Sunset Blvd., E. PH A, L.A.	659-8072
Herb Tannen & Assocs.	6640 Sunset Blvd., Suite 203, Hollywood	466-6191
Herb Tobias & Assocs.	1901 Ave. of the Stars, Suite 840, L.A.	277-6211
Terri Turco Agency	7469 Melrose Ave., Suite 30	653-2520
U.K. Management, Inc.	1052 Carol Dr., L.A.	275-9599
Wilhelmina Artists Representatives, Talent Agency, Inc.	6430 Sunset Blvd., Suite 701A, Hollywood	464-6744 464-8577
Williamson & Assocs.	932 N. LaBrea, L.A.	851-1881
Wormser, Heldfond & Joseph, Inc.	1717 N. Highland Ave., Suite 414, Hollywood	466-9111
Ann Wright & Assocs. Ltd.	8422 Melrose Ave., L.A.	655-5040
Writers & Artists Agency	11726 San Vicente, Suite 300, B.H.	550-8030

COLORADO

Aspen Production Services	Aspen	(303) 925-1031
Brittney Modeling & Talent	7 E. Bijou, Colorado Springs	(303) 633-5411
Illinois Talent	2664 L. Krameria, Denver	(303) 757-8675

J.F. Images, Inc.	3600 S. Yosemite, Denver	(303) 779-8888
Light Co. Talent Agency	1443 Wazee St., Denver	(303) 572-8363
M.T.A.	4615 N. Park Dr., Colorado Springs	(303) 599-3533

HAWAII

Commercial Casting Services	Honolulu	(808) 538-6731
Ann Karelon	Kalau	(808) 988-2188
Greg Kendall & Associates, Inc.	2003 Kalia Rd., Honolulu	(808) 946-9577
Nui Nani Productions	Kipa No. 4, Lahaina, Maui	(808) 669-5017

LAS VEGAS, NEVADA

Universal Models	953 E. Sahara, Las Vegas	(702) 732-2499

PORTLAND, OREGON

Character Actors	935 N.W. 19th Ave.	(503) 223-1931
Ewe-Me & Company	921 S.W. Morrison	(503) 224-5351
Media Talent Centre	4315 N.E. Tillamook	(503) 281-2020

THE SOUTH*

BIRMINGHAM, ALABAMA

Elan	1025 Montgomery Hwy.	(205) 822-5032

FLORIDA

Act 1	1460 Brickell Ave., Miami	(305) 371-1371
Jay Brown Music & Talent Agency	221 W. Waters Ave., Tampa	(813) 933-2456

*Alabama, Arkansas, Florida, Georgia, Kentucky, Louisiana, Mississippi, North Carolina, Oklahoma, South Carolina, Texas, Tennessee, Virginia

Dott Burns Talent Agency	478 Severn, Tampa	(813) 251-5882
Russ Byrd Ent., Inc.	1005 Woodbrook South	(813) 586-1504
Cassandra Model & Theatrical Agency	P.O. Box 6305, Orlando	(305) 423-7872
Coconut Grove Talent Agency	3525 Vista Ct., Coconut Grove	(305) 858-3002
Travis Falcon Modeling Agency	17070 Collins Ave., Miami Beach	(305) 947-7957
Florida Talent Agency	2631 E. Oakland Pk. Blvd., Ft. Laud.	(305) 565-3552
Gold Coast Model Agency	4056 Estepona Ave., Miami Beach	(305) 592-1130
Jerry Grant Agency	2741 N. 29th Ave., Hollywood	(305) 944-1011
Glyne Kennedy, The Jockey Club	11111 Biscayne Blvd., Suite 3161, Miami	(305) 899-0260
MarBea Talent Agency	104 Crandon Blvd., Key Biscayne	(305) 361-1144
Sarah Parker Models & Talent	425 S. Olive Ave., W. Palm Beach	(305) 659-2833
Marian Polan Talent Agency	411 N.E. 11th Ave., Ft. Laud.	(305) 525-8351
Michelle Pommier Models, Inc.	1501 Sunset Dr., Coral Gables	(305) 667-8710
John Robert Powers Agency	828 S.E. 4th St., Ft. Laud.	(305) 467-2851

GEORGIA

Atlanta Models and Talent	3030 Peachtree Rd. N.W., Atlanta	(404) 261-9627
Chez Agency	922 W. Peachtree St., Atlanta	(404) 873-1215
Bonnie Reeve	545 Pharr Rd., Atlanta	(404) 523-3700
Serindipity Talent	3130 Maple Dr. N.E., Suite 19, Atlanta	(404) 237-4040

Take One	3330 Peachtree Rd. N.W., Atlanta	(404) 231-2315
The Talent Shop	3379 Peachtree Rd. N.E., Atlanta	(404) 261-0770
Tamca	4540-F Memorial Dr., Decatur	(404) 292-4207

KENTUCKY

Faces Ltd.	2915 Frankfurt Ave., Louisville	(502) 893-8840
Vogue of Lexington, Inc.	3347 Tates Creek Rd., Lexington	(606) 269-8407

LOUISIANA

Artists' Reps. of N.O., Inc.	1416 Webster St., New Orleans	(504) 524-4683

NORTH CAROLINA

The Fetter Agency	605 Forum VI, Greensboro	(919) 852-4883
Signature Talent, Inc.	4600 Park Rd., Charlotte	(704) 523-1001
Jan Thompson Agency, Inc.	1800 East Blvd., Charlotte	(704) 377-5987

OKLAHOMA CITY, OKLAHOMA

Accent, Inc.	901 Office Pk. Plaza	(405) 843-1303
Crème de la Crème	5643 N. Pennsylvania	(405) 840-4419
JoAnn Fullerton	923 W. Britton	(405) 840-4636

TENNESSEE

Bruce Agency	1022 16th Ave. S., Nashville	(615) 255-5711

TEXAS

Tanya Blair Agency, Inc. Blair/Casablancas	3000 Carlisle, Suite 102, Dallas	(214) 748-8353

Marquerite Burns Agency	2639 Walnut Hill La., Suite 211, Dallas	(214) 350-0544
Dallas International Agency	8383 Stemmons, Suite 148, Dallas	(214) 630-8888
Kim Dawson Agency	1643 Apparel Mart, Dallas	(214) 638-2420
Images Model & Talent Agency	2639 Walnut Hill La., Suite 154, Dallas	(214) 353-9858
K-Hall Agency	503 W. 15th St., Austin	(512) 476-7523
Mad Hatter Agency	7349 Ashcroft Dr., Bldg. B., Houston	(713) 995-9090
The Norton Agency	3023 Routh St., Dallas	(214) 749-0900
Peggy Taylor Talent, Inc.	2 Dallas Comm. Complex, Suite 120, 6309 N. O'Connor at Royal La., Irving	(214) 869-1515
Professional Artists of Texas, Inc.	2829 W. Northwest Hwy., Suite 141, Dallas	(214) 350-4844
Stars Over Texas	4330 N. Central Expwy, Dallas	(214) 522-2030
Sherry Young, Inc.	6420 Hillcroft, Suite 319, Dallas	(713) 981-9236
Joy Wyse Agency	6318 Gastron Ave., Dallas	(214) 826-0330

Fashion and Modeling Agents

NEW YORK		*(212 Area Codes)*
About Faces Model Mgmt., Inc.	250 W. 57th St., 10107	582-7035
Sue Charney Models Ltd.	641 Lexington Ave., 10022	751-3005
Click	881 7th Ave., 10019	245-4306
D.M.I. Talent Assoc.	250 W. 57th St., 10107	246-4650
Elite Models	150 E. 58th St., 10022	935-4500

Pat Evans Model Mgmt., Inc.	3850 HMT, Riverdale	884-4785
Ford Model Agency	344 E. 59th St., 10022	753-6500
Foster-Fell Agency	26 W. 38th St., 10018	944-8520
Gilla Roos Ltd.	527 Madison Ave., 10022	758-5480
Ellen Harth (women only)	149 Madison Ave., 10016	686-5600
Legends	40 E. 34th St., 10016	684-4600
L'Image	667 Madison Ave., 10021	758-6411
Mannequin	730 5th Ave., 10019	586-7716
Perkins Talent	156 E. 52nd St., 10022	582-9511
Wallace Rogers, Inc.	160 E. 56th St., 10022	755-1464
Charles Ryan Agency	200 W. 57th St., 10019	245-2225
Sabrena Artists Corp.	1650 Broadway, 10019	757-8354
Stewart Artists Corp.	140 E. 63rd St., 10021	249-5540
Summa Models, Inc.	250 W. 57th St., 10107	957-9866
Wilhelmina Model Agency	9 E. 37th St., 10016	532-6800
Zoli Mgmt., Inc.	146 E. 56th St., 10022	758-5959

Agents for Children

NEW YORK (*212 Area Codes*)

Agents for the Arts	1650 Broadway, #306, 10019	247-3220
J. Michael Bloom	400 Madison Ave., 10017	832-6900
Bonnie Kid Assoc.	250 W. 57th St., 10107	246-0223
Brats	527 Madison Ave., 10022	752-6090
Rosemary Brian Agency	250 W. 57th St., 10107	546-8616
Francis Dilworth Agency	496 Kinderkamack Rd., Oradell, N.J.	661-0070

D.M.I. Talent Agency	250 W. 57th St., 10107	246-4650
Marje Fields, Inc.	250 W. 57th St., 10107	581-7240
Ford Talent Group	344 E. 59th St., 10022	753-6500
Jan J. Agency	222 E. 46th St., 10017	490-1875
Joe Jordan Talent Agency	200 W. 57th St., 10019	582-9003
KMA Assoc.	303 W. 42nd St., #606, 10036	
Sanford Leigh Agency	527 Madison Ave., 10022	752-4450
Marge McDermott	216 E. 39th St., 10016	889-1583
Mary Ellen White, Inc. (MEW)	370 Lexington Ave., 10017	889-7272
Marcia's Kids	250 W. 57th St., 10107	246-4360
Fifi Oscard Assocs.	19 W. 44th St., 10036	764-1100
Dorothy Palmer Talent	250 W. 57th St., 10107	765-4280
Honey Sanders Agency	229 W. 42nd St., 10036	947-5555
William Schuller Talent/New York Kids	667 Madison Ave., 10021	758-1919
Gloria Troy Talent	1790 Broadway, 10019	582-0260
Bob Waters Agency	510 Madison Ave., 10022	593-0543
Ann Wright Rep.	136 E. 57th St., 10022	832-0110

Managers for Children

NEW YORK

Norma Belsky/New Personalities	18 Fairway Dr., Great Neck, 11020	423-1762 582-8868
Cuzzins Mgmt.	250 W. 57th St., 10019	586-1573
Kathy Dowd	331 Madison Ave., 10017	661-4966
Betty A. Geffen	17 W. 71st St., 10023	874-6374
Barbara Jarrett & Paula Lindstrom	220 E. 63rd St., 10021	355-7500

Muriel Karl Talent Mgmt.	888 8th Ave., 10019	245-3770
Selma Rubin Talent Mgmt.	104-60 Queens Blvd. #1-D, Forest Hills, 11375	896-6326
Millie Spencer Theatrical Mgmt.	1697 Broadway, 10019	765-1210
Kuno Sponholz Mgmt.	350 W. 55th St., 10019	265-3777

Special Sizes

NEW YORK   *(212 Area Codes)*

Big Beauties (plus sizes)	159 Madison Ave., 10016	685-1270
Little Women (5'4" & smaller)	159 Madison Ave., 10016	685-1270
12 Plus—Ford Women (plus sizes)	344 E. 59th St., 10022	753-6500
Plus Model Mgmt. (plus sizes)	49 W. 37th St., 10018	997-1785

Animal Agents

NEW YORK

All-Tame Animals, Inc.	37 W. 57th St., 10019	(212) 752-5885
Canine Academy of Ivan Kovach	3725 Lynn Ave., Brooklyn	(212) 682-6770
Chateau Theatrical Animals	608 W. 48th St., 10036	(212) 246-0520
Dawn Animal Agency	160 W. 46th St., 10036	(212) 575-9396
Long Island Game Farm & Zoo	Chapman Blvd., Manorville, L.I.	(516) 878-6644

NEW JERSEY

Animal Actors, Inc.	RD #3, Box 221, Washington, N.J.	(201) 689-7539 (212) 586-3700

FLORIDA

| Studio Animal Renters, Inc. | 70 W. 64th St., Hialeah, Fla. | (305) 558-4160 |

CALIFORNIA

Carriage Charter	3225 Hwy. 116 N., Sebastopol	(707) 823-7083
Critters of the Cinema	11307 Eastwood Ave., Inglewood	(213) 412-0470
Gentle Jungle, Inc.	1238 N. Highland Ave., Hollywood	(213) 469-2213
Studio Dog Training School		(213) 457-7528

LAS VEGAS, NEVADA

| Studio Animal Rentals, Inc. | | (702) 369-0114 |

Index